Sweet Swan of Avon

Well then, must I work otherwise what I may

Mary Sidney Herbert, the Countess of Pembroke / 1603

Sweet Swan of Avon

Did a Woman Write Shakespeare?

Robin P. Williams

WILTON CIRCLE PRESS

USA

Sweet Swan of Avon: Did a Woman Write Shakespeare?
©2006 Robin P. Williams

Library of Congress copyright 2002 in the category
of "original research that reaches a new conclusion";
TXu 1-071-346

2002 WGA registration of screen treatment: 91888

All illustrations © 2006 by John Tollett
www.MarySidney.com
www.MarySidneySociety.org

Wilton Circle Press

www.WiltonCirclePress.com
Wilton Circle Press is an imprint of Peachpit Press, a division of Pearson Education

Peachpit Press
1249 Eighth Street
Berkeley, CA 94710
510.524.2178 voice
510.524.2221 fax

Credits

Cover design and production: John Tollett
Formal portrait of Mary Sidney and of Wilton House: John Tollett
Interior design and production: Robin Williams
Index: Robin Williams
Editor: Barbara Riley
Proofreader: Ted Waitt
MarySidney.com and MarySidneySociety.org websites:
    Brian Forstat, John Tollett, Robin Williams

Notice of rights

The literary paper trail chart by Diana Price is used with permission: *Shakespeare's
Unorthodox Biography, New Evidence of an Authorship Problem*, Diana Price, ©2001
by Diana Price. Reproduced with permission of Greenwood Publishing Group, Inc.,
Westport, CT.

All quotes from plays are from *The Complete Works of Shakespeare*, 5th ed., edited by
David Bevington. This book not only has lots of background material, excellent glosses,
and thoughtful editing, it also has the most considerate typography, nicest paper, and
is the easiest and most pleasant collected works to read.

ISBN

0-321-42640-1
Printed and bound in the United States of America

10 9 8 7 6 5 4 3 2 1

Mary Sidney Herbert

Countess of Pembroke

1561–1621

*He remains, in fact,
the most anonymous
of our great writers.*

Alvin Kernan
*Shakespeare,
The King's Playwright*

*In fact, we probably know more
about the daily life of a dinosaur
than we do of the man W. H.
Auden dubbed "The Top Bard."*

Norrie Epstein
"Who Wrote Shakespeare"
*Living in a
Shakespearean World*

Contents

Part Six - THE ANTAGONIST

Part Seven - THE PUBLICATION

Part Eight - THE POSSIBILITY

Part Nine - THE APPENDICES

Note: *I occasionally repeat information in the book. This is for two reasons: People enter books in different ways and don't always read front to back. Also, there are so many details in this book that I do not expect you to actually remember everything from one chapter to another! So where information is critical for understanding, I repeat it.*

In an effort to reflect the breadth of scholarship around both the Shakespearean canon and Mary Sidney, I quote extensively from published material. This also assures you that I am not speculating or inventing ideas to make my point—I am merely making connections between people, events, and opinions that are already well established.

I have great cause to give great thanks *Coriolanus*

This book has been a long time in the making. I thank the founding members of the Mary Sidney Society and especially the dedicated board of directors for their enduring and endearing support as this project unfolded; Peachpit Press for believing in me once again and turning Wilton Circle Press into an imprint, especially Nancy Davis and Nancy Ruenzel for going to great lengths to make it happen; Mary Grady for her early editing; Jim'Bo Norrena, Laura Egley Taylor, and Dana Evans for their eager participation on our grand adventure in England, filming a pilgrimage to places where Mary Sidney had been and getting dizzy in roundabouts along the way; Mr. Ray Stedman, Nigel Bailey, Carole Druce, and Deborah Evans at Wilton House for their patient cooperation with us when we show up every year; Mark Rylance for his warm acceptance and encouragement at Shakespeare's Globe Theatre in London; Claire van Kampen at the Globe Theatre for her invaluable insights into the possible musical work of Mary Sidney, and for her genuine appreciation of this woman; for the many friends who have enthusiastically read and provided great critiques on early versions, especially Amy Meilander, Ross and Danby Carter, Elizabeth Thornton, Jeanne Bahnson, Martha Callanan, Joannie Starbuck, Kathleen Bradbury, Carmen Sheldon, Barbara Sikora, Tim Taylor, Reeve Taylor; my mother, Pat Williams, and her friends; my dad, who would have been proud; my sibs Jeff, Shannon, Cliff, and Julie Williams; my uncle Merv Williams and my "Ant Jean" Williams; the First Friday Club and Sundays with Sidney, readers who have spent years reading the plays out loud with me; Barbara Riley, dear friend and skillful editor who really pulled the book together; Ute, Steven, and Malte Forstat for the elegant German translation, and Brian Forstat for his elegant web site work; the wonderful Peachpit staff who have put up with me for so many years and are now working on this very different book, especially Sara Todd and Zigi Lowenberg for publicity, and Ted Waitt and David Van Ness for final proofing and pre-press. To my incredible kids, Ryan, Jimmy, and Scarlett, who have been unconditionally encouraging, bless their hearts. And many loving thanks to John Tollett, my man of men, my knight in shining technogear.

To JT, my stalwart supporter, who says, "There's more evidence that a spaceship crashed in Roswell than that the man named William Shakespeare wrote those plays."

Who Wrote Shakespeare?

To a certain type of mind, all fresh evidence is so extremely distasteful.

W. W. Greg, 1931

SINCE THE MID-1700S, experts and amateurs have been debating what may seem like an absurd question—on the order of "Who is buried in Grant's tomb?" The debate has its own title, "The Authorship Question."

It's a surprise to many people that there is even a question of the true authorship of the Shakespearean works. Some insist adamantly that there is no question at all. But the query isn't going away. If the arguments for William Shakespeare's authorship were sound, two hundred years' worth of books, articles, debates, and films about the issue would not exist. No one quibbles over who wrote the works attributed to Ben Jonson or Sir Francis Bacon, written in the same era. But because the language of these plays shapes the very patterns of our speech and colors our standards of literary excellence worldwide, the Authorship Question is more than a quibble.

Even if you've never seen or read a Shakespeare play in your life and don't intend to, I hope you'll find this presentation to be thought-provoking. I'll explain some of what we know about the author derived from the plays and why William Shakespeare's authorship is a problem. With that in place, I'll introduce you to the documented evidence pertaining to Mary Sidney Herbert, the Countess of Pembroke, and ask you to consider this question:

> *Might this woman have written the plays and sonnets attributed to the man named William Shakespeare?*

The purpose of this book is not to *prove* that Mary Sidney wrote the works attributed to Shakespeare—I only hope to present enough documented evidence to elicit the curiosity of others to pursue further research into this possibility. Most of all, I hope to create an expectation of using *only* documented evidence in future scholarship regarding the Authorship Question.

Robin

Prologue

To catalogue Shakespeare's largest gifts is almost an absurdity: where begin, where end? He wrote the best poetry and the best prose in English, or perhaps in any Western language. That is inseparable from his cognitive strength; he thought more comprehensively and originally than any other writer. . . . he went beyond all precedents (even Chaucer) and invented the human as we continue to know it.

Harold Bloom, *Shakespeare: The Invention of the Human*, 1999

THE PLAYS AND SONNETS OF SHAKESPEARE are considered by many to be the most impressive literary works in the English language; by others, the greatest in any language. Understanding the importance and influence of this playwright will show why it is important to know who the author was and at the same time, perhaps, provide a glimpse into what this person was like.

The Impact of Shakespeare

THIS AUTHOR WRITES ABOUT A WIDER RANGE of human experience than any other writer before or since. Over a period of less than thirty years, the plays explore and present insights into hate, revenge, politics, jealousy, relationships between children and parents, many kinds of love, battles between good and evil, ambition, nature and nurture, passion, melancholy, old age, youth, justice, loyalty, marriage, fidelity and perfidy of all sorts, innocence, wonder, stupidity, war, forgiveness, time, madness, patience, tyranny, guilt, magic, fate, free will, friendships, deception, competition, racism—struggles large and small. The playwright doesn't judge these frailties and nobilities, but presents them to us as part and parcel of our humanity—a mirror that simply reflects and illuminates what it is to be human.

THE DEPTH OF THE PLAYS AND SONNETS is astonishing. While the first introduction to the work can be difficult, as many complex things in life can be, spending time to become familiar with the canon frequently leads to wonder and awe.

Each time we read or see a particular play, our appreciation deepens. The first time through a play we often get the gist of the plot, a sense of the language, and we can answer specific questions like, How old is Juliet? Why is Romeo melancholy in Act I? To which town did Romeo run away?

As we spend more time with a play, we're compelled to look at other questions, such as, Why would the nurse suddenly change her support of Romeo? Why are there so many references to dark and light?

And after the whos and whats are out of the way, we start to ponder the deepest questions of love, commitment, revenge, defiance—what does it mean to truly love your daughter or your father, where should one's allegiance lie, how does this play reflect our present society? Each play presents moral quandaries to which characters must respond, and their reactions force us to regard our own choices.

THE PLAYWRIGHT USES A VAST RANGE OF POETIC TECHNIQUES and rhetorical devices that emphasize and enrich the concepts and human themes explored in the plays. The author did not simply pour heart and soul onto the page as a stream of consciousness, but was instead a classically trained poet who displays a very skilled use of formal devices such as as alliteration, onomatopoeia, anaphora, analepsis, anadiplosis, doublets, epistrophe, epanalepsis, hendiadys, synecdoche, isocolon, stichomythia, oxymorons, parison, litotes, antanaclasis, ploce, assonance, epizeuxis, chiasmus, polyptoton, paradoxes, puns, personifications—and so many others that entire books are devoted to the subject.

Of course, many good writers instinctively use a particular technique, unconsciously understanding its inherent effect. But this author's apparently effortless mastery of techniques taught in poetry and rhetoric, even in the least critically successful of the plays, reveals a person who respected the craft and consciously manipulated the English language to achieve specific emotional responses from the reader or viewer.

THE PLAYWRIGHT EXCELS IN CREATING IMAGES that develop in our minds and reinforce not only individual lines, but the stories as a whole. To this end, clusters of particular images appear in the plays. For instance, *Romeo and Juliet* is filled with contrasting visions of dark and light, old and young, hate and love, night and day, death and life—each image strengthening the individual lines while building toward a powerful, cohesive whole.

Hamlet is filled with images of sickness: infection, maggots, weeds, ulcers, disease, and corruption; *Measure for Measure* with justice, balancing, weighing, and comparing; *The Tempest* with master/servant and bondage references, the moon, water, ebbing and flowing, language, dreaming, sleeping, and death. These clusters are treasures of imagery that become richer with repeated readings and viewings.

Provocative and multiple levels of meaning in thousands of lines add to the elegance and depth of the language. For instance:

> *O powerful love, that in some respects makes a beast a man;*
> *in some other, a man a beast.*
> Falstaff in *The Merry Wives of Windsor,* 5.v.4

Taken *out* of context, the lines are rich in multiple meanings; *in* context, with Falstaff dressed in chains and stag horns to meet two married women whom he plans to woo, even more meanings bubble to the surface.

It is astonishing how many words and lines in the plays and sonnets resonate with multiple rich, subtle (and not so subtle) meanings—it is one of this writer's greatest gifts.

ON A PERSONAL LEVEL, in every play we are struck by thoughts and ideas that accurately mirror our place in the world at that moment. Rereading the plays at different times in our lives, the following might be more or less true for each one of us:

> *Out of my sight! Thou dost infect mine eyes.*
> Anne in *Richard III,* 1.ii.151

> *Would that my tongue were in the thunder's mouth!*
> *Then with a passion would I shake the world.*
> Constance in *King John,* 3.iv.38–39

> *My tongue will tell the anger of my heart,*
> *Or else my heart, concealing it, will break,*
> *And rather than it shall, I will be free*
> *Even to the uttermost, as I please, in words.*
> Kate in *The Taming of the Shrew,* 4.iii.77–80

And whether we shall meet again I know not.
Therefore our everlasting farewell take:
For ever, and for ever, farewell, Cassius!
If we do meet again, we shall smile;
If not, why then, this parting was well made.
Brutus in *Julius Caesar*, 5.i.118–122

SUCH A WIDE VARIETY OF DISPARATE CHARACTERS, each with a unique voice, has never been equaled by any other writer. There are more than a thousand characters in the collection of plays; more than one hundred are major personalities. Individual characterizations unfold with startling richness and depth through their words and actions.

AND SPEAKING OF LANGUAGE, not only is this the medium through which the author excels in reaching our hearts, but the language itself has been a forceful influence for 400 years. The poet had a 30,000-word vocabulary.[1] A college graduate today has a vocabulary of about 10–15,000 words (no wonder we don't understand every line!), and most of us actually use only 3–4,000 of the words we know. This writer contributed about 1,500 new words to the English language, from *addiction* and *assassination* to *wild-goose chase*, *worthless*, and *zany*. Entire phrases have become part of our everyday lives. As Bernard Levin eloquently explains in *The Story of English:*

> If you cannot understand my argument, and declare "It's Greek to me," you are quoting Shakespeare; if you claim to be more sinned against than sinning, you are quoting Shakespeare; if you recall your salad days, you are quoting Shakespeare; if you act more in sorrow than in anger, if your wish is father to the thought, if your lost property has vanished into thin air, you are quoting Shakespeare; if you have ever refused to budge an inch or suffered from green-eyed jealousy, if you have played fast and loose, if you have been tongue-tied, a tower of strength, hoodwinked or in a pickle, if you have knitted your brows, made a virtue of necessity, insisted on fair play, slept not one wink, stood on ceremony, danced attendance (on your lord and master), laughed yourself into stitches, had short shrift, cold comfort,

or too much of a good thing, if you have seen better days or lived in a fool's paradise—why, be that as it may, the more fool you, for it is a foregone conclusion that you are (as good luck would have it) quoting Shakespeare; if you think it is early days and clear out bag and baggage, if you think it is high time and that that is the long and short of it, if you believe that the game is up and that truth will out even if it involves your own flesh and blood, if you lie low till the crack of doom because you suspect foul play, if you have your teeth set on edge (at one fell swoop) without rhyme or reason, then—to give the devil his due—if the truth were known (for surely you have a tongue in your head) you are quoting Shakespeare; even if you bid me good riddance and send me packing, if you wish I were dead as a door-nail, if you think I am an eyesore, a laughing stock, the devil incarnate, a stony-hearted villain, bloody-minded or a blinking idiot, then—by Jove! O Lord! Tut, tut! for goodness' sake! what the dickens! but me no buts—it is all one to me, for you are quoting Shakespeare.[2]

What Did the Playwright Value?

Based on close readings of the plays, we can make some educated speculations as to what this author valued.

MUSIC: In 37 plays, there are more than 500 references to music, the depth of which indicates the author was probably a trained musician.

LITERACY: "In every one of the 37 plays attributed to Shakespeare, within the first act of each there are references to some aspect of literacy or media (reading, writing, letters, documents, books, etc.); furthermore, 28 of the plays contain such references in the first scene. . . . Letters are so common that they are exchanged in all but six of the plays."[3]

POLITICAL STATEMENTS: The plays satirize leading political figures and the royal court itself, with its fawning servility and superficiality—an insider's view of the court. The author had a thorough understanding of the feudal aristocracy, its death cries, and the voice of the emerging middle class. "The plays concern themselves with such

In every man's writings, the character of the writer must lie recorded.
Thomas Carlyle
1795–1881

sensitive issues as the abuse of royal power, political hypocrisy, courtly vanity, monarchical madness, and regicide." [4]

IMAGERY: In Caroline Spurgeon's book, *Shakespeare's Imagery and What It Tells Us*,[5] she categorizes every image in every play. Based on the preponderance of various images, she concludes that the author disliked bad smells and hated war (although none of the imagery suggests a direct knowledge of war or fighting). The author loved the garden and orchard (but did not farm); was a keen observer of birds; knew the names of flowers, weeds, and herbs, as well as their medicinal uses and emotional symbolisms. The author's favorite sport was lawn bowling, second was archery, and had a familiarity with soccer (football) and tennis. Fluent knowledge of alchemy, astrology, and legal terms is evident. The unforced vocabulary of the equestrian, falconer, and hunter suggests lifelong exposure. Although very class-conscious, the playwright had more empathy for the downtrodden of every species than did any other writer of the time. While enjoying the occupations of daily indoor life, there is also obvious pleasure in nature and the English countryside. Though the images and references to the sea, ships, and seafaring "are generally a landsman's images, a few of them drawn from the management of a ship show that he had some knowledge of technical language and the sailor's craft, which indeed is sufficiently proved in the opening of *The Tempest*." [6]

Ms. Spurgeon surmises that "His interest in and acute observation of cooking operations are very marked all through his work,"[7] "and there is clear evidence of his observation of and interest in needlework."[8] The knowledge of medicine, treatment of disease, and actions of medicines on the body became more important as the writer grew older.[9] A dislike of overeating and drunkenness is noticeable,[10] and the writer has a remarkable interest in and observation of children and child nature from babyhood.[11] And, "In general it would seem Shakespeare does not rebel against death, but accepts it as a natural process . . . ."[12]

What Did the Playwright Favor?

You might ask how we know that the playwright favored particular recreations. For instance, it is often said that the author was an experienced falconer or hawker, yet there is only one short scene about this sport in the entire canon.

Falconry

While a writer today might study falconry to describe a hunt or to add color to dialogue, this author was so familiar with the sport that technical terms are integrated into speeches that have nothing to do with hawking or falconry. For instance, from *Romeo and Juliet*:

> *O for a falconer's voice,*
> *To lure this tassel-gentle back again!*
> Juliet in *Romeo and Juliet*, 2.ii.159–160

> Juliet wants to be able to call Romeo as loudly as a falconer calls
> to her hawks. A tassel-gentle (tiercel-gentle) is the peregrine,
> the noblest of the falcons. The peregrine is also a bird to whom a
> falconer must make a long-term commitment to train and keep.

The laws of ownership established in the 15ᵗʰ century stipulated that certain birds were allocated to certain social ranks, and a person could not hawk with a bird that was allocated to a higher rank. Thus in the quotation above, the writer also indicates the lover's social status— a person of the lower class was forbidden to hunt with a peregrine. (He would be allowed to hunt with a kestrel, which catches rodents and bugs.)

Or as Juliet says to the night while waiting for Romeo to arrive to consummate their marriage:

> *Hood my unmann'd blood, bating in my cheeks,*
> *with thy black mantle.*
> *Romeo and Juliet*, 3.ii.14–15

> When a bird is unaccustomed to being handled by a human, it
> is "unmanned." When a bird is nervous, it "bates," or flutters its
> wings. When a bird bates, a hood is placed over its head to calm it
> down. The "mantle" is the dark cloak of night that will hide Juliet's
> blushing face so Romeo won't notice how immodestly she awaits
> his arrival, but it is also a pun on how a bird mantles, or stands over
> its kill with its wings wide open to hide it.

Romeo calls Juliet his "nyas" (an obsolete term for "eyas," 2.ii.167), which is a young hawk taken from its nest in preparation for training.

In *Othello*, the Moor says of Desdemona,

> *If I do prove her haggard,*
> *Though that her jesses were my dear heartstrings,*
> *I'ld whistle her off and let her down the wind,*
> *To prey at fortune.*
>
> *Othello*, 3.iii.276–279

A "haggard" is a bird that has been caught as an adult, instead of as a young chick; a haggard is harder to train and more easily lost. "Jesses" are the straps that are fastened around the legs of a trained hawk. To recall a hawk on the wing, you "whistle her off"; when a bird turns "down the wind," she cannot maintain her height and so heads to the ground where the prey is usually caught, either on the ground or on the way down.[13]

Lawn bowling

We also suspect the author was very fond of bowls, or lawn bowling, because bowling terms appear often and in surprising places:

> *To die, to sleep;*
> *To sleep: perchance to dream: Ay, there's the rub ...*
>
> Hamlet in *Hamlet*, 3.i.65–66

The term "rub" refers to an obstacle or impediment that hinders the bowl (ball) or diverts it from its proper course.

> *A woman's face, with nature's own hand painted,*
> *Hast thou, the master mistress of my passion—*
>
> Sonnet 20

The terms "'Master' and 'Mistress,' used interchangeably to refer— as here—to something which is an object of passionate interest or a center of attention, come from the game of bowls. They are names for the small bowl thrown out at the beginning of the game."[14]

Alchemy

Alchemy was known as "the royal art," [15] and this playwright was an avid student of metaphysics, based on the imagery and ideas in the plays. Alchemy, closely allied with chemistry and medicine at the time, was a popular study. Queen Elizabeth had her own private alchemist.[16] Carl Jung has argued that alchemy was "a mystical system of spiritual growth, an art of personal transformation." [17]

Numerous distillation images, specific references to alchemical materials and paraphernalia, indeed, entire plays and sonnets based on symbolic death and transmutation with alchemy metaphors, tools, and practices reveal a scholar's fluency with the material.

Romeo remarks on the specific objects he saw in an apothecary's shop:

> *And in his needy shop a tortoise hung,*
> *An alligator stuff'd, and other skins*
> *Of ill-shaped fishes; and about his shelves*
> *A beggarly account of empty boxes,*
> *Green earthen pots, bladders and musty seeds,*
> *Remnants of packthread and old cakes of roses,*
> *Were thinly scatter'd, to make up a show.*
>
> Romeo and Juliet, 3.i.64–65

> The tortoise, alligator, empty boxes, green earthen pots,
> seeds, and roses all have very specific alchemical uses.

Prospero's lines, below, are well-known alchemical references to an experiment that is approaching a critical point and has not yet blown up or failed. *The Tempest* is filled with symbolic references of the sea, the ship as coffin, the island in the sea, the "king being marinated in sea water before he is rescued and taken to dry land,"[18] the wedding of Ferdinand and Miranda that symbolizes the "chemical wedding" of alchemy, death and regeneration, and much more. These knowledgeable images provide clues to the author's understanding of this spiritual and intellectual art form.

> *Now does my project gather to a head:*
> *My charms crack not; my spirits obey . . .*
>
> Prospero in The Tempest, 5.i.1–2

FROM THE PLAYS, an author emerges who seems to have enjoyed various disciplines, sports, and cultural activities as a way of life, possessing a fluency in a broad range of natural interests and pursuits, which in turn facilitated the use of technical terms and expressions in complex yet lucid metaphors.

What Did the Playwright Read?

In creating the plays and sonnets, the author drew on a vast breadth of booklearning. Scholars have relentlessly dissected every word and line in every play and poem to identify the sources of Shakespeare's plots and references (only four plays have original plots,[19] and even those use existing sources for images and ideas). The results are tremendous: "Geoffrey Bullough's *Narrative and Dramatic Sources of Shakespeare* runs to eight volumes. The sources accumulated for [Ben] Jonson [a contemporary of Shakespeare's] could be contained in one."[20]

What scholars have discovered is that this author read *at the very least* the works listed on the following pages, as evidenced by direct plot lines, phrases, or ideas that came from these sources. It is important to remember that a number of the sources did not exist in English translations during Shakespeare's lifetime. According to *The Oxford Companion to Shakespeare,* the playwright "is now generally credited with the ability to read Latin and French, probably Italian and perhaps a little Spanish."[21]

On the following pages is an incomplete list of the books the author of the plays is known to have read—a visual representation of the source materials for the plays.[22] Of course, this does not include any books that the poet might have read simply for pleasure.

Anonymous plays	Children's play about friends Titus and Gisippus at court in 1577
	Life and Death of Jack Straw, 1593–94
	1 Richard II, or Thomas of Woodstock, c. 1592
Anonymous	*Frederyke of Jennen*, Antwerp in 1518; translated from Dutch in 1520 and 1560
Anonymous	*Radulphi de Coggeshall Chronicon Anglicanum*, Latin manuscript
Anonymous	*The Rose of England*
Anonymous	*The Tragedy of Pyramus and Thisbe*, unpublished manuscript
Anonymous	*The Rare Triumphs of Love and Fortune*, acted before Queen Elizabeth in 1582
Anonymous	*The Chronicle History of King Leir*, c. 1590
Anonymous	*Gl'Ingannati*, 1531, Italian with no translation
Anonymous	*Sir Clyomon and Sir Clamydes*, c. 1570
Anonymous	*Caesar and Pompey, or Caesar's Revenge*, c. 1595, pub. 1606–07, performed at Oxford in early 1590s
Anonymous	*The Battle of Agincourt*, c. 1530
Anonymous	*The Jew*, c. 1569 ~79
Anonymous	*The True Tragedy of Richard III*, c. 1591 (or 1594, per Bullough)
Anonymous	*The History of Titus Andronicus*
Anonymous	*A Merry Jest of a Shrewd and Curst Wife Lapped in Morel's Skin for her Good Behaviour*, c. 1550
Anonymous	*The Taming of a Shrew*, 1594
Anonymous	*The Troublesome Reign of John, King of England*, two parts, 1591
Anonymous ms	*Chronicque de la Traison et Mort de Richard Deus*, French manuscript
Anonymous	*Wakefield Chronicle*, Latin manuscript
Anonymous	*Barlaam and Josaphat*, ninth-century Greek, translated into Latin by 13th century
Bible	*Geneva Bible*
Chaplain in HV's army	*Henrici Quinti Angliae Regis Gesta*, Latin manuscript
Appian of Alexandria	*Civil Wars*, translation by W.B., 1578
Apuleius	*Apologia*, in Latin
	The Golden Ass, in Latin
	The Golden Ass, Adlington translation of 1566

Ludovico Ariosto	*Orlando Furioso*, translation of Sir John Harington, 1591
William Averell	*A Marvellous Combat of Contrarieties*, 1588
John Bale	*King John*, a play begun before 1536 and rewritten in 1538 and 1561
Baldwin, ed.	*A Mirror for Magistrates*, 1559 edition
	A Mirror for Magistrates, third edition, 1563
Matteo Bandello	*Novelle (Novella 22)*, 1554, in Italian only AND/OR Belleforest's *Histoires Tragiques*, 1568, the French translation
Richard Barnfield	*The Affectionate Shepherd*, 1594
	Cynthia, 1595
François de Belleforest	*Histoires Tragiques*, 1570
Lord Berners	anonymous *Huon of Bordeaux*, translated by Lord Berners c. 1533–1542
Thomas Blenerhasset et al	*A Mirror for Magistrates*, 1578 edition
Giovanni Boccaccio	*Decameron (Day 2, Tale 9)*, Italian with no English translation (two translations in French)
Jean Bodin	*Six Books of a Commonweal*, 1606, translation by Richard Knolles
Timothy Bright	*Treatise of Melancholy*, 1586
Arthur Brooke	*The Tragical History of Romeus and Juliet*, 1562
George Buchanan	*Rerum Scoticarum Historia*, 1582, no English translation
William Camden	*Remains . . . Concerning Britain*, 1605
Baldassare Castiglione	*The Courtier*, translation by Sir Thomas Hoby, 1561
William Caxton	*The Ancient History of the Destruction of Troy*, 1596 edition, translation of Raoul Le Fèvre
Geoffrey Chaucer	"The Knight's Tale"
	"The Miller's Tale"
	"The Legend of Good Women"
	Troilus and Criseyde
Henry Chettle	*Troilus and Cressida*, 1599 manuscript plot (with Thomas Dekker)
G.B. Giraldi Cinthio	*Epitia*, 1583, Italian with no translation
	Hecatommithi, 1565 edition, Italian with no translation
	Hecatommithi, 1583 edition, Italian with no translation

Gasparo Contarini	*The Commonwealth and Government of Venice*, 1599 translation by Lewis Lewkenor
Sir Thomas Coningsby	*Journal of the Siege of Rouen*, 1591 unpublished manuscript
Henry Constable	*Diana*, 1592
	Diana, enlarged edition of 1594
Thomas Cooper	*Thesaurus Linguae Romanae et Britannicae*, 1573 edition
Jean Créton	*Histoire du Roy d'Angleterre Richard*, French manuscript only
Richard Crompton	*Mansion of Magnanimitie*, 1599
Samuel Daniel	*Delia*, 1592
	The First Four Books of the Civil Wars, 1595
	Complaint of Rosamond, 1592
	Musophilus, 1599
	The Tragedy of Cleopatra, 1599 edition
	Letter from Octavia, 1599
Sir John Davies	*Nosce Teipsum*, 1599
Thomas & Dudley Digges	*Four Paradoxes, or Politique Discourses*, 1604
Richard Eden	*History of Travel*, 1577
Richard Edwards	*Damon and Pithias*, c. 1565
John Eliot	*Ortho-epia Gallica*, 1593
Thomas Elmham	*Vita et Gesta Henrici Quinti*, erroneously attributed to Elmham; in Latin
Sir Thomas Elyot	*The Governor*, 1531
Desiderius Erasmus	*The Praise of Folly*, in Latin
	The Praise of Folly, translation of Thomas Challoner in 1549
	A Modest Mean to Marriage, 1568 translation by N.L.
	A Merry Dialogue Declaring the Properties of Shrewd Shrews and Honest Wives, translation of 1557
Giovanni Fiorentino	*Il Pecorone (First story of Fourth day)*, 1558, Italian only
Edward Forset	*A Comparative Discourse of the Bodies Natural and Politique*, 1606
Robert Fabyan	*Chronicle*, 1533, first English version
	Chronicle, 1559 edition
Lucius Florus	*Roman Histories*, in Latin
Emmanuel Forde	*The Famous History of Parismus*, 1598
John Foxe	*Acts and Monuments of Martyrs*, 1570 edition
	Acts and Monuments of Martyrs, 1583 edition

Jean Froissart	*The Chronicle of England*, Lord Berners' translation of c. 1523–1525
George Gascoigne	*Supposes*, 1566
Geoffrey of Monmouth	*Historia Regum Britanniae*, Latin manuscript
Simon Goulart	*Thrésor d'histoires admirables et mémorables*, French, no translation until 1607 by Grimeston, but *Shrew* was written by 1594
John Gower	*Confessio Amantis*, 1554 edition
Richard Grafton	*A Chronicle at Large*, 1569
Saxo Grammaticus	*Historia Danica*, 1180–1208, in Latin
Robert Greene	*Planetomachie*, 1585
	Pandosto: The Triumph of Time, 1588
	The Second Part of Cony-Catching, 1591
Jakob Gretser	*Timon: Comoedia Imitata*, 1584, German playwright, no English translation
Edward Hall	*The Union of the Two Noble and Illustre Families of Lancaster and York*, 1548
Nicholas Harpsfield	*The Life of Sir Thomas More*, c. 1557 in manuscript only in 16th century
Samuel Harsnett	*Declaration of Egregious Popish Impostures*, 1603
Gabriel Harvey	*Pierce's Supererogation*, 1593
	Ciceronianus, 1577, in Latin
Robert Henryson	*The Testament of Cresseid*, 1532
Pontus Heuterus	*De Rebus Burgundicis*, 1584 in Latin (no translation until 1607)
John Higgins, ed.	*A Mirror for Magistrates*, 1574 edition
	A Mirror for Magistrates, 1587 edition
Ralph Holinshed	*The Chronicles of England, Scotland, and Ireland*, second edition, 1587
Homer	*Iliads (Books I–II, VII–XI)*, 1598, translation by George Chapman
	Achilles' Shield, 1598
King James I	*Daemonologies*, 1597
	The True Law of Free Monarchies, 1598
	Basilikon Doron, 1599
	A Counterblast to Tobacco, 1604
Sylvester Jourdain	*A Discovery of the Bermudas*, 1610
Richard Knolles	*History of the Turks*, 1603

Thomas Kyd	*Hamlet*, 1589 (probably by Kyd)	Thomas More	*Dialogue . . . of the Veneration and Worship of Images*, 1529
	The Spanish Tragedy, play, 1582~89		*The History of King Richard III*, unfinished manuscript in 1513; Latin in 1566; English in 1557
	Cornelia, 1594		
Lewes Lavater	*Of Ghosts and Spirits Walking by Night*, translation of R.H. in 1572	Anthony Munday	*Zelauto, or The Fountain of Fame*, 1580
Thomas Legge	*Richarus Tertius*, manuscript of 1579 (Latin tragedy performed at Cambridge)		*Fedele and Fortunio*, c. 1584 (actually by "M.A."; attributed to Munday)
Gerard Legh	*Accidence of Armory*, 1562		*John a Kent and John a Cumber*
John Leslie	*De Origine, Moribus, et Rebus Gestis Scotorum*, 1578 in Latin	Thomas Nashe	*Have With You to Saffron Walden*, 1596
Titus Livy	*The Roman History*, translation of 1600 by Philemon Holland		*Summer's Last Will and Testament*, performed 1592, pub. 1600
Thomas Lodge	"Truth's Complaint Over England," in *An Alarum Against Usurers*, 1584		*Christ's Tears over Jerusalem*, 1593
			Terrors of the Night, 1593, 1594
	Rosalynde, 1590		*Lenten Stuffe*, 1598–9
Lucca	*La Prima Parte de le Novelle del Bandello (Novella XXII)*, 1554		*Pierce Penniless*, 1592
Lucian	*Timon, or the Misanthrope*, in Greek; or Latin translation by Erasmus, 1506; or Italian translation by Lonigo, 1536; or French translation by Bretin, 1583	Ovid	*Metamorphoses*, in Latin
			Metamorphoses, Golding's translations of 1567 and 1575
			Fasti, 1340 translation by John Gower
John Lydgate	*The Ancient History and Only True Chronicle of the Wars [of Troy]*, 1555 edition, translated by Guido delle Colonne		*Fasti*, 1520, in Latin
		William Painter	*The Palace of Pleasure*, 1566–67, translation of Boccaccio
John Lyly	*Midas*, c. 1589	Matthew Paris	*Historia Major*, 1571 in Latin
	Campaspe, c. 1584	Orlando Pescetti	*Il Cesare*, 1594, Italian
	Euphues: The Anatomy of Wit, 1578/9	Plautus	*Menaechmi*, in Latin; may have known Wm. Warner's translation of 1595
	Gallathea, 1592		
	Endymion: The Man in the Moon, 1591		*Amphitruo*, in Latin manuscript
Thomas Lupton	*Too Good to be True*, 1581	Pliny the Elder	*The History of the World*, 1601 translation by Philemon Holland
Don Juan Manuel	*El Conde Lucanor*, 1350, in Spanish		
Gervase Markham	*How to Choose, Ride, Train, and Diet both Hunting Horses and Running Horses . . . Also a Discourse of Horsemanship*, 1593	Plutarch	*Lives of the Noble Grecians and Romans*, North's translation, 1579
			Lives of the Ancient Greeks and Romans, North's translation, 1603
Christopher Marlowe	*Hero and Leander* (with George Chapman), 1598	Thomas Preston	*Cambyses*, 1569
	Jew of Malta, c. 1589, pub. 1633	J. Rathgeb	*Journal*, 1602
	Tamburlaine, 1590	Barnaby Riche	*Riche, His Farewell to Military Profession*, 1581
	Edward II, c. 1592		
John Marston	*The Malcontent*, 1604		*The Adventures of Brusanus, Prince of Hungaria*, 1592
Masuccio Salernitano	*Il Novellino (fourteenth story)*, 1476, Italian only	Clement Robinson et alii	*A Handful of Pleasant Delights*, 1584
Thomas Moffett	*Of the Silkworms and their Flies*, 1599	Richard Robinson	anonymous *Gesta Romanorum (story 66)*, translation of Richard Robinson, 1577, 1595
Michel Montaigne	*Essays*, original French manuscript		
Jorge de Montemayor	*Diana Enamorada*, Spanish original in 1559; French translations in 1578 and 1587		

Samuel Rowley	*When You See Me, You Know Me*, 1604
Francis Sabie	*The Fisherman's Tale*, 1594
	Flora's Fortune, 1595
Saint Paul	*Acts of the Apostles*
	Epistle to the Ephesians
Flaminio Scala	*Flavio Tradito*, Italian manuscript
Reginald Scot	*Discovery of Witchcraft*, 1584
Nicolò Secchi	*L'Interesse*, 1581
	Gl'Inganni, 1547
Seneca	*Hercules Furens*, Studley translation of 1566 (Bullough says Jasper Heywood translation, 1561)
	Octavia, Studley translation, 1566
	Medea, Studley translation, 1566
	Hippolytus, Studley translation, 1567
	Thyestes, Jasper Heywood translation of 1560
	Oedipus, translation by Alexander Neville, 1563
Mary Sidney	*The Tragedie of Antonie*, 1595
	A Discourse of Life and Death, 1592
Philip Sidney	*The Countess of Pembroke's Arcadia*, 1590
	Astrophel and Stella, 1591
	An Apology for Poetry (A Defence of Poesy), 1595
Robert Sidney	*The Poems of Robert Sidney*, uncirculated manuscript
Alexander Silvayn	*The Orator*, L. Piot translation, 1596
Sir John Smith	*Instructions, Observations and Order Militarie*, 1595
John Speed	*History of Great Britaine*, 1611
Edmund Spenser	*Ruines of Rome: By Bellay*, 1591
	The Shepherd's Calendar, 1579
	The Faerie Queen, 1590 edition
	The Faerie Queen, 1596 edition
William Strachey	"True Repertory of the Wrack and Redemption of Sir Thomas Gates," a letter to the Virginia Company dated July 15, 1610
John Stow	*Annals, or a General Chronicle of England*, 1580
Tacitus	*Annales (Books I and II,)* translation of Richard Grenewey, 1598
Richard Tarleton	*The Famous Victories of Henry the Fifth*, unpublished manuscript; registered in 1594, but ascribed to Tarlton 1587 or 1588
	News Out of Purgatory, 1590

Lawrence Twine	*The Pattern of Painful Adventures*, 1576 and 1607 editions
William Tyndale	*The Obedience of a Christian Man*, 1528
Polydore Vergil	*Anglica Historia*, 1534, in Latin
The Virginia Council	"True Declaration of the Estate of the Colony in Virginia," 1610
Juan Luis Vives	*The Office and Duty of an Husband*, translation of 1555
R.W.	*The Three Ladies of London*, 1584
George Whetstone	*The Rocke of Regard*, 1576
	Promos and Cassandra, 1578 (play based on Giraldi Cinthio's *Hecatommithi*, 1565, and Claude Rouillet's *Philanira*, 1556)
	Heptameron of Civil Discourses, 1582
Sir Thomas Wilson	*The Art of Rhetoric*, 1553
Henry Wotton	*A Courtly Controversy of Cupid's Cautels*, 1578

Note: There are no source materials that were only available in the Greek language. The Greek source for *Timon of Athens* (Lucian's *Timon, or the Misanthrope*) was also available in Latin, Italian, and French translations. A ninth-century Greek source for *The Merchant of Venice*, called *Barlaam and Josaphat*, had been translated into Latin by the 13th century.

"Not of an age, but for all time"

Despite the author's prodigious scholarship, the Shakespearean plays have appealed to a wide range of audiences throughout history. In the author's own time, plays were attended by the lower-class "groundlings" who paid a penny to stand in the roofless courtyard of the theatre, as well as by the wealthy upper-class who paid more to sit in the covered seats that rose around the courtyard. Today, the plays are still enjoyed by people of every age, race, color, religion, political preference, education level, income level, and social status—all over the world. They have been translated into almost every written language (including Klingon).

Shakespeare's contemporary, Ben Jonson, declared in 1623 that these works were "not of an age, but for all time." Little did Jonson know they would not only be for all ages, but also for all humankind.

Alexander Dumas (1802–1870) summed it up:

> Shakespeare contains the whole of humanity. Anybody that studies Shakespeare, studies at once Corneille and Molière, Racine and Regnard—plus Shakespeare. Shakespeare is as much a writer of comedy as Molière and Regnard: look at Falstaff and Mercutio.

> He is as tragic as Corneille and Racine: see Othello and Richard III. Moreover, he's as much a dreamer as Goethe: see Hamlet; as dramatic as Schiller—think of Macbeth. As poetic . . . as ever poet has been: remember Romeo and Juliet.

> It results that, when an actor or actress has studied Shakespeare, they have studied everything . . . Shakespeare has divined everything . . . .

> In conclusion, Shakespeare, in the hands of a capable student, can at one and the same time replace Molière, Corneille, Racine, Calderon, Goethe, and Schiller.

So Who Was This Person?

This author, who was so well-schooled in the craft of writing, so learned, so well-rounded in pursuits and passions, so brilliant at examining and communicating human emotion, so adept at turning a phrase more succinctly and elegantly than anyone before or since—and who has influenced writers, readers, and cultures all over the world for centuries—who *was* this person?

Part One

The Question

The center of this obsession [of Shakespeare-worship], then as now, is the Shakespeare biography, or rather lack thereof. It is by now somewhat cliché to be reminded that we know next to nothing about Shakespeare's life, that our knowledge is confined mainly to dry legal records or unsatisfying contemporary references, and that so little about him is "revealed" in his works.

Michael Keevak [1]

Documented Data

- While he was alive, there is no record of anyone personally meeting William Shakespeare.

- There is no record that William Shakespeare was ever acknowledged by a patron.

- There is no record that he was ever paid for writing.

- There are no documents or even references to hearsay that Shakespeare acknowledged himself as a writer, nor did anyone in his family ever mention he was a writer.

- There is nothing from Shakespeare in his handwriting except six signatures on legal documents. One is illegible (on his will), and all are spelled differently.

- Not one piece of an original Shakespearean manuscript or draft has ever been found.

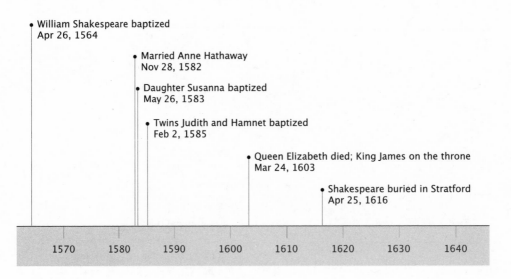

- William Shakespeare baptized
  Apr 26, 1564

- Married Anne Hathaway
  Nov 28, 1582

- Daughter Susanna baptized
  May 26, 1583

- Twins Judith and Hamnet baptized
  Feb 2, 1585

- Queen Elizabeth died; King James on the throne
  Mar 24, 1603

- Shakespeare buried in Stratford
  Apr 25, 1616

1570   1580   1590   1600   1610   1620   1630   1640

1 The Man Named *William Shakespeare*

HUNDREDS OF THOUSANDS OF BOOKS have been written about the man named William Shakespeare, the plays, the sonnets, and the Authorship Question—some say Shakespeare is the most researched subject on earth. Yet there is no other human being so famous about whom we know so little.

We do know these facts:[2] William Shakespeare was born in April of 1564 in Stratford-upon-Avon, England. In 1582, at the age of 18, he married Anne Hathaway, who was eight years older than Shakespeare— and pregnant. They had three children by the time he was twenty. His parents, wife, and two daughters were illiterate[3] (his son died at age eleven).

At some point between the ages of twenty and thirty, Shakespeare left his wife and children to go to London where he was sometimes an actor and a shareholder in various acting companies. He often returned to Stratford-upon-Avon where he bought the second-largest house and other properties; sued people for small sums and was sued; sold a load of stone to a Mr. Chamberlin; illegally held eighty bushels of grain during a shortage; owed a shepherd two pounds which was unpaid on the shepherd's death; and defaulted on his property taxes several times. He died in 1616 in Stratford at the age of 52 and was buried in an unmarked grave at the front of the village church.

What We Don't Know

We don't know if William Shakespeare ever went to school. There was a local grammar school he might have attended from about five to ten years of age. There are no records of the school, Shakespeare's attendance, or the school's curriculum, yet some scholars maintain that "Shakespeare received in the Stratford grammar school a formal education that would daunt many college graduates today . . . ."[4]

With this supposedly remarkable public education in town, it's interesting to note that of the nineteen leaders of the town at the time (aldermen and burgesses), only six of them could write their names.[5] Shakespeare's own father was a high bailiff for a short time; he signed documents with an x.

Not one piece of handwriting exists that was penned by the man named William Shakespeare. Not one letter from him, not one note, not a journal or a diary, not a poem, not one scrap of a manuscript for a play—nothing exists except six signatures on legal documents, and each is spelled differently. All signatures are within the last four years of his life; three of them are on his will.

There is only one letter written to him—a request for a loan—and that letter was never sent.

Because books were so valuable, it was standard practice at the time to put your name or bookplate inside. Ardent Shakespeareans have scoured the land for centuries and never found a book Shakespeare owned or even appeared to have used.

Philip Henslowe was the most important theater owner, manager, and company banker of the time. He recorded letters to and from writers and actors, but not one letter to or from William Shakespeare.

In his account books, called a "diary," Henslowe recorded personal and business contacts from 1592 through 1603. "The importance of his diary and papers to dramatic history cannot be overemphasized."[6] Although Henslowe was most closely associated with the Rose theater (as opposed to the Globe), he recorded a number of performances of five Shakespearean plays,[7] but never mentioned Shakespeare.

Who Met William Shakespeare?

Considering the body of Shakespeare's work during this era of prolific publishing, letter-writing, diary-keeping, gossip-mongering, satires, and recorded comments by everybody about everybody, it is remarkable that "No one who met him made a record during his lifetime of what he was like or what he said or did." [8]

Katherine Duncan-Jones notes that "We do not have a single letter written by Shakespeare, nor even a single incontrovertibly genuine passage of his handwriting, and the Shakespeare biography-industry did not get going until nearly a century after his death. By the time of Nicholas Rowe's biographical essay in 1708 [92 years after Shakespeare's death] oral traditions had proliferated, but there was no one alive who remembered Shakespeare." [9]

Diana Price points out, "Shakespeare is the only alleged writer of any consequence from the period who left no personal contemporaneous records revealing that he wrote for a living." [10]

Shakespeare's own family is never recorded as having mentioned that he was a writer.

There is no record that Shakespeare was personally acquainted with any of the other writers, philosophers, or intellectual thinkers of the time, with the exception of Ben Jonson. Jonson talked about him years after Shakespeare died. [11] (Shakespeare is listed as an actor in two of Jonson's plays; one of these plays was booed off the stage.[12])

Shakespeare himself wrote not one word outside the plays and poems—not a word about anyone's death or life or marriage or beauty, not even a word about himself. John Berryman remarked about this lack, "Through an age brimming with eulogy and lament, his friends will publish and die, his son will die, Essex fall, Southampton languish in the Tower and emerge, the Queen lie speechless sweating and perish, James be crowned, without poems from Shakespeare." [13]

If He Were a Rich Man

It is documented that William Shakespeare held varying portions of the leases of the Blackfriars gatehouse and the Globe theater, that he received 4.5 yards of red cloth as an actor, and once received £20[14] to share with the Lord Chamberlain's troupe for a performance of a play, but there is no evidence that William Shakespeare was ever paid as a playwright.

Nonetheless, Shakespeare became quite wealthy and bought various homes and pieces of property: In 1597 he paid £60 cash for the summary record to transfer the second-largest house in Stratford, called New Place, into his name (we don't know how much he actually paid for the house).[15] He then apparently proceeded to repair and remodel the house. In May of 1602 he paid £320 cash for 107 acres of land. In September that same year he acquired another quarter-acre of land with a cottage and garden. Also in September he paid a fee equal to one-fourth the yearly value of New Place; in July of 1605 he paid £440 cash for a half-interest in a lease of tithes (£20 unpaid several weeks later); in 1613 he paid £140 for the Blackfriars gatehouse,[16] £80 of which was in cash (the gatehouse was a living establishment near the Blackfriars theater in London).

It's remarkable that there are so many financial records for William Shakespeare, yet no record of income. It's a mystery acknowledged by many Shakespearean researchers. "If Shakspere* had sold all 37 known Shakespeare plays, he would have earned somewhere between £185 and £350 during his lifetime (the going rate for plays increased from roughly £5 to £10 after James I came to the throne). There is not one record to verify a penny of that alleged income."[17]

*Some writers use the spelling "Shakspere" to indicate the man from Stratford, since that's the way he spelled it on his will. This is opposed to the spelling "Shakespeare" to indicate the author of the works.

Yet Gerald Bentley, in *The Profession of Dramatist in Shakespeare's Time*, reports, "Fortunately there are a good many records of the financial rewards of the playwright."[18] Not even Bentley's research, however, could find one record referring to William Shakespeare as playwright or as getting paid. And in the records Bentley did find of other writers of the day, none made as much money as Shakespeare spent.

In 1599, Shakespeare became part of the shareholders' syndicate for the Globe; in 1608 the King's Men, of which Shakespeare was a member, assumed the lease of the Blackfriars theater. Shakespeare shared the income from the two theaters during these years, but he also had to help pay the expenses for the leases, upkeep, and operations. This income was not a significant source of wealth for any of the shareholders.

As Diana Price explains in *Shakespeare's Unorthodox Biography*, "All of Shakspere's undisputed personal records are non-literary, and that is not only unusual—it is bizarre. Statistically, it is also a virtual impossibility. Over seventy historical records survive for Shakspere, but not one reveals his supposed primary professional occupation of writing. . . . All the Shakespearean literary allusions are either impersonal, confined to literary criticism, or ambiguous."[19]

Literary References to Shakespeare

Scholars of Shakespeare regularly cite items like the following as "proof" that the person who wrote the reference was a friend of William Shakespeare's and personally knew that he wrote the plays, but no such assurance can be assumed.

> *These may suffice for some Poeticall descriptions of our auncient Poets, if I would come to our time, what a world could I present to you out of Sir Philip Sidney, Ed. Spencer, Samuel Daniel, Hugh Holland, Ben: Johnson, Th. Campion, Mich. Drayton, George Chapman, John Marston, William Shakespeare, & other most pregnant wits of these our times, whom succeeding ages may justly admire.*

> William Camden (1605)
> from *Remaines of a greater Worke concerning Britaine, Poems* [20]

There are twenty-one contemporaneous reviews *of the works attributed to William Shakespeare;* not one mentions the man himself. Here are two examples (a complete list is in Appendix E):

> *Will you read Virgil? Take the Earl of Surrey. Catullus? Shakespeare and Marlowe's fragment. Ovid? Daniel. Lucan? Spencer. Martial? Sir John Davies and others. Will you have all in all for Prose and verse? Take the miracle of our age, Sir Philip Sidney.*[21]

> Richard Carew, 1614

> [Note that Carew considers Sir Philip Sidney to be a better writer than Shakespeare. Sidney had been dead for almost thirty years by this time.]

> *To Master W. Shakespeare.*

> *Shakespeare, that nimble Mercury thy brain,*
> *Lulls many hundred Argus-eyes asleep . . .*
> *Who loves chaste life, there's Lucrece for a Teacher:*
> *Who list read lust there's Venus and Adonis,*
> *True model of a most lascivious letcher. . . .*[22]

> Thomas Freeman, 1614

I wonder whether this is an honorific mention—Mercury bored Argus to sleep by talking incessantly.

These writers were clearly familiar with *the work attributed to* William Shakespeare, but there are no details in their statements that suggest they were *personally acquainted* with the dramatist.

Many critics claim that the most significant proof of his authorship is Shakespeare's name on the title pages of printed editions of the plays. Yet the name "William Shakespeare" is also printed on other plays published during his lifetime, such as *Sir John Oldcastle, A Yorkshire Tragedy, The London Prodigal, Locrine,* and *Thomas Lord Cromwell*—but experts insist Shakespeare did NOT write these other plays.

> Only half of the Shakespearean plays were in print during Shakespeare's lifetime, as explained in Chapter 15.

So is the name on the printed title page proof or not proof? Either it is or it isn't: Either the name proves Shakespeare wrote *A Yorkshire Tragedy* and *The London Prodigal,* or it does NOT prove he wrote *The Merchant of Venice* and *Much Ado About Nothing.* It can't do both.

Millions of books are printed with the name "George Eliot" as author on the covers, and thousands of reviews of George Eliot's work refer to George Eliot as the author. But that does not prove there was a man named George Eliot who actually wrote the work. There was no man named George Eliot, of course—Mary Ann (or Marian) Evans wrote the work attributed to the pseudonym.

If even one written statement existed from anyone during Shakespeare's lifetime that clearly indicated that person personally knew William Shakespeare and referred to him as a great author of plays, we wouldn't have an Authorship Question.

Missing: William Shakespeare

"The allusions to Shakespeare that perhaps speak the loudest are the ones that are not there."[23] So begins Diana Price in a description of some of the contemporaneous documents that do NOT mention the great William Shakespeare.

This includes Thomas Lodge complimenting fellow writers Lyly, Spenser, Daniel, Drayton, and Nashe—but not Shakespeare.

Or the historian William Camden, quoted earlier, in his work of 1607 in which he neglected to mention Shakespeare when discussing the important people in Stratford-upon-Avon. Yet 1607 was the height of Shakespeare's supposed popularity.

The author of *The New Metamorphosis* (1600–1615) did not name Shakespeare in a list of over thirty poets and playwrights of the day.

In a 1613 defense of poetry called *Abuses Stript, and Whipt,* the author George Wyther praises Spenser, Daniel, Sidney, Drayton, Jonson, Chapman—but not Shakespeare.

In 1598, Francis Meres published *Palladis Tamia: Wits Treasury,* in which he mentions eleven known plays of Shakespeare's by name (and one as yet unknown play). Yet when he updated this book in 1634 and again in 1636, Meres did not add any more information regarding Shakespeare's plays.

Especially telling is Ben Jonson's *Timber, or Discoveries,* a collection of thoughts published 24 years after Shakespeare's death in 1616, in which Jonson recommends the best authors to read—Sidney, Donne, Gower, Chaucer, and Spenser—but not Shakespeare. This is most interesting considering Jonson had written the eulogy in the First Folio calling Shakespeare the "Soul of the Age" and the "Star of Poets."

Ms. Price muses, "Most people would rank Shakespeare with the major figures of his day, such as Francis Bacon, Spenser, Jonson, Sir Francis Drake, or Sir Walter Raleigh. Historical records prove that these men interacted with each other or were personally recognized for the activities with which their names are linked. If Shakespeare personally interacted with any of the opinion-setters, decision-makers, or influential personages of the time, the historical record is inexplicably and uncharacteristically silent."[24]

The following page charts this discrepancy: It is true we have more documentation about the man named William Shakespeare than we do of any other dramatist of the time, with the exception of Ben Jonson. But within all the documentation, nothing says Shakespeare was a playwright. We have *less* documentation for the other writers, but in their fewer papers, it is clear they wrote for a living.

The Literary Paper Trail

	1. Evidence of education	2. Record of correspondence, esp. concerning literary matters	3. Evidence of having been paid to write	4. Evidence of a direct relationship with a patron	5. Extant original manuscript	6. Handwritten inscriptions, receipts, letters, etc. touching on literary matters	7. Commendatory verses, epistles, or epigrams contributed or received	8. Miscellaneous records (e.g., referred to personally as a writer)	9. Evidence of books owned, written in, borrowed, or given	10. Notice at death as a writer, within a year of death
Ben Jonson	Yes	Yes	Yes	Yes	Yes	Yes	Yes	Yes	Yes	Yes
Thomas Nashe	Yes	Yes	Yes	Yes	Yes	Yes	Yes	Yes	Yes	•
Philip Massinger	Yes	Yes	Yes	Yes	Yes	Yes	Yes	Yes	•	•
Gabriel Harvey	Yes	Yes	•	Yes	Yes	Yes	Yes	Yes	Yes	•
Edmund Spenser	Yes	Yes	•	Yes	•	•	Yes	Yes	Yes	Yes
Samuel Daniel	Yes	Yes	Yes	Yes	Yes	Yes	Yes	Yes	•	Yes
George Peele	Yes	Yes	Yes	Yes	Yes	Yes	Yes	Yes	Yes	•
Michael Drayton	•	Yes	Yes	Yes	•	Yes	Yes	Yes	•	Yes
George Chapman	•	Yes	Yes	Yes	•	Yes	Yes	Yes	Yes	•
William Drummond	Yes	Yes	•	•	Yes	Yes	Yes	Yes	Yes	•
Anthony Mundy	•	•	Yes	Yes	Yes	Yes	Yes	Yes	•	Yes
John Marston	Yes	Yes	Yes	•	•	Yes	Yes	Yes	Yes	•
Thomas Middleton	Yes	•	Yes	•	Yes	Yes	•	Yes	•	•
John Lyly	Yes	Yes	•	Yes	•	Yes	Yes	Yes	•	•
Thomas Heywood	•	•	Yes	•	Yes	Yes	Yes	Yes	•	Yes
Thomas Lodge	Yes	Yes	•	Yes	•	•	Yes	Yes	Yes	•
Robert Greene	Yes	•	Yes	Yes	•	•	Yes	Yes	•	Yes
Thomas Dekker	•	Yes	Yes	•	•	Yes	Yes	Yes	•	•
Thomas Watson	Yes	•	•	Yes	•	•	Yes	Yes	•	Yes
Christopher Marlowe	Yes	•	•	Yes	•	•	•	Yes	Yes	Yes
Francis Beaumont	Yes	•	•	•	•	•	Yes	Yes	•	Yes
John Fletcher	•	•	Yes	•	•	•	Yes	Yes	Yes	•
Thomas Kyd	Yes	Yes	•	Yes	•	•	•	Yes	•	•
John Webster	•	•	Yes	•	•	•	Yes	Yes	•	•
William Shakespeare	•	•	•	•	•	•	•	•	•	•

Diana Price, *Shakespeare's Unorthodox Biography: New Evidence of an Authorship Problem* (Westport & London: Greenwood Press, 2001), pp. 302–313; updated from her web site: www.Shakespeare-Authorship.com. Used with permission from Greenwood Publishing Group, Inc.

Proof by Patron

All biographies of Shakespeare insist that the Earl of Southampton was his patron, based on the dedication of Shakespeare's two lengthy poems (*Venus and Adonis, The Rape of Lucrece*) to the young Earl, who was nineteen years old at the time, ten years younger than William Shakespeare. Yet there is absolutely no evidence that the Earl ever acknowledged William Shakespeare as a patron—or in any other way.

Of this era, John Berryman affirms that for patronage, "Poets dedicated often at random, fishing."[25] In *Literary Patronage in the English Renaissance*, Michael G. Brennan elaborates: "Generally, aristocratic patronage involved a patron's personal assistance only for a minority of writers, and they were usually those who either lived within the patron's household or were privileged to mingle with members of the nobility on terms of friendly intimacy. For the rest, panegyric dedications brought no guarantee of either acceptance or reward, nor did patrons necessarily consider themselves responsible for the contents or quality of works which were prefaced by their names. Numerous literary tributes were addressed to members of the aristocracy on a purely speculative basis—many of them achieving nothing."[26]

Or as Arthur Marotti points out, "One is well advised to view with some skepticism writers' claims of having special relationships with the patrons whose favors they sought. This is especially so in the case of [Thomas] Churchyard who, in a touching moment of candor, revealed to [Sir Walter] Raleigh that of the sixteen books he had by then published, he was seldom even acknowledged by those to whom they were dedicated."[27]

"Richard Robinson, who published from 1576 to 1600," says Gerald Bentley in *The Profession of Dramatist in Shakespeare's Time*, "set down his receipts for a number of his publications . . . . Apparently he tried for a gift from a patron in connection with each publication, but he was only intermittently successful."[28] For instance, from the Earl of Warwick, Robinson received nothing. For a dedication to the president of the London Archery Society, he received 5 shillings; to the Dean of St. Paul's, 10 shillings; to Sir Philip Sidney, £2, plus 10 shillings more (half a pound) added by his father; the Earl of Rutland and Sir Christopher Hatton both gave him £3 for works dedicated to them.

Neither the Earl of Southampton, anyone who corresponded with the Earl, nor anyone who wrote about him ever mentioned the name William Shakespeare. Charlotte Stopes spent twenty-eight years in research for her book on the life of this Earl,[29] but never found a single reference to Shakespeare. Neither did G. P. V. Akrigg who more recently studied newly discovered archives of the Southampton family.[30]

The two narrative poems, *Venus and Adonis* and *The Rape of Lucrece*, were published in 1593 and 1594, five years before the first printed play appeared with Shakespeare's name on it. Never again did Shakespeare dedicate any written work to the Earl of Southampton (or to anyone)—a difficult proof of patronage, at best.

It is an assumption that Shakespeare had a patron. The idea suits the mythology of Shakespeare, particularly since he would have needed funding in his formative years, so the assumption is usually presented as a documented fact. Even Berryman admits, "He seems not to have known Southampton much." [31]

Traditions vs. Truth

But those who shape the popular imagination usually find fiction more memorable than fact.

Peter W. M. Blayney
1997

Many traditions have been handed down about William Shakespeare, casting him as a schoolmaster or as a butcher in his father's trade killing calves while making speeches in high style. Some maintain he "must have been" a law clerk, or that he poached deer on Sir Lucy's land—all gossip dispensed almost 100 years after Shakespeare's death. We read about Shakespeare drinking with Michael Drayton and Ben Jonson—hearsay almost 40 years after Shakespeare's death. Numerous posthumous anecdotes came into popular belief, but no contemporaneous documentation for any of these events exists.

But there *is* contemporaneous documentation for several anecdotes that we don't hear so much about. For instance, there is a record that "Shakespeare the Player" got his coat-of-arms under false pretenses[32] (having a coat-of-arms gave a man the official title of "gentleman," which in the English social system was a step up the ladder). Shakespeareans make much of the fact that he became a "gentleman" and little of the fact that he came by it dishonestly. Note that when the accusation was made in 1602, at the height of his supposed career, Shakespeare was pejoratively referred to as a "player," not as a dramatist, writer, or poet. (A subsequent hearing defended the eligibility of Shakespeare's *father*, in whose name William had applied.)

There is documentation that Shakespeare was sued along with two women and Francis Langley (owner of the Swan theater) for an incident in which another man was in "fear of death" from Shakespeare. Langley himself is a man whose "biography is a litany of unscrupulous activities, greed, and extortion."[33]

Shakespeare and several other "wicked people" were fined in Stratford for hoarding grain during a shortage; Shakespeare had the second-largest hoard. He is also listed as dodging his property taxes a number of times.

And there's the story that he often stopped at a place called The Tavern on his way to and from London and had an affair with the innkeeper's wife and even had a son by her, named William Davenant, a story perpetuated by the boy himself as he grew up.

William Davenant grew up to become England's poet laureate upon Ben Jonson's death. The cartilage in Davenant's nose was destroyed during third-stage syphilis, but he got married three times, even without his nose.[34]

The only gossip written about Shakespeare as a man while he was alive (as opposed to a reference to the poems or plays) was written in a diary belonging to a law student: A woman told the actor Richard Burbage, after seeing a performance in which he played Richard III, to come to her house that night under the name of Richard III. Shakespeare overheard the invitation, went to the woman's house, and was "entertained, and at his game ere Burbage came." When the message was brought that Richard III had arrived, Shakespeare sent back a message that William the Conqueror came before Richard III. The diarist added a note that "Shakespeare's name William," indicating Shakespeare wasn't so famous that everyone would know his name.[35]

If we collect the contemporaneous, documented events in Shakespeare's life, which are more reliable than the posthumous and apocryphal "traditions" in the law clerk and poacher category, we see: Shakespeare married an older woman whom he had already impregnated, then later abandoned this wife and his three children to run off to London; he was a cheat and a tax evader; he fathered a child with his host's wife, slept around indiscriminately, and while carousing with an extortionist and two women (one of them married), he created such trouble that a man feared for his life; he didn't pay back the shepherd from whom his wife had to borrow two pounds.

Shakespeare's image has been selectively polished with many assumptions. Yet most of what is passed off as truth about his life is fabricated. How did that happen?

The Shakespeare Biography Industry

In the long run it is far more dangerous to adhere to illusion than to face what the actual fact is.

David Bohm, physicist
1948

When you next read a biography of William Shakespeare, take a yellow highlighter and mark every phrase such as "surely," "must have," "doubtless," and "almost certainly," to make obvious how much of what we know about Shakespeare is speculative fiction.

Because there is so little to work from in creating a life of William Shakespeare, biographers have embellished various elements deliberately, thus shaping our image of the man. For example, in 1693 (77 years after Shakespeare died) an antiquarian named Mr. John Dowdall wrote an account of his visit to Stratford. He stated that Shakespeare himself wrote his own epitaph, which reads like a nursery rhyme:

> *Good friend, for Jesus' sake forbear*
> *To dig the dust enclosèd here.*
> *Bles't be the man that spares these stones*
> *And curs't be he that moves my bones!*

Says Oscar James Campbell in *The Reader's Encyclopedia of Shakespeare,* "The attribution does no credit to the poet and is generally rejected."[36]

Yet the same document also states that Shakespeare ran away from his master to London and was received in the playhouse as a servitor. Campbell says, "The most interesting piece of information in this report is that Shakespeare's first position in the theater was that of a servitor or hired man."[37] So Campbell claims one statement in the letter as fact and another in the same letter as fictitious, based on nothing except it "does no credit to the poet."

Unfortunately, this sort of "scholarship" is widely practiced, apparently to compensate for a scarcity of facts. It seems to be irresistible. Alden Brooks, an amateur Shakespearean sleuth, complained in 1937, "As an example of an almost universal procedure, take this statement of principle made by [Canon] Beeching [a highly respected scholar of the time]. 'If the evidence is good enough, if it fits in with the mental picture we have formed of the dramatist from his plays, and is not inconsistent with contemporary testimony, we shall incline to accept it, giving the great man the benefit of any doubt.'"

Brooks is incredulous and continues, "In what other field of study would such a principle have authority? Imagine a scientist accepting as 'good enough' evidence, evidence that must first pass muster by agreeing with a preconceived idea, and that for this acceptance has none the less received the benefit of any doubt."[38]

Unfortunately, some writers don't differentiate between documented facts and speculative fiction. In his 2,500-page *Annotated Shakespeare*, 1943, editor A. L. Rowse claims, "When the actor-playwright met the fascinating half-Italian Emilia Lanier . . . he fell completely under her spell, partly out of pity for her unhappiness." Rowse goes on to explain that Shakespeare begged his dear friend, the nobleman Southampton, to write to the woman on his behalf, "driving the poet to distraction."[39] Shakespeare was "a strongly sexed heterosexual" who couldn't help himself. All of which comes directly from Rowse's colorful imagination, but presented in his ponderous tome as patent facts. The recent books by Michael Wood (*In Search of Shakespeare*) and Stephen Greenblatt (*Will in the World*) are often just as speculative, presenting many of their fanciful notions as if they are confirmed facts.

Don Foster, Vassar professor who recently proved "A Funeral Elegy" to be written by William Shakespeare (and subsequently proven wrong), candidly admitted in his book, *Author Unknown*, "Professors of literature are rarely required to be 'right' about anything. In my academic discipline, we don't usually produce facts—we produce incredibly clever interpretive commentary."[40]

It's no wonder that the entire Authorship Question has often been dismissed as "poppycock." With professional scholars contributing unprofessional interpretation and embellishment, public knowledge of Shakespeare's life remains a field of petrified assumptions.

Oops—He Died

When William Shakespeare died in 1616 there was no mention of his death, no eulogies, and no record of his funeral. Numerous public, documented tributes were made upon the deaths of other literary figures of the time: Philip Sidney, Jonson, Beaumont, Drayton, Spenser, Fletcher, Chapman, Massinger.

"The Renaissance elegy was a form 'accessible to writers of all ages and abilities'. . . . This may have been even more true for women, since the need to commemorate the dead could override gender restrictions, making the elegy one of the few forms of original writing open to women."[41] So even though commemorating the dead was so important that even *women* were *allowed* to write elegies, not one person wrote a poem for the man named William Shakespeare on his death.

In his will, Shakespeare gave away clothes, money, silver, a sword, alms for the poor, rings for friends, and the famous (and only) bequest to his wife, one that was inserted between the lines as an apparent afterthought, of his "second-best bed."

But there is not a single mention of any of the expensive books he had to have read and studied. Nor does his will mention one word about anything he ever wrote—not a poem, play, or written work of any kind.

Shakespeare was buried in an unmarked grave inside the Stratford village church, while other (whom today we consider "lesser") poets and dramatists of his day—such as Jonson, Spenser, Beaumont, and Drayton, as well as Chaucer—were buried in Poets' Corner of Westminster Abbey in London. A statue of Shakespeare was not installed in Poets' Corner until 1740, more than a century after he died.

The Sum of the Whole is Greater than the Parts

In a list of the apparent deficiencies of William Shakespeare as the author of the Shakespearean canon, it is easy to dismiss each item one at a time. For each of the facts (shown below, left), I have heard Shakespeareans' stock responses (on the right).

No appeal to evidence can ever convince true believers, because nothing can disprove their fixed idea.

Scott McCrea, *The Case for Shakespeare*, 2005

Facts	Fast Thinking
There is no indication that William Shakespeare had an education. If he went to school, it was to the local small-town grammar school from about the ages of five to ten years old.	*"**Of course** he attended the local school and had a remarkable education there."* *"He was a genius who didn't need formal schooling."* *"There is no evidence of extensive booklearning in the plays."*
There is no record that he had training in any of the specialty areas of which he writes.	*"He **surely** read about the speciality areas."* *"He **surely** had training; it's just not recorded."*
He owned no books.	*"He didn't put his name in his books."* *"He **surely** studied in the library of a local aristocrat."*
His entire family was illiterate.	*"So what."* *"Just because his daughter Susanna couldn't recognize her husband's handwriting doesn't mean she was illiterate."* *"Just because his father, mother, wife, daughter Judith, and granddaughter Elizabeth each signed with an X doesn't mean they were illiterate."*
He had no friends among the literati.	*"Just because no other writer mentioned him in writing doesn't mean he didn't have any literary friends."*
No one who knew him personally, such as his family and Stratford friends, referred to him as a writer.	*"Merely an oversight on the part of his family and friends."*

Facts	Fast Thinking
There is no record, while he was alive, that anyone mentioned meeting William Shakespeare.	*"Merely an oversight on the part of the gossipy English and Europeans."*
There is no indication that he was ever recognized by a patron or spent time in a noble household.	*"Merely an oversight on the part of his patron and the noble households."*
He never referred to himself as a writer.	*"Merely an oversight on his own part."*
There is no documentation he was ever paid as a writer.	*"It's lost."* *"So what."*
This greatest writer in the English language never wrote a single thing outside the printed works.	*"It's lost. All lost."* *"He was just a working man writing plays to put bread on the table."*
There are no scraps of Shakespeare's handwriting outside of the six signatures on legal documents.	*"They're lost."* *"So what."*
There is no shred of an original manuscript.	*"Manuscripts were regarded as superfluous after printing and the paper they were written on was recycled."* (See Chapter 16.) *"We have no manuscripts of plays written by well-known writers of the time that were performed on the public stage and that were put into printed form."* (See Chapter 16.)
Nobody noticed when he died.	*"This is not unusual."*
He was buried in an unmarked grave in a village church instead of in Poet's Corner in Westminster Abbey, where lesser writers were laid to rest with honor.	*"His unmarked grave is at the front of that village church, which proves he was very important."*
He is not known to have associated with any other great writers or thinkers of his time, nor to have participated in the two most important literary circles of his time.	*"So what."* *"He **surely** associated with writers, thinkers, philosophers, statemen, and participated in the literary circles. It just wasn't documented."*

Each of these items, taken individually, can be dismissed. But when these facts are viewed as a collection, the situation starts to look a little suspect.

What if you come home from work and notice the following:

> A window is broken.
>
> Inside the house there are muddy footprints.
>
> A light is on that wasn't on when you left the house.
>
> A dresser drawer is open.
>
> Clothes have been thrown onto the floor.
>
> Your diamond brooch is not where you left it.
>
> The back door is unlocked and open.

Each of these individual circumstances has a possible explanation: The kids playing ball broke the window; your teenager walked in with muddy feet, your husband came home to get something and left a light on, the housekeeper left a dresser drawer open, etc. But *when you view the facts as a collection,* you might entertain a different possibility, one that needs to be explored.

To be able to credit the most influential literary canon in human history to the man named William Shakespeare, one has to accept a mass of assumptions which range from implausible to bizarre.

Taken all together, the Authorship Question becomes urgent—not only to consider new possibilities, but to insist on valid documentation from original sources.

But Wait . . .

THERE ARE LITERALLY MILLIONS of extant documents from the sixteenth and seventeenth centuries that are still in readable condition.[42] I mentioned that not one document records anyone meeting, dining, or speaking with the great William Shakespeare.

That might not be quite true: There was a letter, written in 1603, that was described in 1865 by a reputable historian and tutor living at Wilton House in England. The letter was from the aristocrat Mary Sidney Herbert, the Countess of Pembroke, to her younger son Philip asking him to bring King James from Salisbury back to Wilton House. She wanted to plead with the king on behalf of Sir Walter Raleigh, who was about to get his head cut off.

It was claimed that Mary Sidney wrote in the letter that the play *As You Like It* was to be presented. And she wrote, "We have the man Shakespeare with us."[43] Unfortunately, the letter is now lost,[44] and many scholars don't believe it ever existed.[45]

But it is known that the King held court at Wilton House for most of the autumn in 1603 to escape the bubonic plague that was making its periodic sweep through London. The Kings Men were paid £30 to perform before the king at Wilton House on December 2, 1603. (Mary did prevent the execution of Raleigh at that time, although he was eventually beheaded.)

Who was this woman, Mary Sidney Herbert, the Countess of Pembroke—possibly the only person to have mentioned meeting the man named William Shakespeare?

Part Two
The Woman

Make the doors upon a woman's wit,
and it will out at the casement;
shut that, and 'twill out at the key-hold;
stop that, 'twill fly with the smoke
out at the chimney.

Rosalind in *As You Like It*, 4.i.154–157

Documented Data

- Mary Sidney was the most educated woman in England of her time, comparable only to Queen Elizabeth.

- She owned an extensive private library and developed a personal alchemy laboratory.

- She hunted, hawked, bowled, sang, played musical instruments, composed music, stitched needlework, and studied medicine.

- She managed several large estates requiring expertise in logistics, accounting, medicine.

- She read, wrote, and spoke multiple languages fluently.

- She developed the most important literary circle in English history.

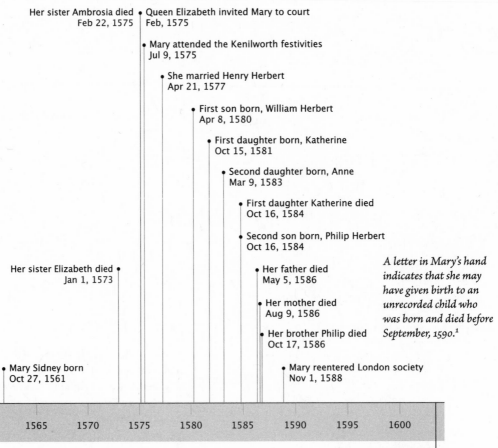

Her sister Ambrosia died • Queen Elizabeth invited Mary to court
Feb 22, 1575   Feb, 1575

• Mary attended the Kenilworth festivities
Jul 9, 1575

• She married Henry Herbert
Apr 21, 1577

• First son born, William Herbert
Apr 8, 1580

• First daughter born, Katherine
Oct 15, 1581

• Second daughter born, Anne
Mar 9, 1583

• First daughter Katherine died
Oct 16, 1584

• Second son born, Philip Herbert
Oct 16, 1584

Her sister Elizabeth died •
Jan 1, 1573

• Her father died
May 5, 1586

• Her mother died
Aug 9, 1586

• Her brother Philip died
Oct 17, 1586

A letter in Mary's hand indicates that she may have given birth to an unrecorded child who was born and died before September, 1590.[1]

• Mary Sidney born
Oct 27, 1561

• Mary reentered London society
Nov 1, 1588

| 1565 | 1570 | 1575 | 1580 | 1585 | 1590 | 1595 | 1600 |

Queen Elizabeth died

2 *Mary Sidney* as a Young Woman

In Tickenhill Manor, near the Severn River on what used to be the border of Wales in Bewdley, Mary Sidney was born.[2] It was October 27, 1561, three years before William Shakespeare was born.

Her mother, Mary Dudley Sidney, was sister to Robert Dudley, the Earl of Leicester (Queen Elizabeth's closest friend; some say, lover). The Dudley and Sidney families had been members of the English royal court for generations. Thus "before Mary was eleven, her family had consolidated so much power in this alliance of faith and blood that it controlled approximately two thirds of the land under Elizabeth's rule: Ireland, Wales, Warwickshire [home of William Shakespeare], and the north, as well as vast holdings scattered throughout England."[3]

Mary Dudley Sidney (the mother) is known historically as the woman who nursed Queen Elizabeth through smallpox, then caught the disease herself, almost died, and was so horribly disfigured that she never appeared in public again without a veil (Mary Sidney, the daughter, was one year old at that time).

Mary grew up mainly on the Sidney family estate in Kent, called Penshurst Place, with many summers spent in Ludlow Castle on the border of Wales. She was exceptionally well educated. While her older brother, Philip, attended Shrewsbury School for his primary education, Mary was tutored at home along with her younger brothers (Robert, who was enrolled in Oxford at about age 12, and Thomas) and her two surviving sisters (Elizabeth and Ambrosia). She read, wrote, and spoke Latin, French, and Italian, probably Greek and Welsh, and possibly some Hebrew and Spanish (her mother interpreted Spanish for the Queen, and Mary had Spanish books in her library[4]).

She was trained in poetry, rhetoric, and the classics, as was expected of every well-bred person, and medicine, as was expected of every female head of household, especially women who were to run large manors. Several medical remedies created in her own laboratory have been preserved, as well as her formula for invisible ink.[5] She created exquisite needlework, sang, read and composed music, and played the lute, virginals (an early spinet or small harpsichord), and possibly the violin. It seems there was always music in the house—it is recorded that her father paid almost £67 for violins "that perhaps represents the initial costs of establishing a violin consort in his household."[6] The family even had their own jester, or fool; it is recorded that her father paid for "3 yards of motley to make his coat."[7]

I am ambitious for a motley coat.

Jacques in
As You Like It, 2.vii.43

She grew up riding horses, hawking, hunting, using a bow and arrow, and later had a lawn bowling green on her own estate.

Mary's father, Henry Sidney, was Lord President of the Marches (border counties) of Wales and later the Lord Deputy Governor of Ireland. "Because Henry Sidney had a particular interest in geography and cartography, his children were probably better schooled in those fields than most."[8]

Mary was exposed to and involved in theater all her life. The account books of the Sidney family indicate that troupes of actors reenacted the adventures of Robin Hood and his merry men, singers celebrated May Day, and minstrels played at midsummer.[9]

The account books at Ludlow Castle during her lifetime recorded performances of children's theater troupes, the Lord of Sussex players, and Lord Stanford players.[10] An elaborate Christmas season at the castle while Mary was in attendance included the nobility performing in a production of King Arthur's Knights of the Round Table.

A regular stream of acting companies are recorded as having performed throughout the years Mary was at Ludlow: Acting troupes sponsored by the Lords Stafford, Bergavenny, Burghley, Berkeley, Hundson, Chandos, Essex, Darcy, the Earls of Worcester, Oxford, Pembroke, and

Leicester, the Queen's Men from both Queen Elizabeth and Queen Anne, the Master of the Revels players, as well as sundry musicians, minstrels, and jesters all provided theater and music.[11]

"Some players [actors] were obviously known to the Sidneys, since Sir Philip [Mary's older brother] later stood as godfather to the son of Richard Tarleton, an actor in Leicester's company."[12] Leicester was Mary's uncle, Robert Dudley.

This active family interest and household participation in theater grew to be a lifelong passion of hers. Even in her 40s, it is documented in court records that Mary Sidney was one of three women who participated in all four masques (plays intended for amateur performance by the nobility in the royal court, not on the public stage) written by Ben Jonson. The other two women were Queen Anne (James' wife) and Mary's daughter-in-law, Susan de Vere (married to Philip).

She grew up surrounded by literary pursuits. Her mother was well-educated and interested in writing—verses penned by her and Mary's father in Latin and English (with French phrasing) are extant. Her mother's female friends were also well educated, such as the five remarkable Cooke sisters who were among the first generation of woman humanist scholars. Her mother's best friend was Mildred Cooke, married to William Cecil Lord Burghley, the Queen's chief minister. Another good friend, Anne Cooke, was the mother of Sir Francis Bacon. Mary's aunt Frances Sidney, the Countess of Sussex, was the founder of Sidney Sussex College at Cambridge in 1589, when Mary was 28 years old. Mary grew up surrounded by intelligent, educated women in a country governed by a remarkable woman.

"There was probably never an age in which women held a greater sway physically and intellectually than during this period."[13]

"One daughter of very good hope"

When Mary was six years old, her seven-year-old sister Elizabeth died, and when Mary was thirteen, her beloved eleven-year-old sister Ambrosia died. Family documents tell us she and Mary often dressed in matching outfits. She was now the only surviving daughter. Queen Elizabeth wrote a condolence letter to the parents and suggested that since God had left them yet "one daughter of very good hope,"[14]

The earth hath swallow'd all my hopes but she— She is the hopeful lady of my earth.

Thirteen-year-old Juliet's father in *Romeo and Juliet*, 1.ii.14–15

she should come to live at court. Thus Mary Sidney became one of the Queen's maids-of-honor at thirteen. (The term "maid-of-honor" is a phrase invented by Mary.[15])

Her first experience of court spectacle was the nineteen-day extravaganza at Kenilworth, the magnificent estate of her uncle Robert Dudley (the Queen's dear friend, or "favorite"). It is documented that she attended with her parents and her older brother, Philip Sidney. The festivities at Kenilworth were an extravagant display of merry-making—allegorical figures, sibyls, and mythological creatures all spouting poetry at every turn, musical concerts, lavish hunting expeditions, dancing, fireworks, bearbaiting, theater, a movable island on the lake, barges carrying musicians, Italian tumblers. "Besides all this, they had upon the pool a Triton riding on a mermaid eighteen feet long; as also Arion on a dolphin's back, with rare music."[16]

Thou rememberest
Since once I sat upon
a promontory,
And heard a mermaid
on a dolphin's back . . .
Oberon in A Midsummer
Night's Dream, 2.i.149–50

After Kenilworth, the royal court progressed to other castles and country estates, then on to Woodstock. Here, "Mary's first notice from a poet appropriately stressed her lineage and her intelligence"[17]:

Tho young in years yet old in wit, a gest due to your race,
If you hold on as you begin, who is it you'll not deface?

paraphrase according to the meanings of the words when they were written:
Though you are young, you are intelligent and quick beyond your
years, a bearing attributable to your family heritage;
If you continue as you've begun, who is it you'll not outshine?

. . . for I never knew
so young a body
with so old a head.
The Duke in The Merchant
of Venice, 4.i.162, referring
to Portia who is disguised
as a judge

At court, Mary's exposure to and involvement in theater continued. "In general [Queen Elizabeth] was one of the theater's most devoted patrons. Numerous plays were put on at court throughout the Christmas holidays, sometimes as many as eleven in one season."[18]

Theater was provided not only by the public acting troupes sponsored by noblemen, but the production of plays was a common pastime among the lords and ladies at court. Noted poets such as Ben Jonson, Francis Beaumont, and John Fletcher wrote masques. Family and court records document that Mary Sidney actively participated throughout her life as an actress in these productions.

At court, Mary caught the eye of Henry Herbert, the second Earl of Pembroke. He was a widower and "the one great Protestant earl who was not a member of the Dudley family."[19] Mary's uncle Robert Dudley arranged her politically motivated marriage with Henry when she was 13 years old; they married when she was 15 and the Earl was 43.

Henry Herbert,
2^d Earl of Pembroke

Not long after their wedding they went to live at his estate, Wilton House, on 14,000 acres in Wiltshire, just outside of Salisbury. The river Avon flowed through her land. The estate was very near to Stonehenge, about 80 miles south of Stratford-upon-Avon, and only a few miles from another town on the Avon called Stratford-sub-Castle.

The Earl indulged Mary in her passion for alchemy, chemistry, mineralogy, and medicine at Wilton House where she developed a complete laboratory. Sir Walter Raleigh's half-brother Adrian Gilbert was an assistant in her lab.[20] Gilbert also acted as a landscape architect and developed the elaborate gardens at Wilton based on symbolic geometry "in such admirable art-like fashion, resembling both divine and moral remembrances."[21]

Mary developed an extensive private library, regarded as an exceptionally large one for its time. Around 1660 John Aubrey mentioned his visit to it in *The Natural History of Wiltshire:* "Here was a noble library of books, choicely collected in the time of Mary Countess of Pembroke. I remember there was a great many Italian books; all their poets; and books of politics and history."[22] Aubrey also noticed a Latin manuscript written in Julius Caesar's time, and *The Book of Hawking and Hunting,*[23] by Juliana Berners, printed in 1486 (yes, an English woman wrote the book).

"Wilton soon established itself as a base away from town not only for the Herberts, but also for the Dudleys and Sidneys. In such a group, so closely knit by familial and marital bonds, it was difficult to spot where a family gathering ended and a political summit began."[24]

Mary and Philip Sidney

To begin to understand Mary Sidney's influence in the literary world developing around her, it is first important to understand her brother Philip's part, as well as Mary's attachment to this brilliant older brother.

The entire Sidney family was known for being devoted to each other. Mary was very close to all three of her brothers—Philip, Robert, and

Thomas—but especially to Philip. He was the quintessential Elizabethan courtier: learned, traveled, cultured, courteous, athletic, intelligent, handsome, and single. "He was the rising sun in the Court of an ageing and childless Queen."[25] He has been compared with the late John Kennedy, Jr., in his charm, charisma, "great expectation,"[26] and tragic early death.

When Philip was a young boy, he was sent to a private school in Shrewsbury for his education. At the age of 13, he entered Christ Church College at Oxford. At 17, Philip left for his European tour, considered to be the finishing school for young aristocrats in preparation for their lives in the service of the Crown.

Philip was welcomed into all the royal courts of Europe, and so impressed the heads of states that while still seventeen years old he was created a Baron by the King of France. (This title did him no good in England, however. Queen Elizabeth disdained foreign titles for her courtiers and had been heard to remark, "My dogs wear my collars.")

Unfortunately, on his return to England Philip still did not receive from the Queen the favors she routinely bestowed upon other courtiers. Whether the Queen was angered by his foreign honors, his meetings in Prague with the English Catholic priest Edmund Campion, his familial relation to Robert Dudley, Earl of Leicester, or any of several other perceived transgressions, she constantly passed him over for honors and even refused to knight him.

"The grandson of a duke, godson of a king, nephew to four earls, brother-in-law of an earl, brother of an earl, and uncle to three earls, he was himself, through nearly all his life, an untitled commoner . . . the only title which he in fact received, that of knight, was granted for the sorriest of reasons and brought him neither commendation nor reward."[27]

Philip was eventually knighted in January, 1583, age 28, but not by the Queen. He became a knight through an old friend, the German Prince Casimir. Casimir nominated Philip as his proxy when he was unable to attend his own installation as a Knight of the Garter, but a proxy had to be someone of equivalent rank so Philip was hastily knighted.

Philip exercised his literary skills in various forms at court. "Sidney played an increasingly public role in Elizabethan high society as a deviser of and participant in . . . 'royal pastimes.'" These included tiltyard appearances, playlets, and allegorical displays ranging from the "pastoral show" at Wilton, the mini-drama "The Lady of May," to the elaborate and mysterious *Triumph of the Four Foster Children of Desire*, "which made use of elaborate machinery, lavish costumes and armor, caparisoned horses, and 'special effects' on a grand scale."[28]

But after Philip wrote his famous letter[29] to the Queen against her proposed marriage with the French Duke of Alençon, and after making an enemy of the nettlesome Earl of Oxford, "Sidney withdrew from the Queen's presence, attaching himself instead to the society of his sister and the increasingly absorbing literary pursuits that he shared with her. . . . Though he was not explicitly banished from Court, he was tied up, if not muzzled, and had for the time being to abandon hopes for advancement in rank or a posting abroad."[30]

In his self-imposed "retirement" from court, Philip turned to writing full-time, along with his worthy and admired sister. "The numerous dedications to her [Mary Sidney] portray a chaste, pious, gracious and intelligent woman, the exact female counterpart of her famous brother: if Philip Sidney was depicted as the ideal Renaissance man, then Mary came to personify the ideal Renaissance woman."[31]

A Life of Literary Pursuits

At Mary's request, Philip composed *The Countess of Pembroke's Arcadia*,[32] which is "the most important work of prose fiction in English of the sixteenth century."[33] "None of the writers of his age approached his influence in the field of prose romance."[34]

Philip also wrote an essay called *The Defense of Poesy*. "Considered the finest work of Elizabethan literary criticism, Sidney's elegant essay suggests that literature is a better teacher than history or philosophy."[35]

His lengthy sonnet sequence, *Astrophil and Stella*, popularized the sonnet form in England.[36] *Astrophil and Stella* "was to be followed by dozens of sonnet sequences in the 1590s, but it must be remembered that when Sidney wrote it there were no other sonnet sequences in English . . . Sidney's is not only the earliest English sonnet sequence properly so described: it is also arguably the best, in terms of assured poetic technique, richness of tone, and subtlety of organization." [37]

It is important to keep in mind that at this time in history, the only place English was spoken was in England—it was rare to hear it spoken even in Wales, Ireland, or Scotland. According to Roma Gill, "At the start of the sixteenth century the English had a very poor opinion of their own language: there was little serious writing in English, and hardly any literature. Latin was the language of international scholarship, and Englishmen admired the eloquence of the Romans." [38]

Yet "When [Philip] Sidney came to devote himself more fully to his 'unelected vocation' as a poet, he wrote entirely in English . . . *he hoped to lay the foundations of a body of literature in his own language which might ultimately stand comparison with the Greek and Latin classics."* [39] [emphasis added]

I want to emphasize the point that there were great works of literature in Greek, Latin, Italian, and French, but few in English; it became Philip Sidney's—and then Mary Sidney's—mission in life to create great literary works in the English language.

The Wilton Circle

Through their own writing, as well as the patronage and encouragement of other writers, Mary and Philip developed the most important and influential literary circle in England, referred to today as the Wilton Circle.

"The developments at Wilton in the 1580s, then, were an attempt on the part of the Sidneys to instigate a revival of English aristocratic culture. For her [Mary's] own part, in providing Wilton's hospitality and its unique atmosphere of these crucial years of Elizabethan literature, the Countess was also re-creating in her own, perhaps typically English, way a pattern of patronage by noble women that had flourished in Italy and France for a century or more." [40]

Scholars agree on the importance of the poetic and dramatic work of Mary and Philip Sidney. As John Buxton said in 1966, "We remember how much the Florentine Renaissance owed to the Medici, but we forget that a similar debt was owed by the English Renaissance to the Sidneys."[41]

It's interesting to note that in his writing, "[Philip] Sidney's development of women who are active and strong without being evil or dominant over men was something new in literary history."[42]

It is even more interesting, in light of the Authorship Question, that "In his portrayal of women as intelligent, capable, and morally responsible human beings, *Sidney very likely paved the way for writers like Shakespeare* who came after him to develop strong, active heroines and to alter, however slightly and gradually, cultural perceptions of women."[43] [emphasis added]

Albert Baugh, in *A Literary History of England*, 1948, summed it up in this way:

> In three directions, to be sure, Sidney's actual achievement ranks him among the very highest of the Elizabethan writers. None but Shakespeare and Spenser produced a finer sonnet sequence. None but Ben Jonson surpassed him as a literary critic. None of the writers of his age approached his influence in the field of prose romance. Yet if *Astrophil and Stella,* the *Defense of Poesy,* and the *Arcadia* had never been published, we should still have to regard Sidney as a cultural landmark. Seconded by his sister, he created through his personal efforts and his personal charm a new artistic atmosphere more stimulating than any other that then existed. Together— or more strictly in succession, for the Countess of Pembroke (1561–1621) was but twenty-five when her brother died— they first produced what in the highest sense may be called the academic spirit in English letters.[44]

Mary and her brother Philip laid a remarkable groundwork for the future of the English language and literature. Devoted to each other and to the literary arts, they stimulated excellence and perfected their craft, while inspiring the writers of the Wilton Circle.

Give Sorrow Words

The early stage of the Wilton literary circle was also the beginning of a devastating period for Mary. Her first son, William Herbert, was born when she was eighteen years old, and she had two daughters in the next three years. Tragically, on the very day Mary gave birth to her second son, Philip Herbert, her little girl Katherine died, the day after her third birthday. In the Sidney family Psalter it is written of this little girl that she was "a child of promised much excellency if she might have lived."[45]

Little more than a year after Katherine's death, Mary's father died. Mary's brother Philip, recently married, was away in the Netherlands fighting for the Queen, who did not allow him to return home to comfort his mother nor to attend their father's funeral.

Three months after her father's death, Mary's mother died.

"[Philip] Sidney could have borne the news of his parents' death, [Dr. Thomas] Moffett thought, if he had received no other bad news: but it was reported to him also that his sister was mortally ill—'such a sister . . . as no Englishman, for aught I know, had ever possessed before.'"[46]

As Moffett mentioned, Mary was near death herself when, two months after her mother's burial, she received news that her beloved brother Philip had been killed in the war, fighting for the Protestant cause in Zutphen, Netherlands—a musket ball shattered his thigh bone during a battle and he died twenty-five days later.

Philip Sidney was the first untitled "commoner" in English history to be given a state funeral at St. Paul's Cathedral. This would not happen again until Lord Nelson (1805) and Sir Winston Churchill (1965) were also so honored.

Forward—in All Directions

Then in November of 1588, two years after Philip's death, Mary returned strong and energetic once again to the London court for the season. She's twenty-seven years old. And she returned in style:

> On Thursday the wife of the Earl of Pembroke made a superb
> entrance into this city. She has been for more than a year on her
> estates in the country. Before her went 40 gentlemen on
> horseback, two by two, all very finely dressed with gold chains.
> Then came a coach in which was the Countess and a lady, then
> another coach with more ladies, and after that a litter
> containing the children, and four ladies on horseback. After
> them came 40 or 50 servants in her livery with blue cassocks.[47]

Fourteen years after her introduction to the royal court as a thirteen-year-old maid-of-honor, Mary's back to court—older, stronger, sadder, wiser, and with a mission. The literary mantle had been passed to her by her beloved mentor, Philip.

Could this be the profile of the author of the Shakespearean canon: Extremely intelligent; superbly educated; literate in a number of modern and classical languages; holder of a celebrated library of books; politically involved; active in the sports, artistic, and intellectual pursuits that appear in the plays; living in the society about which the plays are written?

But that's not enough.

Documented Data

- Mary Sidney's single-minded mission in life was to create great works in the English language. She studied the art and craft of writing.

- She published her own "appropriate" (and pioneering) work: Two translations from French, one of which was the first English play published by a woman; the first original pastoral prose piece published in English by a woman; and several original poems.

- She circulated other work in manuscript form: A translation from Italian; the Psalms of David; other lyrics and poems.

- She was the first English woman who did not apologize for publishing her work.

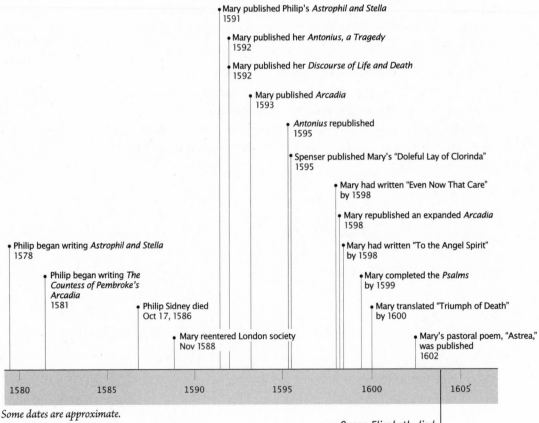

- Mary published Philip's *Astrophil and Stella* 1591
- Mary published her *Antonius, a Tragedy* 1592
- Mary published her *Discourse of Life and Death* 1592
- Mary published *Arcadia* 1593
- *Antonius* republished 1595
- Spenser published Mary's "Doleful Lay of Clorinda" 1595
- Mary had written "Even Now That Care" by 1598
- Mary republished an expanded *Arcadia* 1598
- Mary had written "To the Angel Spirit" by 1598
- Mary completed the *Psalms* by 1599
- Mary translated "Triumph of Death" by 1600
- Mary's pastoral poem, "Astrea," was published 1602

- Philip began writing *Astrophil and Stella* 1578
- Philip began writing *The Countess of Pembroke's Arcadia* 1581
- Philip Sidney died Oct 17, 1586
- Mary reentered London society Nov 1588

| 1580 | 1585 | 1590 | 1595 | 1600 | 1605 |

Some dates are approximate.

Queen Elizabeth died

34

3 Mary Sidney's *Life of Literature*

MARY SIDNEY's most recent biographer, Margaret P. Hannay, describes the countess:

> Mary Sidney, like her brother Philip, was brilliant, learned, witty, articulate, and adept at self-presentation. . . . In an age when women were required to be chaste, silent, and obedient, she may have been chaste—but she was certainly eloquent and assertive. She was able to challenge the norms for women while appearing to follow them, empowered by her own clever self-promotion, her brother's legendary death, and her husband's money.[1]

Mary Sidney—brilliantly educated, passionate about literature, her life informed with marriage, birth, joy, loss, and grief—was determined to take up her brother's literary mantle. Her Wilton estate "became a workshop for poetical experimentation, the seedbed of a literary revolution. Centered upon Wilton's congenial and hospitable lifestyle, on Sidney's example, and on his sister's enlightened enthusiasm, it became the still center of the rapidly turning world of late Elizabethan literature."[2]

Gary F. Waller, in his book, *Mary Sidney, Countess of Pembroke: A Critical Study of her Writings and Literary Milieu*, 1979, remarks:

> After [Philip's] death, it was at Wilton that the Countess gathered the poets and men of letters to continue her brother's work to improve English literature.[3]

> Indeed, it would seem . . . that after Sidney's death in 1586, the Countess took a more active part in the literary experiments of the Circle, and developed a much more highly organized salon, closer to its continental models.[4]

> She presumably felt her duty was to further the revolution begun by her brother—and probably in the process discovered that her own talents lay not merely in enlightened encouragement [of other writers] but in actively writing herself.[5]

Navarre shall be the wonder of the world; Our court shall be a little Academe, Still and contemplative in living art.

King Ferdinand in *Love's Labor's Lost*, 1.i.12–14

In awe and admiration, contemporaries called Wilton House a "little university," an "academie," and Mary Sidney's own "court." She gathered the greatest writers around her, acted as an active patron to many, requested specific works from various poets, and encouraged others to develop their writing talents and expand their skills.

> Wilton did indeed become "like a College"; writers like Spenser, Greville, Daniel, Drayton, Breton, Watson, and Fraunce gathered formally or informally around "the Lady of the plain," dedicating their common efforts to what they saw as the betterment of English letters.[6]

> This circle of Lady Pembroke became one of the most interesting coteries in the history of English literature.[7]

> For almost two decades Mary Sidney and her household at Wilton became one of the most dynamic cultural influences in late Elizabethan England, and at the center of Wilton's life were her writings.[8]

Mary Sidney dedicated herself to the discipline and craft of writing. She also acted as mentor to other writers in her circle. Numerous documents refer to her indirectly or directly educating others. The poet Thomas Churchyard wrote "A Pleasant Conceit" in 1593 in which he celebrated twelve of the young ladies in Queen Elizabeth's court, and says of Mary Sidney:

> *A gem more worth than all the gold of Ind,*
> *For she enjoys the wise Minerva's wit,*
> *And sets to school our poets everywhere,*
> *That doth presume the laurel crown to wear.*[9]

The laurel wreath, or crown, is an ancient symbol of an accomplished or celebrated writer.

The renowned and gentle poet Samuel Daniel was a lifelong friend of Mary's. In 1607 he wrote a dedication to her son and gave credit to Mary for having taught him to write:

> *Having been first encouraged and framed thereunto by your*
> *most worthy and honorable mother, and received the first*
> *notion for the formal ordering of those compositions at Wilton,*
> *which I must ever acknowledge to have been my best school and*
> *thereof always am to hold a feeling and grateful memory.* [10]

The doctor in her employ, Doctor Thomas Moffett, gently chastised Mary for working too hard. Referring to her translations of Petrarch and her work versifying the Psalms of David, he wrote:

> *Vouchsafe a while to lay thy task aside,*
> *Let Petrarch sleep, give rest to Sacred Writ,*
> *Or bow or string will break, if ever tied.*
> *Some little pause aideth the quickest wit.*[11]

Mary was celebrated as a writer of the highest distinction in her own time. An indication of her reputation can be seen in the book of miscellaneous verse titled *Bel-vedére* (1600), in which she is ranked as a writer alongside Edmund Spenser, Philip Sidney, and William Shakespeare with no notice of her gender. Three quotations from one of Mary's works are also cited. Queen Elizabeth is the only other female writer mentioned in the book (but she is, of course, compared only to King James; one would not dare compare the Queen with a mere citizen). "Such presentation of a non-royal woman author was unprecedented in England, for women were admonished to be silent, not to write and publish."[12]

Mary is also the only woman (again, besides Queen Elizabeth) mentioned as a writer in Francis Meres' *Palladis Tamia: Wits Treasury*, the publication so important to literary history because it lists the known Shakespearean plays up to 1598. Meres, comparing Mary to Octavia as a patroness, exclaims that "she is a most delicate Poet," and finds her comparable to Sappho as the Tenth Muse.[13]

> *Octavia . . . was exceedingly bountiful unto Virgil . . . so learned Mary, the honorable Countess of Pembroke, the noble sister of immortal Sir Philip Sidney, is very liberal unto Poets; besides she is a most delicate Poet, of whom I may say, as Antipater Sidonius writeth of Sappho: Dulcia Mnemosyne demirans carmina Sapphus, Quaesivit decima Pieris unde foret.**

> *Sweet Mnemosyne (goddess of memory), amazed at the poems of Sappho, asked from whence she became the tenth muse.

Examples of Her Work

Below are a number of samples from various works of Mary Sidney Herbert, the Countess of Pembroke.

Translations

Most of Mary's known major works are translations, plus original versification of the *Psalms*.

The literary form of translation was an acceptable genre for an Elizabethan noblewoman, especially if she translated what was considered to be "appropriate" works.

> Translations were 'defective' and therefore appropriate to women; this low opinion of translating perhaps accounts for why women were allowed to translate at all. . . . By engaging in this supposedly defective form of literary activity, women did not threaten perceptions of male superiority; any competence they displayed could be dismissed by denigrating the task of translation itself.[14]

The Psalms of David

One of her literary projects was the metaphrasing and versifying of most of the *Psalms of David*. She consulted a French psalter and the 1560 Geneva Bible, among other psalm versions, as well as commentaries in English, French, and Latin. This project was begun by her brother Philip but unfinished at his death in 1586. He had rewritten just 43 of the 150 psalms.

Professor and critic Gary Waller explains that Mary "revised his versions and then finished the remainder herself. She [did so], however, not merely with a mere literal versification; her psalms involve an unprecedented degree of literary experimentation, and are the basis of her claim to literary, as opposed to mere historical, significance." [15]

"At their best the Countess' psalms, even more than [Philip] Sidney's, display a remarkable intensity of poetic evocation, formal inventiveness and intellectual subtlety." [16]

Other experts agree on Mary's achievements of the *Psalms*:

> The Countess' virtuosity in experimenting with stanzaic and metrical forms is most striking. Overall . . . her Psalms contain 164 distinct stanzaic patterns, with only one repeated. There are, as well, 94 quite distinct metrical patterns. [17]

> Indeed, there is no collection of lyrics in English which uses such a wide range of metre. [18]

> This was an unprecedented achievement in English verse, leading Hallett Smith to call the Sidneian *Psalms* a "School of English Versification." [19]

> Pembroke's "technical virtuosity in inventing verse forms can scarcely be exaggerated" and suggests that had she chosen a different "poetic matter" than the *Psalms,* "her accomplishment might be better appreciated today." [20]

> In this work, [Mary] Sidney perhaps found a legitimate means of imitating the language, patterns, and images often used to construct a masculine paradigm of authorship. [21]

> In these *Psalms,* Lady Pembroke's ability as a translator is admirably shown. The consensus of critical opinion seems to

be that her part shows more literary merit than her brother's, especially in the skill and ingenuity of the versification.[22]

And what an ironic statement R.E. Pritchard has made:

> If the Countess, as Elizabethan lady, could not easily speak out publicly, she could at least, as mouthpiece for the Psalmist's (male) voices, and like some of Shakespeare's heroines, speak most for herself when speaking as another.[23]

Short examples of Mary's *Psalms*, alongside the originals, show the inventiveness and skill she used in making the *Psalms* her own verse. The spellings here are modernized.

Psalm 69, first verse, **Geneva Bible:**

> *Save me, O God, for the waters are entered even to my soul.*
>
> *I stick fast in the deep mire, where no stay is: I am come into deep waters, and the streams run over me.*
>
> *I am weary of crying: my throat is dry, mine eyes fail, whiles I wait for my God.*

Psalm 69, first verse, **Mary Sidney:**

> *Troublous seas my soul surround:*
> *Save, O God, my sinking soul,*
> *Sinking, where it feels no ground,*
> *in this gulf, this whirling hole,*
> *waiting aide, with earnest crying:*
> *calling God with bootless crying—*
> *Dim and dry in me are found*
> *Eye to see, and throat to sound.*

Psalm 57, line 4, **Geneva Bible:**

> *My soul is among lions:*
> *I lie among the children of men,*
> *that are set on fire:*
> *whose teeth are spears and arrows,*
> *and their tongue a sharp sword.*

Psalm 57, line 4, **Mary Sidney:**

> *My soul encagèd lies with lion's brood,*
> *villains whose hands*
> *are fiery brands,*
> *Teeth more sharp than shaft or spear,*
> *Tongues far better edge do bear*
> *Than swords to shed my blood.*

Portion of Psalm 58, **Geneva Bible:**

> *Break their teeth, O God, in their mouths:*
> *Break the jaws of the young lions, O Lord.*
>
> *Let them melt like the waters, let them*
> *pass away: when he shooteth his arrows,*
> *let them be as broken.*
>
> *Let him consume like a snail that melteth,*
> *and like the untimely fruit of a woman,*
> *that hath not seen the sun.*
>
> *And men shall say, Verily there is fruit*
> *for the righteous: doubtless there is a*
> *God that judgeth in the earth.*

Portion of Psalm 58, **Mary Sidney:**

> *Lord crack their teeth,*
> *   Lord crush these lions' jaws,*
>
> *So let them sink as water in the sand:*
> *   When deadly bow their aiming fury draws,*
> *   Shiver the shaft ere past the shooter's hand.*
>
> *So make them melt as the dishoused snail,*
> *   Or as the embryo, whose vital band*
> *   Breaks ere it holds,*
> *   And formless eyes do fail to see the sun,*
> *   Though brought to lightful land.*
>
> *While all shall say, the just rewarded be,*
> *There is a God that carves to each his own.*

Even without the advantage of training in rhetorical devices and poetic analysis, one can see that these comparisons provide a sense of the mastery, art, and experimentation of Mary Sidney's superb translations.

"The Doleful Lay of Clorinda"

The Renaissance elegy was another literary form open to women. This is one of several elegies Mary wrote for her brother, although she wasn't allowed to publish them in the university collections upon his death in 1586.

"The Doleful Lay of Clorinda," a ballad, was published in Edmund Spenser's "Astrophel" in *Colin Clouts Come Home Again* in 1595 and attributed by Spenser to Mary Sidney. Below are the first four stanzas of the sixteen-stanza lay.

To whom should I complain? Did I tell this, who would believe me?

Isabella in
Measure for Measure,
2.iv.172

AY ME, to whom shall I my case complain
That may compassion my impatient grief?
Or where shall I unfold my inward pain,
That my enriven heart may find relief?
  Shall I unto the heavenly powers it show?
  Or unto earthly men that dwell below?

To heavens? ah they alas the authors were,
And workers of my unremedied woe:
For they foresee what to us happens here,
And they foresaw, yet suffred this be so.
  From them comes good, from them comes also ill,
  That which they made, who can them warn to spill.

To men? ah, they alas like wretched be,
And subject to the heavens ordinance:
Bound to abide what ever they decree,
Their best redress, is their best sufferance.
  How then can they like wretched comfort me,
  The which no less, need comforted to be?

Then to my self will I my sorrow mourn,
Sith none alive like sorrowful remains:
And to my self my plaints shall back return,
To pay their usury with doubled pains.
  The woods, the hills, the rivers shall resound
  The mournful accent of my sorrow's ground.

A Discourse of Life and Death

In 1590, Mary translated from French Philippe de Mornay's *A Discourse of Life and Death*. She first published it in 1592. About this work, Diane Bornstein notes that

> [Mary] Sidney's most notable additions are her continuations or expansions of metaphors that appeared in the original. . . . At a time when English syntax was still in an unsettled state, the countess translated Mornay's sophisticated French prose into a smooth, idiomatic English that fully reflected its rhetorical ornaments. A comparison with Edward Aggas' translation [the first English translation], with its awkward phrases and excess words, shows how skillful the Countess' work was. Her changes even improved the original by making it more concise, more specific, and more metaphorical. One can only regret that the Countess limited herself to the silent art of translation and did not write her own meditations.[24]

The following pages present the opening paragraphs of *A Discourse of Life and Death*. On the left-hand page you'll see the translation by Edward Aggas, a contemporary of Mary's, and on the right-hand page is Mary's version from the French original.

published in 1577 ## Edward Aggas, opening of *A Discourse of Life and Death*

It is a strange matter wherat I cannot sufficiently marvel, to behold how the laborer to the end to cease from his labors doth even in manner hasten the course of the Sun. The Mariner for the attaining unto the desired Haven, saileth forward amain, and from as far as he can espy the coast, to shout out for joy. And the Pilgrim or traveler, to take no rest before his journey be ended. And yet that man in the meantime being bound to perpetual labor, tossed with continual tempests, and tired with many rough and miry paths, is nevertheless unwilling to look upon or come near to the end of his journey, sorrowful to see the Haven of his assured rest, and with horror and fear to draw toward his lodging and peaceable dwelling place.

Our life resembleth a right Penelope's web, which still must be woven and woven again, a Sea abandoned to all winds, which sometime inwardly sometime outwardly tormenteth it, and a troublesome path, through frost and extreme heat, over steep mountains and hollow valleys, among deserts and thievish places.

This is the communication that we do use, being at our work, pulling at our oar, and passing through this miserable path and rough way. And yet when death cometh to finish our labors, when she stretcheth forth her arm to help us in to the Haven, and when after so many passages and troublesome hostelries, she seeketh to bring us into our true habitation; into a place of comfort and joy, where we should take heart at the view of our land, and drawing toward our happy dwelling place, should sing and rejoice; we would if we might have our own wills, begin our work again, return our Sails into the wind, and voluntarily retire back into our journey.

Mary Sidney, opening of *A Discourse of Life and Death*   published in 1592

It seems to me strange, and a thing much to be marvelled, that the laborer to repose himself hasteneth as it were the course of the Sun; that the Mariner rows with all force to attain the port, and with a joyful cry salutes the descryed land; that the traveller is never quiet nor content till he be at the end of his voyage; and that we in the meanwhile tied in this world to a perpetual task, tossed with continual tempest, tired with a rough and cumbersome way, cannot yet see the end of our labor but with grief, nor behold our port but with tears, nor approach our home and quiet abode but with horror and trembling.

This life is but a Penelope's web, where we are always doing and undoing; a sea open to all winds, which sometime within, sometime without never cease to torment us; a weary journey through extreme heats, and colds, over high mountains, steep rocks, and thievish deserts. And so we term it in weaving at this web, in rowing at this oar, in passing this miserable way.

Yet lo when death comes to end our work, when she stretcheth out her arms to pull us into the port, when after so many dangerous passages and loathsome lodgings she would conduct us to our true home and resting place; instead of rejoicing at the end of our labor, of taking comfort at the sight of our land, of singing at the approach of our happy mansion, we would fain (who would believe it?) retake our work in hand, we would again hoist sail to the wind, and willingly undertake our journey anew.

Ending Mary's translation:

Neither ought we to fly death, for it is childish to fear it; and in fleeing from it, we meet it. . . . It is enough that we constantly and continually wait for her coming, that she may never find us unprovided. For as there is nothing more certain than death, so is there nothing more uncertain than the hour of death, known only to God, the only Author of life and death, to whom we all ought endeavor both to live and die.

> *Die to live,*
> *Live to die.*

To sue to live,
  I find I seek to die,
And, seeking death,
  find life.

Claudio in *Measure for Measure*, 3.i.42–43

The Tragedy of Antonie

Mary's published writings include *Antonius* or *The Tragedy of Antonie*, a translation from French of Robert Garnier's *Marc Antoine*. It was first published in 1592 with *A Discourse of Life and Death*, then separately in 1595.

> *Antonie* was the first public expression of the Countess'
> dedication to her brother's literary ideals; it was a deliberate
> step to further the literary revolution he had started. . . . *She*
> *was deliberately taking up the matter of raising literary standards*
> *in a form which was becoming increasingly popular—the drama.*[25]
> [italics added]

Below are two examples from Mary's translation:

ANTONIUS:
> *Well; be her love to me or false, or true,*
> *Once in my soul a cureless wound I feel.*
> *I love, nay burn in fire of her love:*
> *Each day, each night her image haunts my mind,*
> *Her self my dreams: and still I tired am,*
> *And still I am with burning pincers nipt.*

Antonius, lines 919–924

CLEOPATRA:
> *Ah, weeping Niobe, although thy heart*
> *Beholds itself enwrap'd in causeful woe*
> *For thy dead children, that a senseless rock*
> *With grief become, on Sipylus thou stand'st*
> *In endless tears: yet didst thou never feel*
> *The weights of grief that on my heart do lie.*

Antonius, lines 1909–1914

Regarding Mary's *Antonie*, Cerasano and Wynne-Davies point out:

> ...recent criticism suggests that we should interpret the play
> as an innovative and important contribution to a radical form
> of historical drama which employed the past as a veiling device
> for acute comment upon the contemporary political situation.
> Instead of closeting herself within a classical and Sidneian past,
> the Countess of Pembroke explored new forms of theater which
> allowed her to offer covert criticism of the government of her
> own day.[26]

This is particularly interesting in regard to the Authorship Question in that scholars continually note the political agenda of many of the Shakespearean plays, especially the histories, and of their covert criticism of the government of the day.

But Mary went beyond the step of merely writing—for an Elizabethan noblewoman, she took an unusually aggressive path and actually published her own work. She had *Antonie* printed in 1592 and "thus became the first woman in England to publish a play. *Antonie* was reprinted in 1595, 1600, 1606, and 1607; although unacted, it was widely influential."[27] Mary was one of the first dramatists in English to use blank verse, the form that is used in the Shakespearean plays.

This play, a closet drama, was meant to be read out loud by aristocrats at their social gatherings in great houses, rather than acted on a public stage—thus it was on the edge of what was acceptable for a woman to publish.

But just as important as the act of publishing are the dedications with which Mary Sidney prefaced her books. Typically the few other women who published wrote dedications that were apologies for being so brazen as to publish, and included assurances that the woman was still a good wife and a good mother. Often they laid the "blame" on God. However,

> Pembroke [Mary Sidney] never apologizes for or even mentions
> her own role as a woman writer, thereby making her most
> powerful statement on gender.[28]

A woman write a Play! Out upon it, out upon it, for it cannot be good . . . . If it be good, they will think she did not write it . . . for men will not allow women to have wit.

From the introduction to a collection called *Playes*, written and published in 1662 by Margaret Cavendish, Duchess of Newcastle, also known as "Mad Madge."

Triumph of Death

In the late 1590s, Mary Sidney translated from Italian a "magnificent version of Petrarch's *Trionfo della Morte*" [29] called *Triumph of Death*.

Gary Waller's analysis of *Triumph of Death* is particularly pertinent as he notes Mary's expertise in the art of writing. After describing the clumsy and wordy earlier translations of Lord Morley and William Fowler, Waller states:

> Her translation is, however, undoubtedly the finest rendition into English of any part of the work before Ernest Hatch Wilkin's modern version, and *the only one* to reproduce Petrarch's terza rima in English. . . . The most outstanding technical feature of the Countess's translation is her reproducing Petrarch's original stanzaic pattern. Petrarch's poem is written in terza rima, where the middle line of one stanza rhymes with the outer lines of the next tercet: *aba, bcb, cdc,* etc. In the Countess's version, each of Petrarch's terzine is, almost without exception, rendered by an equivalent in English, yet as D. G. Rees remarks, "in spite of this close adherence to her originals she succeeds in maintaining that fluency and naturalness which version translations often lack." It is a remarkable performance. She shows constant ingenuity in changing the original eleven-syllable line into English iambic decasyllables and her determined practice to adhere closely to the original is remarkably successful demonstrating, as with so many of her psalms, that she had both an acute ear for the movement and tone of both the English poetical line and that of her original, and a consistent grasp of the high emotional level required. [30]

Several critics notice in Mary Sidney's translation that the speech of Petrarch's Laura is enhanced, more regal, and she speaks with more authority and eloquence than in the work of other translators, such as Lord Morley's. Mary Sidney presents Laura as a "vibrant figure of joy and power." [31]

Below are the opening lines to Mary's translation of Petrarch's *Triumph of Death*.[32] Two other pieces follow from the lengthy work.

> That gallant lady, gloriously bright,
>> The stately pillar once of worthiness,
>> And now a little dust, a naked sprite,
> Turn'd from her wars a joyful conqueress,
>> Her wars, where she had foil'd the mighty foe
>> Whose wily stratagems the world distress,
> And foil'd him not with sword, with spear, or bow,
>> But with chaste heart, fair visage, upright thought,
>> Wise speech, which did with honour linked go.
>>> lines 1–9, first chapter

> Alive am I, and thou as yet art dead,
>> And as thou art shalt so continue still,
>> Till, by thy ending hour, thou hence be led.
> Short is our time to live, and long our will:
>> Then let with heed thy deeds and speeches go,
>> Ere that approaching term his course fulfil.
>>> lines 23–28, second chapter

> That life's best joy was almost bitter cheer
>> Compared to that death, most mildly sweet,
>> Which comes to men, but comes not everywhere.
> For I that journey pass'd with gladder feet
>> Than he, from hard exile, that homeward goes;
>> (But only ruth of thee) without regret.
>>> lines 71–76, second chapter

Mary Sidney never published this work. It exists only in a "corrupt" scribal manuscript copy, held at London's Inner Temple.

Other Written Work

Mary also produced other original poems, among them a dedication of her manuscript book of *Psalms* to Queen Elizabeth, and another elegy for her brother, "To the Angel Spirit of the most excellent Sir Philip Sidney."

Around 1599, Mary wrote a poem entitled "Thenot and Piers in Praise of Astrea." It's actually a singing match between two shepherds and was created for presentation to the Queen on her proposed summer progress, or tour, of the Wiltshire area. Typically the aristocrat who was entertaining the visiting monarch commissioned and paid a professional poet to write glorious accolades, but Mary Sidney boldly broke convention once again to write her own pastoral dialogue for the Queen.

"Thenot and Piers" was published in 1602 in a collection called *A Poetical Rhapsody*, edited by Francis Davison. Thus it was "the first original dramatic verse written by a woman to appear in print." [33]

> Far from the light froth expected from a lady, "Astrea" (as it was also known) is a tightly constructed dialogue between the Neoplatonic Thenot and the Protestant Piers, one that questions the very nature of language. [34]

Even her personal letters were praised. There are fourteen extant letters from Mary Sidney, three of which were included in a volume printed in 1660 to provide models of elegance in epistolary prose. [35]

Gary Waller remarks on her overall body of work:

> The Countess' technical virtuosity is, then, important and remarkable for her time; with few models available in English, she extends the technical range of English versification, and thus contributed to the revolution in both form and sensibility observable in poetry over the next forty years or so. . . . What is more important is the impressive range of appropriate tones and the variations in stylistic level that her virtuosity affords. [36]

Newly Discovered

A book printed in Germany in 1755 claims to be translated from an English manuscript. The writer of the English manuscript professes to have known Mary Sidney and her brother, Philip. He describes what was apparently a popular parlor game in Germany that was invented by Mary—an elaborate game in which spirits (named Auriel, Barthiel, Curiel, Daphniel, Ephtiel, Frugiel, Gaziel, and Honiel) tell your fortune in rhyme. But don't worry, the translator assures the reader, the spirits will not actually appear.

The English Countess
Mary of Pembroke
rare
Secrets
preserved
in a
Melodic Written Script
of the art of painting and stippling.
Thus
exploring in rhymes
the unfathomable future fate
of human beings.

Nürnberg
Publisher Gabriel Nicolaus Raspe 1763

An expanded edition of this book (due to popular demand, it claims), was printed in 1763, shown above, and includes not only the parlor game, but three other "secret procedures." One describes how Mary could remember long strings of numbers and repeat the same string days or weeks later, and could even repeat the list backwards. She wouldn't tell the author the secret, but her brother Philip disclosed to him the mnemonic device:

Translated from my copies by Ute, Steven, and Malte Forstat in Germany.

> Imagine, gracious lady, how could I play the role of teacher
> of *Mnemonica arithmetica* since Mary of Pembroke never

revealed this secret to me. To tell the truth, if I hadn't had the good fortune to have been on a journey to Germany, Hungary, and Italy with Philip Sidney, a brother of this learned Countess, it would have remained forever a hidden secret. He had learned this art from his sister, and having a gregarious and pleasant personality, finally revealed it to me, after I had continuously questioned him.

The book also provides a musical code supposedly developed by Mary. Each letter of the alphabet is represented by a particular measure:

I once paid a visit to this English Sappho, when she actually had a violin in her hands, and was performing a piece of music. As you probably know, this Countess has gained as great a fame among her fellow countrymen through her music as through poetry. I almost went into raptures while listening to it. I could not think of enough praise to compliment the Countess on this piece of music, which in fact was enchanting. She laughed, however, and told me that by no means was this a perfect work of musical art, but nothing other than the transcription of a melodic missive, which she had sent off to Count M. one hour earlier.

The third procedure is a recipe for invisible ink, "the secret and disappearing art of drawing." You can paint or write with it, and when the ink dries, it is invisible. But hold the page over a candle, and the heat makes the ink reappear:

It is my intention to reveal this Countess' art of secret and disappearing drawing, which to this hour has been known to only some of her best friends. I am in possession of two such works of art which she created with her own hand. The first depicts a perspective view of the Tower or the citadel of London. The second is a floor plan of a fortress. Each is in the center of a sheet of fine Dutch writing paper. These artistic representations are invisible unless the paper is held near the heat of a fire for a short time. Soon thereafter they become visible, all green, in fact to such an extent as the "Green of Saxony" is marvelled at. For this reason, the Countess of Pembroke called this method the secret art of drawing.

After two or three hours, the drawing disappears from the paper and is no longer visible, unless it is held to the fire again. This is the reason why in England this technique is called *pictura evanescens* or the art of disappearing drawing.

It's not clear yet what we can consider as factual in this author's account, but it is intriguing to think of an impressive young woman with these diverse and creative pursuits.

On the right-hand page is the recipe for invisible ink made with bismuth and salt.

Conventional Yet Covert

Professional scholars regard Mary as being subversive, covert, shocking, and unprecedented, such as in this typical remark from S.P. Cerasano and Marion Wynne-Davies:

> Throughout her life and work Mary Sidney appears to have been able to sustain a balance between what was customarily expected of a Renaissance noblewoman and what could have been considered shocking and subversive. . . . In this way, the Countess of Pembroke's own work should be viewed, not as a simple continuation of Philip's greater genius, but as a point of transition, *signalling a shift from male to female creativity and heralding a new age for women playwrights in her own family and beyond.* [37] [italics added]

In Margaret P. Hannay's words:

> Mary Sidney herself, by remaining within the established limits, became the most important woman writer and patron of the Elizabethan period, *one who demonstrated what could and what could not be accomplished in the margins.* [38] [emphasis added]

How did Mary Sidney balance this combination of apparent conventionality and subtle subversion? From the studies of Cerasano and Wynne-Davies:

> First, after her marriage she chose to retain the Sidney coat of arms as a form of identification, thereby asserting her familial inheritance and suggesting that the link with them was more important to her sense of self than the alliance with her husband. In other words, Mary Sidney presented herself to the court as a woman of culture, and not as a wife and mother.

> Second, the year 1586, in which her parents and her brother all died, proved a watershed for the Countess, and it is from this point that she seems to have taken on the Sidney mantle, transforming her home, Wilton House, into an academy for artists of all kinds, and reconstructing herself as a Sidneian scholar, fully capable of continuing the textual endeavors initiated by her brother.

However, rather than interpreting, as many commentators have done, Mary's post-1586 literary activity as a refuge from grief, it is more perceptive to discern a brilliant woman who, having been nurtured within the safety of a cultured familial group and then suddenly finding herself that family's most potent representative, rose to the challenge with exemplary skill and an extraordinary sense of purpose.[39]

Louise Schleiner concurs: "To sum up the observations here of how the Countess of Pembroke, uniquely among Elizabethan women, developed the sustained authorial identity that allowed her to speak with this voice, she did so through interacting with a fairly consistent circle of committedly Protestant writers and other contemporaries. And she had essential advantages that no other woman of her time and place possessed in such measure . . ."[40] including wealth and position, a literary group, support from other poets, and her passion for continuing and developing the ideology she had first established with her brother.

A spirited, courageous woman is revealed. An extraordinarily gifted writer, she used her skill to expand boundaries without apologies. As Schleiner notes, Mary Sidney had advantages that no other woman of the time possessed. But she was still a woman of that time, inexorably held to "honorable" behavior and responsible for upholding the reputation of her entire family.

Wilton House "Under heaven it was my greatest happiness that of this world I ever found, to light into the courtlike house of a right worthy honorable Lady. . . . For in her eye was the seat of pity, in her heart the honor of virtue, and in her hand the bounty of discretion. . . . Her house being in a manner of kind of little Court, her Lord in place of no mean command, her person no less than worthily and honorably attended, as well with Gentlewomen of excellent spirits, as diverse Gentlemen of fine carriage. . . . where first, God daily served, religion truly preached, all quarrels avoided, peace carefully preserved, swearing not heard of, where truth was easily believed, a table fully furnished, a house richly garnished, honor kindly entertained, virtue highly esteemed, service well rewarded, and the poor blessedly relieved, might make much for the truth of my discourse."

drawing of Wilton House
©2003 John Tollett,
used with permission

Nicholas Breton, *Wits Trenchmour*, 1597

And Where Was William Shakespeare?

Gary Waller has noted:

> Wilton and the spirit it embodied and furthered were
> central to late Elizabethan high culture, and there were few
> major poets who were not in some way connected with it.[41]

William Shakespeare, the man purported to be the greatest writer in England, was never mentioned by the greatest literary circle or the people in it.

Besides the Wilton Circle, the Mermaid Tavern in London "was Elizabethan London's literary and dramatic venue.... The membership of the Mermaid Club reads like a roll-call of famous Elizabethans."[42] The writers, philosophers, and thinkers who belonged called themselves the First Friday Club because they met on the First Friday of each month, and the tavern was located on Bread and Friday Streets.

In all the stories and documentation about the Mermaid Tavern, William Shakespeare's name is never mentioned.

Many of the most celebrated contemporary literary works were dedicated to Mary Sidney. Scholar and critic John Buxton exclaims:

> There are indeed few poets of the time who, whether or not
> they received any favours from her, failed to insert some praise
> of her in their poems. Myra, Amaryllis, Urania, Clorinda,
> Miriam, Pandora, Pembrokiana, Poemenarcha—she is
> addressed by countless names, and addressed always as
> the living inspiration of the English Renaissance.[43]

One writer who never dedicated a work to Mary Sidney is William Shakespeare.

Documented Data

■ Shortly after the turn of the century, Mary Sidney's life became much more difficult.

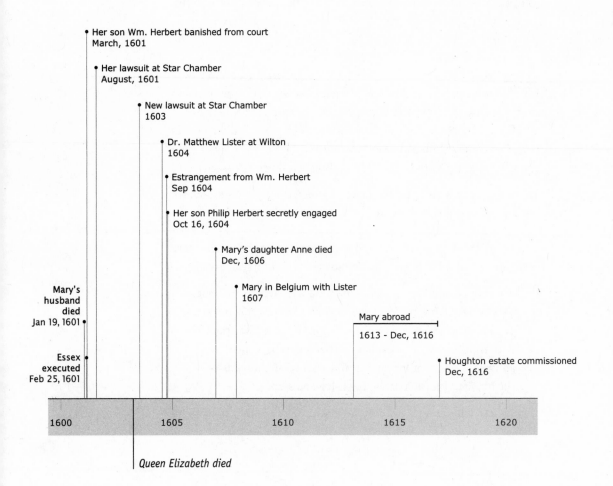

• Her son Wm. Herbert banished from court
March, 1601

• Her lawsuit at Star Chamber
August, 1601

• New lawsuit at Star Chamber
1603

• Dr. Matthew Lister at Wilton
1604

• Estrangement from Wm. Herbert
Sep 1604

• Her son Philip Herbert secretly engaged
Oct 16, 1604

• Mary's daughter Anne died
Dec, 1606

• Mary in Belgium with Lister
1607

Mary abroad

1613 - Dec, 1616

• Houghton estate commissioned
Dec, 1616

Mary's
husband
died
Jan 19, 1601 •

Essex •
executed
Feb 25, 1601

1600   1605   1610   1615   1620

Queen Elizabeth died

4 Mary Sidney as an Older Woman

Well then, must I work otherwise what I may.

Mary Sidney in a letter to Sir Julius Caesar, July 14, 1603

THE EARLY YEARS OF MARY SIDNEY'S LIFE were rich in education, languages, court life, childbirth, grief, travel, literary experimentation, alchemical studies, a literary salon, day to day administration of several large estates, acting in court masques and aristocratic closet dramas, singing, publishing, playing instruments, composing music, hunting and hawking, and more. Even as she grew older, Mary never settled into a mundane existence. Her last twenty years were as lively and abundant as the first forty—if not always as comfortable.

Knowledge regarding her married life with Henry Herbert is difficult to ascertain. For the last five years of her husband's life, it appears that he was "a sick and melancholy man. On Christmas Eve, 1595, he sent a poignant note to his friend, Sir Francis Hastings, in which his seasonal greetings were tempered with the sad lament: 'I dream of nothing but death, I hear of little but death, and (were it not for others' further good) I desire nothing but death.' His condition steadily worsened until he was by late 1599 little more than a semi-invalid." [1]

A Change for the Worse

When Mary's husband died in January of 1601, her life changed. "Pembroke's death was a severe blow to Mary Sidney. As soon as he took his last breath, she lost not only her husband, but also her position, much of her wealth, the writers who sought her patronage, and most of her influence at court." [2]

This is intriguing, as for many years scholars have noted the shift that takes place in the Shakespearean plays around the turn of the century, from history and light, joyous comedy to a more melancholic and tragic perception of life. What might have caused this shift in William Shakespeare's life is impossible to determine, but in Mary Sidney's we see a string of upsetting events over the next several years.

By 1601, not only was her husband gone, but by this time all of her influential relatives at court were gone: her parents, her two brothers (Thomas had died in 1595 at the age of 26), her powerful uncles (the earls of Leicester, Warwick, and Huntingdon), Sir Francis Walsingham (her brother Philip's father-in-law). Her younger son Philip was only seventeen and her older son William was about to be banished from court.

Mary was 39 years old. At Henry Herbert's death she inherited, among other holdings, the town of Cardiff.

> Left with the responsibility for administering the extensive properties she retained under her jointure and [the Earl of] Pembroke's will, she contended with jewel thieves, pirates, and murderers, finally bringing them to trial after two and a half years of complex political and legal maneuvers. She continued to administer her castle and town of Cardiff, despite violent local attempts to shake off the seigneurial rule of the Pembrokes. Each time she was crossed, this indomitable woman found a way to "work otherwise." [3]

Trouble with William

Shortly after her husband died, Mary's older son started giving her trouble. William, not yet twenty-one, was discovered to have impregnated Mary Fitton. This young Mary was 23 years old and had been a maid-of-honor to Queen Elizabeth for five years. A contemporary reference tells us that "during the time that the Earl of Pembroke favored her she would put off her head tire [headdress] and tuck up her clothes and take a large white cloak and march out as though she had been a man to meet the said Earl out of the Court." [4]

William admitted paternity but unconditionally refused to marry her. The Queen threw William in the Fleet prison for a month, then banished him to Wilton House where he was thoroughly miserable. It

LUCIO: *I was once before him for getting a wench with child.*

DUKE: *Did you such a thing?*

LUCIO: *Yes, marry, did I. But I was fain to forswear it; they would else have married me to the rotten medlar.*

Measure for Measure, 4.iii.169–72

wasn't until Queen Elizabeth died two years later that William was able to go back to the royal court. Mary Fitton's baby, a boy, died at birth.

Trouble with Essex

About the same time as William's difficulties, Mary's younger brother Robert was involved with storming the house of the Earl of Essex and negotiating with Essex and his small band of rebels during their ill-fated uprising against the Queen. This must have been difficult for Mary as Essex was a close friend of the family. He was one of her brother Philip's dearest friends—Philip had willed him his best sword, and Essex married Philip's widow. He was executed on February 25, 1601.

Trouble in civil court

By August of 1601, Mary was writing to William Cecil, Lord Burghley, regarding administrative problems at Cardiff Castle, an estate she owned. She entered a complaint with the Star Chamber against a number of citizens of Cardiff who had pulled down parts of her castle, arrested several of her men, and beaten her servants. She went through lengthy legal battles over this.

In 1603 she went once again to the Star Chamber when one of her employees, Hugh David, was brutally attacked while transporting the Countess's money and jewels to London. David's skull was broken in six places with a cudgel, and the assailant escaped with the goods on a horse belonging to the justice of the peace of Cardiff. This justice of the peace then represented Edmund Mathew, one of the accused, who happened to be a former employee of Mary's whom she had fired and replaced with Hugh David.

The Star Chamber was the highest court in England, controlled by the monarch. The court met in a room in Westminster Hall in London; the ceiling of this room was decorated with stars.

This same man, Mathew, had been prosecuted years earlier by the Star Chamber for cruelly and unlawfully embezzling, taking bribes, and levying illegal fines. According to the documentation studied by Margaret P. Hannay, Mathew was able to convince the civil court that Mary was merely a hysterical woman.[5]

Sir Hugh, persuade me not; I will make a Star Chamber matter of it.
Shallow in *The Merry Wives of Windsor*, 1.1.1

Hugh David languished for three months in horrific pain before dying. The other accused man (Philip Llen, an accomplice of Mathew's) was asked if he did this dreadful deed, the accused man said no, and the court told Mary Sidney to go home—illustrating the particular vulnerability of a single woman under English law at the time.

Trouble with the boys

Inferences in several extant letters imply that Mary's oldest son William Herbert was not speaking to her at this time, even though many of the legal battles she fought were for the advantage of his inherited estate.

Mary's second son, Philip Herbert, was an irresponsible playboy who also caused her much grief. He left Oxford University after only a few months of school and entered the royal court when 15 or 16 years old. "As one of [King] James's favorite young men, he achieved wealth and position not by service to the state—as had his uncle, father, and grandfathers—but by hunting, tilting, gambling, and performing in masques." [6]

By his twentieth birthday in 1604, Philip had secretly engaged himself to Susan de Vere, daughter of the Earl of Oxford. Although Oxford was dead by the time the lovers negotiated their own marriage, it's hard to say how Mary felt about this since her brother Philip Sidney had shared "the uncomfortable distinction of being one of those the Earl of Oxford said he wanted to kill." [7] The girl's great-uncle, Robert Cecil, was disturbed about the match and it was only the King's intervention that allowed Philip Herbert and Susan to marry at the end of the year. Philip went on to openly keep a mistress, as did his older brother.

After one particular scene where Philip did not behave as befitted a nobleman, Francis Osborne recorded in his *Historical Memoirs* that "I have been told the mother of [Philip] Herbert tore her hair at the report of her son's dishonour." [8]

Death leads to love

In 1604, the estate physician at Wilton House, Dr. Moffett, died and was buried at Wilton. He had been an integral part of her family and even her literary circle for many years. His place was taken by Dr. Matthew Lister. This must have been a bright spot during these difficult years, because Mary and Lister developed an ardent and romantic relationship that lasted for the rest of her life, although marriage was out of the question because of the difference in social status. In 1604, Mary was 43 years old; Lister was 33, only nine years older than Mary's son, William Herbert. Was this the cause of her estrangement from William—an affair with a younger man who was in a considerably lower social class?

Death of Anne, her adult daughter

Then in late 1606, Mary's 23-year-old unmarried daughter Anne died in Cambridge, apparently after a recurring illness. Records exist of Mary and her daughter participating in masques and dances at court together. Anne is described as taking part in storytelling evenings that Mary sponsored at Wilton House, and Mary Ellen Lamb believes that Anne was also a writer.[9] Of Mary's four children, she now had only two sons; of her six siblings, she and her younger brother Robert were the only survivors.

Traveling and hosting again

In 1607 she was in Spa (the original Forest of Ardennes in *As You Like It*) with Dr. Lister. From 1613 to 1616, Mary sailed, traveled abroad, and lived in Nérac, Amiens, and Calais in France; Flushing in the Netherlands; Flanders, Antwerp in Belgium, as well as Spa, where she held a noted literary salon. She spent part of one winter in Mechlen, the lace-making capital of Europe.

In Spa, aged 52, Mary Sidney shot pistols with her great friend the Countess of Barlemont. Their lodgings became the central "court" for the visiting English for entertaining, dancing, and playing. In a town where people gathered from all over Europe to take the waters for their health, Mary Sidney "complains chiefly of a common disease and much troublesome to fair women, *senectus* [old age], otherwise we see nothing amiss in her."[10]

She smoked cigarettes, danced, sang, played cards, and consorted with her younger lover. She had such a grand time in Europe that she wrote to her friend, Sir Toby Matthew, "For if you saw me now, you would say, it [Spa] had created a new creature. Therefore, let all Pictures now hide themselves; for, believe me, I am not now, as I was then."[11]

In 1616, once again back in England, Mary built an estate with her lover, Matthew Lister, called Houghton House—now in elegant ruins near the town of Ampthill, Bedfordshire.

The stately ruins of Houghton House.[12]

Writing again

And she continued to write. Letters from Mary to her friends Sir Edward Wotton and Sir Toby Matthew intriguingly mention manuscripts that are now presumed lost.

Gabriel Harvey's question in his 1593 work, *Pierces Supererogation*, also implies there were other works of hers:

> And what if she can also publish more works in a month than [Thomas] Nashe hath published in his whole life, or the pregnantest of our inspired Heliconists [those who call on the Grecian Muses] can equal? [13]

What were all these pieces, published or not? Missing manuscripts are newly discovered nearly every year. In 1973, a bound manuscript containing sonnets written by Mary's younger brother Robert was sold at auction. It had been in the library at Warwick Castle for the previous hundred years, mistakenly ascribed to his uncle.

Mary Sidney has only recently been rediscovered—who knows what works of hers are quietly sitting on an old library shelf, waiting to be found?

Still Within the Margins

In Mary Sidney we find an exceptionally intelligent, strong, assertive, and dedicated woman who developed the most important literary circle in England's history and whose single-minded mission in life was to create great works in the English language. As forward-thinking as she was, however, the barriers for women were still formidable, and what was considered acceptable behavior was strictly defined. Inappropriate conduct could affect entire families, and in Mary Sidney's case, could directly impact the fortunes and futures of both her sons.

Before we look at Mary's connections with the Shakespearean plays and what might have prevented her from publishing them, let's first look at the documented evidence that ties her so closely to the Shakespearean sonnets.

Part Three

The Sonnets

Never durst poet touch a pen to write
Until his ink were tempered with Love's sighs.

Berowne in *Love's Labor's Lost*, 4.iii.320–21

Documented Data

- Scholars believe the sonnets were taken to the printing press without the poet's permission.
- The first seventeen sonnets implore a handsome, unmarried man to have a baby to carry on his beauty.
- Most of the other sonnets are passionate love poems written to a younger man.
- The poet thinks the younger man is having an affair with a dark-haired, dark-eyed, newly married woman.

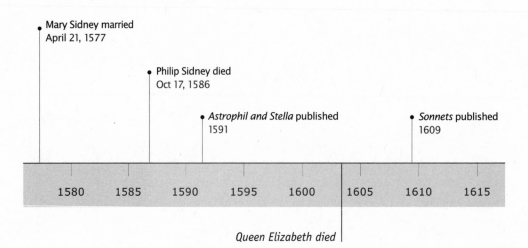

Mary Sidney married
April 21, 1577

Philip Sidney died
Oct 17, 1586

Astrophil and Stella published
1591

Sonnets published
1609

1580   1585   1590   1595   1600   1605   1610   1615

Queen Elizabeth died

5 Introduction to the Sonnets

AHH, THE SONNETS. This collection of 154 poems presents the most perplexing mystery about the man named William Shakespeare. Many are difficult to understand, and there has never been consensus on what an individual sonnet actually means: "Editors and commentators have violently disagreed about the meaning of various words, phrases, and passages."[1]

Most experts agree that the sonnets seem intensely autobiographical. Harold Bloom remarks on their sense of the intimate, "Perhaps the extraordinary voice we hear in the Sonnets is as much a fiction as any other voice in Shakespeare, though I find that very difficult to believe."[2]

But no one can explain how the sonnets fit into Shakespeare's life. "After nearly two hundred years of speculation and scholarship, we have made remarkably little progress toward uncovering the 'true story' behind Shakespeare's Sonnets, if indeed there is a story to be uncovered."[3] Experts also agree the sonnets were not meant for publication and were taken to press without the poet's cooperation. The publisher (not the poet) dedicated the collection, "To the onlie begetter of these ensuing sonnets, Mr. W. H."

And this is the biggest problem with these passionate and often desperate love poems: most of them are written to a man.

Shakespeareans generally believe Henry Wriothesley, Earl of South-ampton, ten years younger than Shakespeare, is the younger man to whom the sonnets were written. Why Southampton? Because the narrative poems published in 1593 and 1594, *Venus and Adonis* and *The Rape of Lucrece* (see Appendix D), each had a dedication to South-ampton from the poet. Sixteen years later, in 1609, the dedication in the book of sonnets from the *publisher* is "to Mr. W.H." Shakespeareans (and the proponents of other authorship candidates as well) believe that W.H. is really *supposed* to be H.W. and therefore *must be* Henry Wriothesley. There is no documented evidence to support this theory.

In *A Literary History of England*, Brooke and Shaaber discuss the sonnets:

> Of all the Elizabethan sonnet sequences, Shakespeare's is the least typical. It celebrates not the idealized love of an idealized mistress but the affection of an older man for a gilded and wayward youth. Even the 25 sonnets addressed to a dark lady express repulsion as well as fascination. On the showing of the sonnets Shakespeare's experience of love and friendship was turbid and disheartening. They abound in meditations on estrangement, failure, and death. They bewail the poet's outcast state, death's dateless night, the anxieties of separation, time's giving and taking away, even world-weariness. The conclusion, however, is triumphant—an uncompromising affirmation of the transcendence of love. The later sonnets (100–126) assert and reassert that love, and love alone, withstands the onslaught of time, eternal amidst the world's ruin and decay.[4]

Depending on how homophobic an individual scholar is, he or she might give you one of the four excuses written by John Boswell, Jr., printed in 1821 in Edmond Malone's version of the collected works of Shakespeare.[5] About these excuses, Peter Stallybrass says in a recent essay, "The final page of Boswell's introductory remarks on the Sonnets are dedicated to proving that Shakespeare was not a pederast. In the process he produces, as hysterical symptom, the lines of defence that have governed nearly all subsequent readings of the Sonnets."[6]

In the following table is the essence of Boswell's excuses for the sonnets, followed immediately by responses from more recent scholarship.

Excuse	Response
1] During the English Renaissance, men talked to each other like this.	James Schiffer says, "No serious reader can any longer make the facile assumption that the relationship between poet and friend is nonsexual or assume as Malone did (and as many have argued since) that the amorous tone of so many of the Sonnets is typical of the way Neoplatonic male friends spoke to one another in Elizabethan times."[7]
	David Bevington says, "His [Shakespeare's] emphasis on friendship seems new, for no other [sonnet] sequence addressed a majority of its sonnets to a friend rather than to a mistress . . . ."[8]
	Bevington also says, "Still, the bond between poet and friend is extraordinarily strong, and certainly there is a danger that traditional scholarship has minimized the erotic bond between the poet and his friend out of a distaste for the idea."[9]
	Michael Keevak says, "The main issue, then as now, is the (apparently undeniable) fact that most of the 154 poems are addressed to a man. This has always been the Sphinx's riddle of Shakespeare sonnet criticism. Was Shakespeare engaged in a sodomitical relationship with another man?"[10]
	Keevak also says, "It is remarkable how many of the controversies that surround the sonnets are inextricably bound up with the issue of sexuality, and with sodomy between men in particular. . . . Whether or not Shakespeare 'himself' was (or should have been) 'gay,' the sonnets are nonetheless queer, and perhaps a lot queerer than most modern critics have been willing to allow."[11]

Excuse	Response
2] Shakespeare wrote like this to get patronage (money and political support) from a nobleman ten years younger.	Joseph Pequigney states, "There is no evidence to support the idea that the young friend is an aristrocratic patron, or a patron of any kind."[12]
	E.K. Chambers says, "The case for him [the Earl of Southampton] as the friend of the sonnets is now very generally accepted. . . . I do not think it a convincing one. If it were sound, one would expect to find some hints in the sonnets of the major interests of Southampton's early life; his military ambitions, his comradeship with Essex, the romance of his marriage. There are none."[13]
	John Dover Wilson says, "A.C. Bradley, again, Shakespeare's most penetrating modern critic, finds it quite impossible to take the language of many of the sonnets as that of interested flattery."[14]
	Wilson also says, "A poet who rebukes, however gently, a young man for loose living (Sonnets 95, 96), for making himself cheap (69), for his love of flattery (84, line 14), for self-satisfaction (67, line 2), for keeping the said poet up for hours waiting for an appointment he fails to observe (57, 58), is going a queer way about to curry his favour."[15]
	Colin Burrow says, "For a printed poem by a commoner to address an Earl as the 'master mistress of my passion' would be audacious beyond belief."[16]

Excuse	Response
3] The poems are merely conventional—they're not really about "being in love," but about the transcendent state of love itself.	James Schiffer says, "The fact that the Sonnets exploit conventional images and themes does not in itself prove that the poems are 'literary exercises' rather than the key to Shakespeare's heart."[17]
	Stanley Wells says, "Athough the sonnet sequence was a fashionable and conventional form, I have been struck by ways in which Shakespeare's poems differ from other sequences. A very obvious one is that, like some of Barnfield's but none, so far as I know, by any other sonneteer of the period, many of Shakespeare's sonnets are explicitly addressed to, or concern, a man. And all of them idealize him. On the other hand the woman, in another reversal of convention stretching back to Petrarch and beyond, is reviled."[18]
4] The poems are simply experiments in writing.	Stanley Wells says, "These surely are poems in which the poet is talking to himself, trying to work through and to gain control over an emotional crisis by imposing poetic form upon an expression of feelings that no words can ultimately assuage."[19]
	I repeat Harold Bloom's statement, "Perhaps the extraordinary voice we hear in the Sonnets is as much a fiction as any other voice in Shakespeare, though I find that very difficult to believe."

Richard Barnfield wrote very homo-erotic poems in the late 1590s.

The scholar L.P. Smith sums it up: "The story Shakespeare recounts of his moral—or rather his immoral—predicament ... must certainly, in the interests of the British Empire, be smothered up; the business of proving and re-proving, and proving over again ... that our Shakespeare cannot possibly mean what he so frankly tells us, has become almost a national industry."[20]

Was Shakespeare Gay?

Homosexuality is certainly not out of the question if the man named Shakespeare actually did write the sonnets. It's just not a very plausible theory because there are no other indications that the man named William Shakespeare from Stratford was gay. Besides being married with three children, we have more documented gossip about his escapades with women than about his acting: In 1596, when Shakespeare was charged with deadly assault, he was out with two women and another man. In 1602, there is a third-hand story in a diary about Shakespeare having a tryst with a female fan from the theater. William Davenant, the poet laureate of England from 1638–68, claimed he was an illegitimate child of Shakespeare's.

Homosexuality is not a modern invention—it has been a fact of life throughout all recorded history. We know that other men of this time were gay, such as Christopher Marlowe and Sir Francis Bacon (his mother complained about it in letters). The "good King Richard" of Robin Hood tales, Richard the Lionheart, was gay. King Edward II, who ruled England from 1307–1327, was also famously gay.[21] King James I (of the *King James Bible*), 1603–1625, openly nuzzled his favorite young men in public, including his greatest love, the Duke of Buckingham.[22]

If Ben Jonson had noticed Shakespeare was gay, scholars assume he surely would have added that comment to the other disparaging remarks he made about Shakespeare after his death.

Babies and Lovers

The first seventeen of the Shakespearean sonnets—often called the "procreation" sonnets—implore a handsome man to marry and have a baby, an heir, a child to carry on his beauty and his name.

Most of the other sonnets are intensely passionate (not just warm) letters to a younger man (younger than the poet), the "friend." The word "friend" is used in the plays to refer to a lover of either sex.

Eventually, the famous "Dark Lady" appears, so called because the poet mentions her dark eyes and hair. The sonnets assumed to be written about the woman, this Dark Lady, are not love poems, but are negative and sometimes hateful—the poet believes the Dark Lady and the young man are having an affair. Eventually the poet and the young man get back together and continue their intense emotional and (apparently) sexually consummated relationship. There is also mention of a rival poet, a male, in several of the sonnets.

Intriguingly, in an essay titled "The Silent Speech of Shakespeare's Sonnets," George T. Wright observes the following:

> Sidney [Mary's brother, Philip] and Shakespeare are "the only two love poets to make central to their sonnet sequences the issue of showing in verse what is truly in the heart." [23]

> It is so much the more curious, then, that, as the only playwright among those Elizabethans who participated in the sonnet-writing vogue of the 1590s, he [Shakespeare] alone should have written sonnets in a style that stresses the solitude of the poet-speaker and the silence of his speech . . . . [24]

> But Shakespeare, following Sidney, moves toward the charging of an inner verbal current, with what sounds like authentic "autobiographical material . . . ." [25]

Hundreds of books that focus on the sonnets as authored by William Shakespeare raise more questions than they answer. My questions are:

> What if the sonnets were not written by a gay or bisexual man to his male lover, but by a woman, Mary Sidney?

> Could some of the sonnets be written to her adored and single brother encouraging him to procreate, to have an heir to carry on his name and beauty?

> Could the love sonnets be written to her younger lover who, for a time, she suspected of having an affair with her dark-haired, dark-eyed, newly married niece?

In the following chapter we'll first look at the documented evidence that demonstrates how Mary's romantic life was fully mirrored in the sonnets that were about or addressed to a younger, male lover and at times lamented his supposed affair with the dark woman.

Documented Data

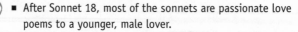

- After Sonnet 18, most of the sonnets are passionate love poems to a younger, male lover.

- The poet thinks the younger man is having an affair with a dark-haired, dark-eyed, newly married woman.

- After her husband died, Mary Sidney had a younger lover for the rest of her life.

- There is documented evidence that for a time she believed her younger lover was having an affair with a dark-haired, dark-eyed, newly married woman.

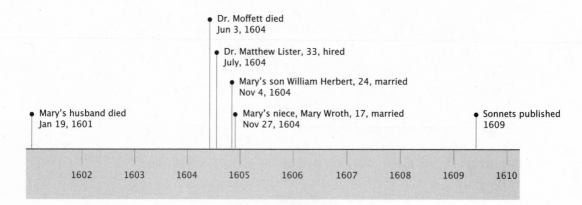

Katherine Duncan-Jones states, "Recent stylometric studies point to 1603–04 as a plausible time for the composition or completion of most of the 'fair youth' sonnets after [sonnets] 1–17."[1]

6 The Love Sonnets

SCHOLARS AGREE that the poet who wrote the Shakespearean sonnets was in love with a younger man.

In the later sonnets, the poet apparently thinks this younger man is having an affair with a dark-haired woman, even though the dark-haired woman is married to someone else, someone who seems to be named "Will." The sonnets that address this "Dark Lady" are not love poems, but verses berating the woman for lust and betrayal. It's very interesting to see how these details mirror documented details of Mary Sidney's life.

In 1601, when Mary was 40 years old, her husband died (at 67 years of age). In 1604, Dr. Moffett, the estate physician, died and a month or so later Dr. Matthew Lister, who was to become a prominent doctor to the nobility and royalty, began to live at Mary's estate as the resident physician.

Matthew Lister was ten years younger than Mary—she was 43 and he was 33—yet they fell deeply in love and stayed together for the rest of her life (Lister lived on to the age of 86). Understanding that most single men his age married nubile 15-year-old girls, we can appreciate that Mary (as a mistress) is considerably older than her lover by the standards of the time.

Mary and Matthew were never allowed to marry because of the differences in their social classes "for all responsible persons accepted that it was inappropriate for individuals of unequal wealth and status to marry one another."² Also, the land and properties Mary inherited from her husband in his will stipulated that they were only hers until she remarried.

With this in mind, consider these excerpts from the love sonnets below as though a beautiful, widowed noblewoman is writing to her younger lover. Then read them again with the standard scholarship in mind—as if the baseborn tradesman named William Shakespeare is writing to a highborn, aristrocratic, younger, male patron, assumed by many Shakespeareans to be Henry Wriothesley, Earl of Southampton.

> *O, let me, true in love, but truly write,*
> *And then believe me, my love is as fair*
> *As any mother's child.*
>
> Sonnet 21

> *Now see what good turns eyes for eyes have done:*
> *Mine eyes have drawn thy shape, and thine for me*
> *Are windows to my breast, wherethrough the sun*
> *Delights to peep, to gaze therein on thee.*
>
> Sonnet 24

> *O know, sweet love, I always write of you,*
> *And you and love are still my argument.*   [*argument* = subject matter]
>
> Sonnet 76

> *Those lines that I before have writ do lie,*
> *Even those that said I could not love you dearer;*
> *Yet then my judgment knew no reason why*
> *My most full flame should afterwards burn clearer.*
>
> Sonnet 115

> > [paraphrase]
> > *The poems I wrote earlier are lies,*
> > *Especially when I said I couldn't love you more*
> > *   than I already do.*
> > *But at the time I couldn't imagine*
> > *That my love for you would grow even stronger.*

The following is Sonnet 108 in full with my paraphrase following.

What's in the brain that ink may character
Which hath not figured to thee my true spirit?
What's new to speak, what new to register,
That may express my love, or thy dear merit?

Nothing, sweet boy; but yet, like prayers divine,
I must each day say o'er the very same,
Counting no old thing old; thou mine, I thine,
Even as when first I hallowed thy fair name:

[The term "boy" was used as a familiar term in addressing or speaking of a grown person.]

So that eternal love, in love's fresh case,
Weighs not the dust and injury of age,
Nor gives to necessary wrinkles place
But makes antiquity for aye his page,

> *Finding the first conceit of love there bred,*
> *Where time and outward form would show it dead.*

[paraphrase[3]]

What is in the mind that I can write in ink
Which has not already portrayed to you how faithful I am?
What else can I say, what else can I record
> *That can express how much I love you,*
> *or how I value your precious worth?*

Nothing more can be said, sweet boy; but yet, like divine prayers
Every day I must say it over and over again
Appreciating all old and repeated thoughts as new,
> *you are mine and I am yours*
Just like the first time I enshrined your beautiful name.

Eternal love, expressed as new once again
Ignores the way our bodies change as we grow older
And pays no attention to the inevitable wrinkles,
But love makes old age the paper upon which it writes,
> *for eternity,*

> *Having discovered the first passions of love in the body*
> *Even though time and our aged bodies might be expected*
> > *to give love and affection the appearance of being dead.*

"The course of true love"

Mary Sidney is the only authorship candidate with *documented evidence* of a younger, male lover, but what about the Dark Lady?

The poet, Shakespeareans claim, was writing sonnets to Henry Wriothesley (some say William Herbert), but then Wriothesley (or Herbert) began having an affair with the Dark Lady. This dark-haired, dark-eyed woman is newly married and her husband seems to be named "Will," based on the text of the sonnets. The Dark Lady in Shakespeare's life (or in the life of any other authorship candidate) has never been documented, although many fantastic theories abound. This is a visual representation of the traditional theory:

William Shakespeare *Henry Wriothesley, the Earl of Southampton* *Mary Fitton, one of the candidates for Dark Lady*

However, Mary Sidney, a strawberry-blonde, had a dark-haired god-daughter and niece (her brother Robert's daughter) named Mary Wroth. This young Mary, whose nickname as a child was "Little Moll," spent a great deal of her childhood in Mary Sidney's home.

Wroth (pronounced "worth") is her married name. This Mary's maiden name was also Sidney, but that gets very confusing. Portraits of Mary Wroth show her dark hair and dark eyes.

Mary Wroth is well known in today's academic circles as a writer.[4] One of the pieces she wrote is an unpublished play called "Love's Victory"[5] that might provide a clue to the story that seems to play out in the Shakespearean sonnets. Scholars who have studied the work of Wroth say, "Indeed, an awareness of Mary Wroth's biography is essential to the understanding of her work, for the characters in her romances, poems, and play represent the people she knew, those she loved and those she despised."[6]

In her play, "Love's Victory," Mary Wroth used a popular technique of the time in which she substituted quasi-anagrams for the names of Mary Sidney and her younger lover, Matthew Lister, as well as for herself and Mary Sidney's oldest son, William Herbert.

Mary Wroth included William Herbert, her first cousin, in this play because she was in love with him, even though they were both married to other people. She eventually had two illegitimate children with William Herbert after her husband died.

In her play, the character who (according to Waller[7] and other scholars) represents William Herbert is in love with the character of Mary Wroth. The character representing Matthew Lister, Mary Sidney's lover, swears he will never fall in love, but the goddess Venus brings him together with Mary Sidney. They fall fiercely in love with each other, but soon their relationship is deeply troubled by an unfounded rumor that breaks them apart—the rumor is that Matthew Lister (the younger lover) is in love with the dark-haired, dark-eyed Mary Wroth (Mary Sidney's niece), and she with him.[8]

But Mary Wroth herself discovers the trouble and helps to reunite Mary Sidney and Lister with vows of eternal love. "The other half of Act 4 presents [Mary Wroth] as a loyal and effective friend, intervening in a quarrel between [Mary Sidney] and [Matthew Lister]."[9]

And they become, as a character named Musella says, "the couple Cupid best doth love."

The historical events that Mary Wroth incorporated into her play may be seen as the same events that surface in the Shakespearean sonnet sequence (after Sonnet 18): Mary Sidney easily becomes the author/poet of the sonnets, Matthew Lister the younger lover, and Mary Wroth the Dark Lady.

Are these the poems that Mary Sidney, in love with Matthew Lister, wrote when she thought her adored niece, Mary Wroth (19 years old), whom she helped raise and who was recently married, was having an affair with Matthew Lister?

Excerpts from the "Dark Lady" sonnets:

> *That thou hast her, it is not all my grief,*
> *And yet it may be said I loved her dearly:*
> *That she hath thee is of my wailing chief,*
> *A loss in love that touches me more nearly.*
>
> *Loving offenders, thus I will excuse ye:*
> *Thou dost love her because thou knowst I love her,*

And for my sake even so doth she abuse me,
Suff'ring my friend for my sake to approve her.

Sonnet 42; is this directed at Matthew Lister?

Thou art as tyrannous, so as thou art,
As those whose beauties proudly make them cruel;
For well thou knowst, to my dear doting heart
Thou art the fairest and most precious jewel . . .
　　In nothing art thou black save in thy deeds
　　And thence this slander, as I think, proceeds.

Sonnet 131; directed at her beloved niece, Mary Wroth?

Beshrew [curse] that heart that makes my heart to groan
For that deep wound it gives my friend and me.

Sonnet 133; directed at Mary Wroth? The word "friend"
is used in the plays to refer to a lover of either sex.

O call not me to justify the wrong
That thy unkindness lays upon my heart;
Wound me not with thine eye, but with thy tongue;
Use power with power, and slay me not by art.
Tell me thou lov'st elsewhere; but in my sight,
Dear heart, forbear to glance thine eye aside.

Sonnet 139; see note below.

O me! What eyes hath love put in my head,
Which have no correspondence with true sight?
Or if they have, where is my judgment fled,
That censures falsely what they see aright?

　　. . .

O how can love's eye be true,
That is so vexed with watching and with tears?

Sonnet 148; is this and Sonnet 139, above, written to Lister,
thinking he is "changing eyes" with Mary Wroth?

It turns out Wroth wasn't having an affair with Lister after all (just as Mary Wroth wrote in her play). But Mary Sidney does discover that her niece (Mary Wroth) is actually in love with her son (Will Herbert), who is also newly married. This, of course, presents an emotional quandary of another kind for Mary Sidney.

> *Whoever hath her wish, thou hast thy Will,*
> *And Will to boot, and Will in overplus....*
> *So thou, being rich in Will, add to thy Will*
> *One will of mine to make thy large Will more.*

[The word "will" can also mean "desire" or "lust."]

Sonnet 135; written to Mary Wroth?

> *In loving thee thou knowst I am forsworn*
> [I have sworn falsely on your love, thinking it true]
> *But thou art twice forsworn, to me love swearing;*
> *In act thy bed-vow* [marriage vow] *broke and new faith torn ...*

Sonnet 152; written to Mary Wroth?

Here is a documented love story that matches the story of the sonnets:

Mary Sidney   Dr. Matthew Lister   Mary Wroth   Will Herbert

It wasn't discovered until 1935 that Mary Sidney's son William had two illegitimate children with his first cousin Mary Wroth.[10] Gary Waller, author of *The Sidney Family Romance*, says, "The modern discovery of the affair is a fascinating one of an almost total cover-up by the Sidneys for nearly three hundred years." [11] The cover-up, which included destroying documentation, was perpetrated by the same man to whom the First Folio (the collection of Shakespearean plays) is dedicated, and possibly the sonnets, "Mr. W. H."—William Herbert. Was this a precedent for handling subsequent family secrets?

Documented Data

- The sonnet mania in England was started by the publication of the sonnet sequence written by Mary's brother, Philip Sidney, called *Astrophil and Stella*.

- With no home of his own, Philip often lived at Mary's Wilton House estate, writing and developing the literary circle with her.

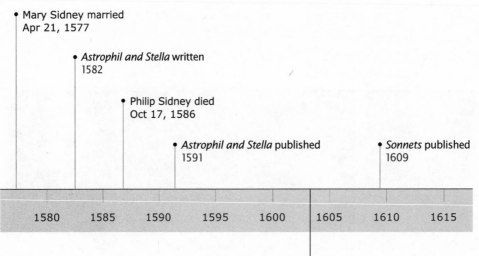

Mary Sidney married
Apr 21, 1577

Astrophil and Stella written
1582

Philip Sidney died
Oct 17, 1586

Astrophil and Stella published
1591

Sonnets published
1609

| 1580 | 1585 | 1590 | 1595 | 1600 | 1605 | 1610 | 1615 |

Queen Elizabeth died

7 The Procreation Sonnets

More folly has been
written about the
sonnets than
about any other
Shakespearean topic.

Sir Edmund Chambers
1866–1954

THE SHAKESPEAREAN SONNETS WENT TO PRESS in 1609. Scholars say the height of the public passion for sonnet writing and reading was about fifteen years earlier, which is one reason they think this particular collection was not meant for publication (besides the fact that the "man" who wrote them was apparently gay and probably wouldn't want his "relationship" exposed through publication).

As Hardin Craig says, "Sonneteering was the rage in the early and mid 1590s. It began in 1591, with the publication of Sir Philip Sidney's *Astrophil and Stella* . . . . "[1] Philip wrote this sonnet sequence around 1582; he died in 1586. An unauthorized and corrupt version was printed in 1591, then recalled by the Sidney family, corrected, and immediately reprinted.[2] So the passion for English sonnets started with the poems of Mary's brother Philip, work that was published by Mary Sidney herself.

"The first [sonnet series] to follow was Samuel Daniel with his *Delia* (1592). Daniel was the protégé and neighbor of Lady Pembroke, to whom his sequence was dedicated. . . . He uses almost exclusively the easy Shakespearean form."[3] Samuel Daniel was employed in Mary's home, most likely as a tutor for her daughter.[4] Daniel credits Mary Sidney as having taught him to write, as evidenced in a dedication he wrote to her oldest son:

Having been first encouraged and framed thereunto by your most worthy and honorable mother, and received the first notion for the formal ordering of those compositions at Wilton, which I must ever acknowledge to have been my best school and thereof always am to hold a feeling and grateful memory.[5]

The first seventeen Shakespearean sonnets implore a man to have a baby, which is why they are called the "procreation sonnets." Over and over and over, the poet gives impassioned reasons for this man to marry and have a child.

Reading these sonnets, keep in mind the thought expressed by Shakespearean scholar John Dover Wilson, whose discussion of the procreation poems includes the following: "One recalls the weeping crowds in February 1587 when Sir Philip Sidney was carried to his grave leaving no son to perpetuate his name." [6]

In the same discussion Wilson also notes a remarkable coincidence: "But this marriage section had a source peculiar to itself . . . namely a famous passage in the *Countess of Pembroke's Arcadia*, which Sir Philip Sidney wrote for his sister . . . which consisted of a series of arguments virtually identical with those Shakespeare advances to the youth."[7] *The procreation sonnets of "Shakespeare" are virtually identical to the sonnets Philip Sidney wrote for his sister Mary.*

What if the first seventeen sonnets (some are excerpted below) were written by a young woman to her beloved brother who is educated, worldly, handsome, charming, almost 30 years old, unmarried, childless, and the sole heir to the entire fortunes of his uncles Robert Dudley, the Earl of Leicester, and Ambrose Dudley, the Earl of Warwick? If a nobleman died without heirs, his fortune and lands went back to the crown so there was an extremely practical side to the desire for an heir, as well as the natural desire of a woman (who is herself a mother) to see the brother she cherishes fulfilled in this way.

> *Is it for fear to wet a widow's eye*
> *That thou consum'st thyself in single life?*
> Sonnet 9

> *Make thee another self for love of me,*
> *That beauty still may live in thine or thee.*
> Sonnet 10

Oh, that you were your self! But, love, you are
No longer yours than you yourself here live.
Against this coming end you should prepare,
And your sweet semblance to some other give.
Sonnet 13

If I could write the beauty of your eyes
And in fresh numbers number all your graces,
The age to come would say, "This poet lies;
Such heavenly touches ne'er touched earthly faces."

But were some child of yours alive that time,
You should live twice, in it and in my rhyme.
Sonnet 17

Dear my love, you know
You had a father; let your son say so.
Sonnet 13

It's interesting to note in these last two examples that the poet refers to both the man's father and mother.

Thou art thy mother's glass [mirror], *and she in thee*
Calls back the lovely April of her prime.

Sonnet 3. Perhaps a reference to their mother who, as an adult, was horribly scarred by smallpox?

The author C. S. Lewis wrote of the sonnets:

His language is too lover-like for that of ordinary male friendship; and though the claims of friendship are sometimes put very high in, say, the *Arcadia,* I have found no real parallel to such language between friends in sixteenth-century literature. Yet, on the other hand, this does not seem to be the poetry of full-blown pederasty. . . . The incessant demand that the Man should marry and found a family would seem to be inconsistent . . . with a real homosexual passion. It is not even very obviously consistent with normal friendship. It is indeed hard to think of any real situation in which it would be natural. What man in the whole world, except a father or a potential father-in-law, cares whether any other man gets married? Thus the emotion expressed in the Sonnets refuses to fit into our pigeonholes.[8]

The sonnets do not fit into pigeonholes. They do not fulfill any of the pat explanations of Renaissance male friendship. They do not resemble the sonnets written by any other man of the time. Perhaps a man did not write these sonnets.

At almost 30 years of age, Mary's brother Philip did finally marry 16-year-old Frances Walsingham, the daughter of Sir Francis Walsingham, the Queen's Secretary of State. It's ironic that so many of these first sonnets implore the man to have a child before he dies, and Philip did indeed die very early in his life, not long after his daughter Elizabeth was born. (His wife Frances was pregnant with a second child when Philip died, but she miscarried at about five months.)

Is it possible that Mary Sidney wrote these early sonnets, the procreation sonnets, to express her feelings to and about her brother Philip (who at the time had yet to get married and have a child)? Might they also be studies in her craft, experimenting in the sonnet form alongside her brother as he wrote the sequence of *Astrophil and Stella*, *Certain Sonnets*, and the book *The Countess of Pembroke's Arcadia*?

"Death shall not brag"

If the first seventeen sonnets are Mary writing to Philip, encouraging him to have a child and heir before he dies, then Sonnet 18, one you might be familiar with, may be read as a shattered goodbye to a youthful Philip upon his death in war.

As Wilson said, "And then comes sonnet 18; and there is no talk of marriage in it, or for ever afterwards."[9]

Regarding the third line, Katherine Duncan-Jones notes in the Arden collection of *Shakespeare's Sonnets*, "The image of often-spoiled spring blossoms hints at early death."[10]

Shall I compare thee to a summer's day?
Thou art more lovely and more temperate:
Rough winds do shake the darling buds of May,
And summer's lease hath all too short a date.

Sometime too hot the eye of heaven shines,
And often is his gold complexion dimmed;
And every fair from fair sometime declines,
By chance, or Nature's changing course untrimmed:

But thy eternal summer shall not fade,
Nor lose possession of that fair thou owest,
Nor shall Death brag thou wand'rest in his shade,
When in eternal lines to Time thou growest.

So long as men can breathe or eyes can see,
So long lives this, and this gives life to thee.

[paraphrase of Sonnet 18]

> Shall I compare you to a summer's day?
> You are lovelier than a summer's day and more even-tempered.
> In summer, rough winds shake the sweet new buds that sprouted
>   in May;
> And the summertime itself is much too short.
>
> Sometimes on a summer's day the sun shines too hot,
> And often it doesn't shine much at all;
> And everything that is beautiful eventually becomes less so,
> Either by chance, or simply from the progression of Time and Nature.
>
> But the eternal summer of your soul shall not fade,
> Nor will you lose the beauty that you have,
> Nor will Death brag that he has overtaken you.
> I have written about you in these lines of my poem, and so
>   the memory of you will be as eternal as Time.
>
> > As long as men can breathe or eyes can see,
> > This poem about you lives just as long, and this poem
> >   gives life to you, long after you are gone.

Philip's Influence

In Anne Ferry's book, *The "Inward" Language: Sonnets of Wyatt, Sidney, Shakespeare, Donne*, she explores the remarkable influence that Philip Sidney had on the author of the Shakespearean sonnets:

> 'O let me true in love but truly write' is the plea of the speaker in Shakespeare's Sonnet 21. The deliberate echo of the opening of [Philip Sidney's] *Astrophil and Stella* is verified by the poem as a whole, which assimilates many characteristic means invented by Sidney for representing Astrophil's struggle to show the truth of his love in verse. The issues involved in that effort about the relation of poetic language to inward experience are first raised in Shakespeare's sequence in this sonnet, which is so closely, complexly, and successfully patterned after a characteristic Sidneian model as to prove that Shakespeare there understood the issues in Sidney's terms, and learned his means for exploring them.[11]

Anne Ferry continues, "Shakespeare, *alone among English writers of love sonnets after Sidney*, [emphasis added] followed him in making these questions a central concern, assimilating their most far-reaching implications for what amounts to a new conception of human nature. Other poets, by contrast, borrowed only details of phrasing from Sidney, or imitated his motifs and manner." [12]

Ms. Ferry explores Philip Sidney's influence in shared themes and motifs, his vocabulary about art, imitations of specific personifications "like a quarrelsome personal Muse, or a neglectful Cupid," and even echoes of individual lines.[13] She shows that the poet of the Shakespearean sonnets "repeatedly turned to *Astrophil and Stella* for models," adapted individual poems, borrowed simultaneously from multiple poems, and combined "specific echoes with adaptations of devices more generally characteristic of Sidney's style." [14]

Beyond influences of writing style and subject, Ms. Ferry demonstrated that this poet absorbed "fundamental assumptions about human nature which are new to English poetry in *Astrophil and Stella*."[15] "The fullness and power of Shakespeare's adaptations show how profoundly he understood what were Sidney's different assumptions."[16]

It is curious, inconsistent, and unlikely that William Shakespeare, who never met Philip Sidney, "understood" him and his work so intimately and completely.

Only Mary Sidney among all the authorship candidates was in such close collaboration with Philip Sidney as to be able to explore and develop so deeply these new ideas in literature.

8 Sonnet Miscellany

O! let my books be
  then the eloquence
And dumb presagers
  of my speaking breast.
Sonnet 23

THERE ARE A NUMBER OF OTHER INTRIGUING PIECES of information about the Shakespearean sonnets. For instance, not all of the sonnets in the collection are love poems. It's puzzling to note how often the poet laments of obscurity, frustration, and disgrace. But why would William Shakespeare complain of obscurity and disgrace when the sonnets were written and published during the supposed height of his achievements and popularity?

David Honneyman remarks that "there is a persistent sense of failure, of disappointment, and of complaints against Fortune which are out of phase with Shakespeare's accelerating prosperity."[1]

The sonnets were published in 1609. By this time all but five of the plays had been written. (Shakespeare died in 1616.)

Could these be the laments of a brilliant woman?

> Let those who are in favor with their stars
> > [those who are born male?]
> Of public honor and proud titles boast
> > [men who can publish openly?]
> Whilst I, whom fortune of such triumph bars . . .
> > [because she is a woman?]
>
> Sonnet 25

"Stars" can refer to fortune or fate, and they can also refer to the members of the royal court.

When, in disgrace with Fortune and men's eyes,
I all alone beweep my outcast state,
And trouble deaf heaven with my bootless cries,   [useless cries]
And look upon myself and curse my fate,
Wishing me like to one more rich in hope,
Featured like him, like him with friends possessed,
Desiring this man's art and that man's scope,
With what I most enjoy contented least . . .

Sonnet 29   "What I am most gifted with gives me the
least satisfaction," because she cannot claim
her art to the world?

So I, made lame by Fortune's dearest spite . . .

Sonnet 37   "I am handicapped by a grievious spite
of fortune," by being born a woman?

My name be buried where my body is,
And live no more to shame nor me nor you . . .

Sonnet 72

Sonnet 81 is another melancholy complaint. If there is a connection between Mary Sidney and William Shakespeare, could she have written this with him in mind?

Or I shall live your epitaph to make,
Or you survive when I in earth am rotten,
From hence your memory death cannot take,
Although in me each part will be forgotten.

Your name from hence immortal life shall have,
Though I, once gone, to all the world must die:
The earth can yield me but a common grave,
When you entombed in men's eyes shall lie.

Your monument shall be my gentle verse,
Which eyes not yet created shall o'erread;
And tongues to be your being shall rehearse.
When all the breathers of this world are dead:

> *You still shall live (such virtue hath my pen)*
> *Where breath most breathes, even in the mouths of men.*

[paraphrase of Sonnet 81]

> *Whether I live long enough to write your epitaph,*
> *Or if you're still living when I'm long dead,*
> *From here on out, death cannot take the memory of you*
>   *from this world,*
> *But me, all of my accomplishments will be forgotten.*
>
> *From now on your name will have immortal life,*
> *But me, once I'm dead, the entire world will forget me.*
> *I will have an ordinary grave of no particular distinction,*
> *But you shall be seen forever, even after you're dead, in men's eyes.*
>
> *Because my ennobling compositions will be your memorial,*
> *And people who aren't even born yet will read them over and over,*
> *And people who aren't even born yet will speak of you.*
> *When everyone now alive in the world is dead:*
>
> > *You shall live on forever, for my writing has that much power*
> > *You shall live on where spoken words are most spoken,*
> >   *especially in the mouths of men.*

The Publication Issues

Another of the mysterious elements about these sonnets is that there is no dedication from the author. Rather, the dedication is from the publisher, "to Mr. W. H." as "the only begetter of these ensuing sonnets."

Experts believe the poet did not authorize the printing because typically an author would check the finished pages as they came off the press and make corrections. When multiple copies of a finished book are compared, one can see the corrections; in the book of Shakespearean sonnets, the mistakes went uncorrected.

The book was a flop. Katherine Duncan-Jones compares the success of the Shakespearean narrative poems printed in 1593 and 1594, *Venus and Adonis* and *The Rape of Lucrece,* with the book of sonnets: "Whereas the early narrative poems were received with immediate enthusiasm, prompting dozens of early allusions, citations and imitations, the 1609 Q [quarto, or small book of sonnets] seems to have been greeted largely in silence—a silence the more surprising given Shakespeare's literary celebrity in 1609, in contrast to his relative obscurity in 1593–94."[2]

John Dover Wilson noticed this: "That Thorpe engaged two booksellers to unload his treasure trove on to the public suggests that he anticipated a brisk sale. Yet no second edition was called for."[3]

In a recent book of essays, James Schiffer concurs that "these poems were virtually ignored for their first 170 years of existence."[4]

Wilson wonders about the failure of the book. "The usual explanation given is that by 1609 the poetry-reading public had grown tired of sonnets: the sonnet craze, dating from the appearance in 1591 of [Philip] Sidney's *Astrophil and Stella*, being supposedly exhausted eighteen years later. It was declining, no doubt, but Drayton's *Idea's Mirror* had been reprinted six times since its appearance in 1590 and was reprinted three times after 1609."[5]

Once again we have conflicting information—traditional Shakespearean scholarship assures us that the "sonnet craze" had passed and no one wanted to read sonnets anymore, an excuse used to explain the failure of Shakespeare's book. But even Wilson has to question this, since records show that the sonnets of other authors continued to be popular and reprinted for many years.

Why were these sonnets so demonstrably unsuccessful? Why was this book not circulated? Apparently someone other than the poet sent the sonnets to press under Shakespeare's name. When William Shakespeare saw the homosexual implications of the poems with his name on them, did he demand their suppression?

Schiffer says, "Various explanations have been offered as to why the 1609 Quarto did not achieve more initial success. The most dramatic theory, offered by John Dover Wilson and others, is that the 'unauthorized' volume was suppressed by Shakespeare, with the help of a powerful friend (in Dover Wilson's theory, that friend is William Herbert, the Earl of Pembroke), presumably because of the embarrassing true-life story the Sonnets presumably reveal."[6]

Responding to the theory that someone beseeched William Herbert (Mary Sidney's son) to suppress the sale of the sonnets, the *Reader's Encyclopedia of Shakespeare* notes that the publisher, Thomas Thorpe, did something unusual: "In this connection, it is interesting to note that in the next year Thorpe published a volume which he dedicated, in extremely obsequious terms, to William Herbert, Earl of Pembroke and one of the candidates for the title of Mr. W. H."[7]

Is Mary's son, William Herbert, the "Mr. W. H." whom the publisher, Thorpe, acknowledged as "the only begetter" of these poems? We do know that it was during this time that Mary and her son William were estranged. Was it because of her affair with the doctor? Was it over his affair with his cousin Mary Wroth? Had William Herbert discovered by this time that his mother was writing plays for the public theater? Did he take this collection of sonnets to press and have them published under William Shakespeare's name, as a number of the plays had been?

A Puzzling Epigram

Shortly after the publication of the Sonnets, an English poet named John Davies of Hereford wrote a short and cryptic epigram titled:

"To our English Terence, Mr. Will. Shake-speare."

Terence was an impoverished writer in ancient Rome who made a living by publishing the works of noblemen under his own name. "It is commonly said that Scipio [a Roman aristocrat] and Laelius [tribune, legate, governor] assisted the author in his plays; and indeed, Terence himself increased that suspicion by the little pains he took to refute it . . . ." To remove the aspersion of plagiarism, Terence took a boat to Greece and was never heard from again. "Some ancient writers relate that he died at sea."[8]

An engaging connection between Mary Sidney and this epigram is that its author, John Davies of Hereford, was Mary's secretary.[9]

Did John Davies quietly suspect that she was writing the plays for which William Shakespeare was getting credit, as Terence received credit for the plays of the noblemen?

Below is the first half of Davies' epigram, which has been interpreted in a wide variety of ways by a diverse group of scholars, which indicates that no one really knows what it means. "In fact, biographers find Davies' poem almost incomprehensible."[10]

To our English Terence, Mr. Will. Shake-speare.

Some say, (good Will)—which I, in sport, do sing—
Hadst thou not played some Kingly parts in sport,
Thou hadst been a companion for a King,
And, been a King among the meaner sort.[11]

Davies' epigram was published in 1610, the year following the publication of the sonnets. The sonnets suggest that the "author" William Shakespeare was gay. Was Davies making a snide comment (in sport) connecting Shakespeare with King James, knowing the King preferred male lovers? Was he saying that if Shakespeare hadn't been a baseborn actor, playing kingly parts on stage (in sport), he might have been a good companion for the King James? And if he had been a companion for King James, he would have been his own king among the "meaner" sort (low class, like himself) because King James bestowed great gifts upon his lovers.

A Sonnet Collection?

Many scholars believe that not all of the sonnets published in the collection are by the same author, including the lengthy poem that was printed at the end of the book, *A Lover's Complaint*. Mary was surrounded by writers in her family—her parents wrote eloquently, her brothers Philip and Robert published books of sonnets, her son William published a book of sonnets, her daughter is believed to have been a writer, her niece was a writer. Might she have encouraged her lover, Matthew Lister, to write sonnets? Did the published book of sonnets that went to press against her will inadvertently include poems from others in her close circle?

If Mary Sidney was the author of most of the sonnets, there are still unanswered questions, but she is the only one who even begins to have personal, documented evidence to connect her life to the story line of these poems.

Part Four
The Sources

My library was dukedom large enough.

Prospero in *The Tempest*, 1.ii.109

Documented Data

- More than 200 books have been acknowledged by experts as sources for the Shakespearean plays. Often several editions of the same book were used.

- About two dozen of the French, Italian, and Latin sources had not been translated into English during Shakespeare's lifetime.

- No book owned or used by William Shakespeare has ever been found.

The Sources *of the Plays*

9

FOR MORE THAN A HUNDRED YEARS scholars and critics have acknowledged not only contemporary references to current events incorporated into the Shakespearean plays, but specific plot lines, literary motifs, characterizations, and word-for-word lines taken from existing books. The lengthy list of books that we know the author consulted is shown in the Prologue on pages xxiii–xxvi.

But not one book has ever been found that was owned by William Shakespeare or anyone in his family, and there were no public libraries.[1] Nor have documented connections been made between Shakespeare and any of the source books or authors.

Mary Sidney, on the other hand, is intimately associated with quite a few of the sources for the plays. Either she wrote the source material herself, her brother wrote it, someone in her literary circle wrote it, it was dedicated to her or her brother, or the book included information about or connected with her family.

Source research to date[2] is presented on the following pages with Sidney and Shakespeare connections paralleled.

Source	Mary Sidney	Shakespeare
About two dozen of the reference books used in the plays were available only in French, Italian, or Latin,[3] with no English translations during Shakespeare's lifetime.	Mary translated works from French and Italian, is known to have been proficient in Latin, and owned books in those as well as other languages.	There is no evidence that Shakespeare was fluent in any foreign language.
Raphael Holinshed's book, *The Chronicles of England, Scotland, and Ireland*, was used in twelve plays.[4] Specifically, the second edition was used, printed in 1587.	The 1587 edition includes a memorial account of Mary's brother Philip, as well as an account of the "excellent" death of Mary's mother, Mary Dudley Sidney.	No recorded connection.
Arcadia, which Bevington calls "this greatest of all Elizabethan prose romances," was used as a source for five plays,[5] including the story of an "unkind king" and a father being blinded by his ungrateful son in the depths of a cold winter. Regarding the several debts to *Arcadia* in King Lear, Bevington also says, "Albany's speeches about anarchy . . . recall one of [Philip] Sidney's deepest concerns."[6]	This book was written by Mary's brother Philip, for Mary, at Mary's request. It was written mostly in Mary's home and Mary published it. In 1685, John Aubrey said about *Arcadia*, ". . . but many or most of the verses in the *Arcadia* were made by her Honour [Mary], and they seem to have been writt by a woman."[7]	No recorded connection.
The works of Samuel Daniel, including *The First Four Books of the Civil Wars* (1595), were used as sources for five plays.[8]	Samuel Daniel was Mary's protégé. As mentioned on page 37, Daniel credits Mary with having been his best teacher of writing.[9] This particular work about the Civil Wars was begun at Wilton. The expanded edition of 1609 was dedicated to Mary.	No recorded connection.
Thomas Kyd's *Cornelia*, translated from the French Senecan tragedy *Cornélie*, by Garnier, is a source for *Julius Caesar*.	"She [Mary Sidney] diverted Thomas Kyd from his true vocation as a writer for the popular stage by persuading him, about 1594, to translate another play of Garnier's, *Cornélie*."[10]	No recorded connection.

Source	Mary Sidney	Shakespeare
As a source for *Antony and Cleopatra*, "Most important for Shakespeare were *The Tragedy of Antony*, translated from Robert Garnier's *Marc Antoine* by Mary [Sidney] Herbert, Countess of Pembroke . . . and *The Tragedy of Cleopatra* by Samuel Daniel." [11] Bevington also states, regarding these sources, "Shakespeare certainly gained from such works as these a sense of tragic greatness in his protagonists." [12]	Mary wrote *The Tragedy of Antony*, also called *Antonius* or *Antonie*. "The influence of her translation may be seen in Shakespeare's *Antony and Cleopatra*, which echoes structural and thematic elements of *Antonius* as well as occasional phrasing. "Both [Mary] Pembroke and Shakespeare emphasize Antony's cross-dressing, a detail absent in Garnier." [13] "Verbal parallels establish that Shakespeare knew Garnier in [Mary] Pembroke's translation. . . . the parallels are too numerous to be coincidental." [14] Samuel Daniel's book *Cleopatra* was written at Mary's request and under her tutelage, "'the work the which she did impose,' for she bade him 'To sing of State, and tragic notes to frame.'" [15] It was "designed as a companion piece to *Antony* and dedicated to the Countess of Pembroke." [16] "*Cleopatra* had been a closet drama, designed only for reading to the highly cultured ears of the Wilton art circle." [17]	No recorded connection.
The Reader's Encyclopedia states, "Romeo's last speech in the tomb contains echoes of *Astrophil and Stella* and Daniel's *Complaint of Rosamond*." [18]	*Astrophil and Stella* was written by Mary's brother, Philip Sidney. As mentioned above, Daniel was a protégé of Mary's and credits her with teaching him how to write.	No recorded connection.
The original Latin version of Ovid's *Metamorphoses* and the 1567 translation by Arthur Golding were used in four plays. [19]	Arthur Golding was personally known to Mary; he completed one of Philip's unfinished translations after Philip died. This particular 1567 translation was dedicated to Mary's uncle, Robert Dudley, the Earl of Leicester.	If he went to grammar school (although undocumented, Shakespeareans assume he did), he may have read Ovid.

Source	Mary Sidney	Shakespeare
Scholars recognize not only the number of references in the plays to Seneca, an early Roman tragedian, but also the elements throughout the plays that are inspired by his style.	"In 1590 Mary Sidney, Countess of Pembroke, initiated the courtly Senecan movement which led several members of her circle to write Roman tragedies within the next ten or fifteen years."[20] "The genre [Senecan closet drama] was also particularly suited for women who desired to write plays but would not be permitted to write for the public arena."[21] [emphasis added]	No recorded connection.
"Shakespeare . . . seems to be indebted to [Mary's translation of] Discourse for some of the Senecan elements in Measure for Measure."[22]	As noted above, Mary initiated the Senecan literary movement, and of course she is the author of this source, A Discourse of Life and Death.	No recorded connection.
Both the 1570 and the 1583 editions of John Foxe's Acts and Monuments of Martyrs were sources for five of the history plays.[23]	In 1573, "The Sidneys purchased a copy of 'two books of Martirs' (the two volumes familiarly known as Foxe's Book of Martyrs) when Mary Sidney was a child. The book included tales of heroic death, including that of her aunt Lady Jane Grey."[24]	No recorded connection.
A book by Matteo Bandello called Novelle (1554) was the source for three plays.[25] "Shakespeare seems to have relied more on the Italian version by Matteo Bandello and its French translation by Belleforest, Histoires Tragiques."[26]	This book is known to have belonged to Mary's brother Philip. "It is a copy of the French version of Bandello's romances, Histoires Tragiques."[27] Philip's copy of this book still survives, complete with its inscription. Also, a writer named Geoffrey Fenton dedicated a collection of translations of Novelle to Mary's mother.	No recorded connection.

Source	Mary Sidney	Shakespeare
John Stow's books, *The Chronicles of England* (1580) and particularly *The Annals of England* (1592 edition) were used in three of the English history plays.[28]	The 1592 edition of *The Annals of England* includes an account of a spectacular entertainment for the Queen that Mary's brother Philip helped write and design and also participated in. This book also includes an account of the battle in which Philip died; in fact, "The description in Stow's *Annals* tells of [Philip] Sidney's gathering his men before the attack and addressing them in terms similar to King Henry's before the walls of Harfleur."[29] "John Stow tells of how Philip, a mile away from their destination, made a speech to the soldiers—which, to the modern ear, might eerily prefigure Shakespeare's Henry V before Agincourt.... This oration, according to Stow, 'did so link the minds of the people that they desired rather to die in that service than to live in the contrary.'"[30]	No recorded connection.
Ariosto's *Orlando Furioso*, originally written in Italian in 1516, translated into English by Sir John Harington in 1591, was consulted for *Much Ado About Nothing*.	In Harington's translation of *Orlando Furioso*, he praises Mary in an allegory.[31] Harington was a good friend of both Mary and her brother Robert, was several times at Wilton, and praised Mary's *Psalms* as "precious leaves" that "shall outlast Wilton walls."[32]	No recorded connection.
Edmund Spenser's book *The Faerie Queene* was a source for three of the plays.[33]	Spenser was a protégé of Philip's and is considered to have been a member of the Wilton Circle. Spenser praised Mary in a dedicatory sonnet in *The Faerie Queene* and again in *Colin Clouts Come Home Again*. He dedicated *The Ruins of Time* to her and dedicated *Shepherd's Calendar* to Philip.[34]	No recorded connection.

Source	Mary Sidney	Shakespeare
Sir Thomas North's 1579 English translation of *Plutarch's Lives of the Noble Grecians and Romans* was the most-often used source for the Shakespearean plays after 1600.	In discussing Mary's translation of *The Tragedy of Antonie*, Hannay says, "In her 'Argument,' she mentions only Plutarch, which she used primarily in Sir Thomas North's 1579 English translation of *Plutarch's Lives of the Noble Grecians and Romans*, the work that was also the basis for Shakespeare's Roman History plays."[35]	No recorded connection.
Thomas Moffett's book, *Of the Silkwormes and their Flies,* was not in print until 1599, about five years after it was used as a source in *A Midsummer Night's Dream.* The author of the play read the unpublished manuscript.	This book was dedicated to Mary Sidney and refers to Mary (as "Mira") in the book. She would have read the unpublished manuscript because the author, Dr. Moffett, was her estate physician and lived at Wilton until his death.	No recorded connection.
A Journal of the Siege of Rouen, written by Sir Thomas Coningsby, was used as a source for *1 Henry VI,* according to *The Riverside Shakespeare.* This manuscript was not printed until 1847.	Sir Thomas Coningsby was a good friend of Mary's brother Philip. Coningsby accompanied Philip on his European tour. Later he married Mary's cousin Philippa.	No recorded connection.
"It was natural that England's greatest living playwright, William Shakespeare, in penning his dramas, should make use of the *Geneva Bible,* rather than the official translations urged on the English people by the church authorities."[36]	Mary used the *Geneva Bible* as one of her main sources while versifying the *Psalms.*	No recorded connection.
Four Paradoxes, or Politique Discourses by Thomas and Dudley Digges was used as a source for *Coriolanus.*	This book honors Mary's brother Philip. Thomas Digges was with Philip in Zutphen during the battle in which Philip was fatally wounded.[37]	No recorded connection.

Source	Mary Sidney	Shakespeare
In 1599, Lewis Lewkenor translated Gasparo Contarini's Italian book into *The Commonwealth and Government of Venice*. "The first book in English to deal exclusively with Venice, it may have been read in manuscript by Shakespeare and used for the legal background of Shakespeare's *Merchant of Venice*. The book was definitely used by the poet for *Othello*, not only for information about Venice, but for Othello's defense against the charge of witchcraft."[38] *The Merchant of Venice* was registered as a play in July, 1598, a year before the publication of Lewkenor's translation.	Philip Sidney owned a copy of Contarini's original, probably purchased in Venice in 1574.[39] Lewkenor wrote two books that included Philip Sidney's actions during the war in Flanders in 1586. *A Discourse of the Usage of the English Fugitives, by the Spaniards* includes Philip's involvement in taking Axel, and it details the cruel and tyrannous butchering of the men whom Philip had sent into the town of Gravelines.[40] When Lewkenor returned to England from the European continent in 1590, he was one of the first to appeal to Mary's younger brother Robert Sidney for patronage.[41]	Sir Lewkenor had a "remote kinship with the Combe family of Stratford with whom Shakespeare was friendly."[42]
The most important source for *The Tempest* was a letter written by William Strachey, the secretary to the Virgina Company, describing the shipwreck in the Bermudas. The letter was not made public until 1625 (nine years after Shakespeare died) to prevent unpleasant publicity about the Virginia Company's explorations. *Why look you pale? Sea-sick, I think, coming from Muscovy.* Rosaline in *Love's Labor's Lost*, 2.v.393–394	Mary, her brother Robert, her husband, and both sons were all founders and stockholders of the Virginia Company,[43] to which the Strachey letter was written. Robert had an active part in the management of the organization. Intriguingly, Strachey's letter was specifically addressed to an unidentified "Excellent Lady." Mary had a lifelong interest in New World exploration—she helped finance Sir Martin Frobisher's voyages in the 1570s and Edward Fenton's voyage in the 1580s as well.[44] Her father, as well as Adrian Gilbert, had been involved with the Muscovy Company years earlier.	Shakespeare had a friend who had a stepson who was involved with New World exploration who "could have been the playwright's source for the 1610 letter by William Strachey," although this stepson was not connected with the Virgina Company, nor did he have a speaking relationship with his stepfather. During the time of the Strachey letter, the stepson had been harassing his stepfather "for years with a long, acrimonious lawsuit."[45]

Source	Mary Sidney	Shakespeare
Also regarding *The Tempest*, scholars agree that the author kept up with the New World travel accounts of Sir Walter Raleigh.	Sir Walter Raleigh was a close friend of Mary's. At one point she successfully appealed to the King to prevent Raleigh from being executed for another few years.[46]	No recorded connection.
There are several references to Richard Tarleton (also spelled Tarlton) as a source. Scholars attribute Tarleton's *News Out of Purgatory* as a source for *The Merry Wives of Windsor*. *The Riverside Shakespeare* also attributes the unpublished manuscript of *The Famous Victories of Henry V*, generally ascribed to Tarleton, as a source for *Henry V*.[47] *The Reader's Encyclopedia of Shakespeare* states that "Hamlet's advice to the players (*Hamlet*, 3.ii.42–50) may have been prompted by Tarlton's practice."[48] Also, "Scholars have conjectured that Tarlton was the model for Yorick whose skull Hamlet recovers from the graveyard . . . ."[49]	Richard Tarleton, the famous comic genius with the Queen's Men, was a servant of Mary's uncle Robert Dudley, the Earl of Leicester. Tarleton was an actor and playwright, and a member of Leicester's Men, the acting troupe sponsored by Dudley. For years Tarleton worked and traveled with her uncle. Mary grew up with these acting companies providing entertainment in the great houses. Mary's brother Philip was godfather to Tarleton's son in 1582.[50]	No recorded connection. Richard Tarleton died in 1588, several years before William Shakespeare is believed to have gone to London.
Two plays[51] use John Florio's translation of Montaigne's *Essays*. "Shakespeare could have read Montaigne in the French original or, if he had access to a manuscript, in John Florio's English translation published in 1603."[52]	Mary could have read the French original, of course, but she also had access to the unpublished manuscript of this translation of Montaigne because Florio was closely connected with the Wilton Circle. In fact, he attacks Mary's literary judgment in the dedication to Book II. His second volume of *Essays* is dedicated to Mary's niece (Philip's daughter Elizabeth) and to Lady Rich (Penelope Devereux), who was raised by Mary's aunt Katherine Dudley, Countess of Huntington.	No recorded connection.

Source	Mary Sidney	Shakespeare
For *Richard II*, the author used a French eyewitness account available only in manuscript, Jean Créton's *Histoire du Roy d'Angleterre Richard*. John Dee is known to have had a copy.[53]	John Dee was a good friend of Mary and her entire family; he lived with her family for a while. Her brother Philip was considered one of his best pupils. The manuscript was in French and Mary was fluent in French.	No recorded connection.
Several of George Whetstone's literary works were used in *Much Ado About Nothing* and as a chief source in *Measure for Measure*.	Whetstone was a member of the Wilton Circle. He published a contemporary account of the battle in which Philip died, based on information from his own brother Bernard who had fought at Zutphen with Philip. And "it has been suggested that the main characters of his work may reflect something of Philip and Mary Sidney themselves."[54]	No recorded connection.
One of the probable sources for *Two Gentlemen of Verona* is a children's play presented at Elizabeth's court in 1577, a play about two friends, Titus and Gisippus.[55]	Mary was living at court in 1577.	No recorded connection.
Two of the few songs that have definite sources (in *As You Like It* and *Twelfth Night*) are in music books by Thomas Morley, one of the greatest Elizabethan composers of madrigals and lute songs.[56]	Morley dedicated his manuscript score *Canzonets* to Mary, not requesting patronage for the dedication, but merely for the honor of her acceptance of his songs.[57]	For several years Shakespeare lived in the same area of London as Thomas Morley.[58]
The 19-day royal extravaganza in July, 1575, at Kenilworth Castle has long been thought by many scholars to have supplied several images for *A Midsummer Night's Dream*.[59]	Mary attended the 1575 extravaganza at Kenilworth, home of her uncle Robert Dudley, Earl of Leicester, along with her parents and her brother Philip.[60]	No recorded connection.

Source	Mary Sidney	Shakespeare
E. K. Chambers identifies the source of several images in *A Midsummer Night's Dream* as a water fête presented by Edward Seymour, the Earl of Hertford to the Queen in 1591 at his Elvetham estate.[61]	The Earl of Hertford had long been associated with Mary and her family. A few years after the water fête, the Earl made an unsuccessful attempt to marry Anne Herbert, Mary's daughter (Anne was 16, the Earl 62). The Earl of Hertford was previously married to Catherine Grey, Mary's husband's first—but annulled—wife.	No recorded connection.
"Many scholars have argued that Burghley [William Cecil, Lord Burghley] is being satirized as Polonius in *Hamlet*. Evidence of this view is believed to be found in Burghley's 'Certain Precepts, or Directions' (1616) which he wrote for his son, Robert Cecil, and which Shakespeare may have seen in manuscript."[62]	Robert Cecil (Burghley's son) was a close friend of Mary's. They had grown up together because Burghley's wife, Mildred Cooke, was the best friend of Mary's mother. There are extant letters from Mary to both Burghley and his son Robert. Another close friend of Robert Cecil was Mary's oldest son, William Herbert. Mary's brother Philip was almost engaged (at age 14) to Burghley's daughter, Anne, but Anne ran off instead with Edward de Vere, the Earl of Oxford, "who made her and her family thoroughly miserable."[63] Years later Mary went through extensive marriage arrangements for her older son, William, with Burghley's granddaughter Bridget. Since the girl's father (Oxford) had abandoned her long ago, grandpa Burghley was the one making arrangements. That deal fell through, but Mary's younger son Philip, after Oxford died, secretly arranged to marry Burghley's other granddaughter, Susan.	No recorded connection. The letter wasn't published until the year Shakespeare died, which was fifteen years after *Hamlet* was written.

Source	Mary Sidney	Shakespeare
In an article in the *Sidney Journal,* Katherine Duncan-Jones writes, "By the mid-1590s, then, it seems that Shakespeare was beginning to be importantly influenced by [Philip] Sidney's writings, both in terms of their verbal and metaphoric detail, and in terms of their literary ideals. It seems likely that he [Shakespeare] had some access to Sidney's writings in manuscript, in advance of their print publication."[64]	In *Literary Patronage in the English Renaissance: The Pembroke Family,* Michael Brennan states, ". . . during the decade following Sidney's death [in 1586], the Countess's households at Wilton and Baynard's Castle, along with those of Robert Sidney, Fulke Greville [Philip's best friend] and the Countess of Rutland [Philip's daughter], remained the most likely locations where writers might gain access to Sidney's literary works before they became generally available in print."[65]	No recorded connection.
"The only instruments not used in the theatre were the organ and the virginals . . . . That Shakespeare knew this instrument [the virginals] is indicated by the jealous Leontes' 'Still virginalling upon his palm' [*The Winter's Tale*, 1.ii.125– 126] as he observes Polixenes caressing his wife's hand."[66]	Mary played the virginals (which is like a small harpsichord), as evidenced by the family household records that detail the maintenance of her virginals.[67]	No recorded connection.
The constable in *Much Ado About Nothing* is one of the few illiterate characters in the plays.	The constable in Wiltshire, where Mary lived, was illiterate. In 1616 he pleaded to be released from his office: ". . . forasmuch as I am unlearned, and by reason thereof am constrained to go two miles from my house to have the help of a scrivener to read such warrants as are sent unto me."[68]	No recorded connection.
Regarding the sonnets, scholar Claes Schaar says, "The thesis that Shakespeare as a writer of sonnets was indebted to Daniel's *Delia* has become widely accepted in English literary history."[69]	Samuel Daniel dedicated his sonnet sequence *Delia* to Mary in 1592. Most scholars believe the woman named "Delia" in the poems refers to Mary herself. It was at Wilton, where Daniel lived for years, that he learned to compose poetry under Mary's tutelage.[70]	No recorded connection.

Source	Mary Sidney	Shakespeare
The Shakespearean plays and sonnets contain approximately 1,500 words that were new to the English language. These new words were either freshly created, or were existing words combined into new words or used with new meanings.	"Pembroke [Mary] is inventive in coining new words and recycling old ones."[71] (and all below) "The OED [Oxford English Dictionary] credits Pembroke with the first recorded use of twenty-seven words," including *sea-monster*, as used in the plays (also *maid-of-honor*). "More than forty words are cited as instances of the first use in particular senses," including *eternize, measure, shallow,* and *winged,* and used in the same sense in the plays. "In addition are words used by the countess before the earliest citations in the OED . . . (such as *thunderstrike*, as used in the plays) and words used in particular senses before the earliest citation in the OED," such as *candy, oblivion, unsounded,* and *void,* as used in the same senses in the plays. These are just a few of the words invented by Mary found in the Shakespearean works.	We have nothing in writing by the man named William Shakespeare (except a few signatures) with which to compare the vocabulary or usage in the plays and sonnets.
Regarding the fictional Captain Fluellen in *Henry V*, "Shakespeare may have found his inspiration for Fluellen in a member of Elizabeth's court," one of Essex's companions named Roger Williams.[72]	This same Roger Williams was a very close friend of Mary's brother Philip, who spent most of his adult years at Mary's home.	No recorded connection.
"It has been suggested that David Gam is the original of Shakespeare's Fluellen. This is not at all an improbable conjecture, as Fluellen is plainly a corruption of Llewelyn, and David was generally called David Llewelyn, or ab Llewelyn."[73] Davy Gam himself is listed as dying on the battlefield at the end of Act 4 in *Henry V*.	Davy Gam was the great-great-great grandfather of Mary Sidney's husband. Gam's daughter became the mother of William Herbert, 1st Earl of Pembroke in the Herbert house. (*"Gam" is a nickname meaning "squinty-eyed."*)	No recorded connection.

Source	Mary Sidney	Shakespeare
In *A Literary History of England*, Brooke and Shaaber state, "Similar farcical characters, Lalus and Rombus, in [Philip] Sidney's masque, "The Lady of May" (1578), appear to be prototypes of Don Armada and Holofernes in *Love's Labor's Lost*." [74]	Although "The Lady of May" was handwritten for the Queen in 1578, Mary did not publish it until 1598, several years after *Love's Labor's Lost* was written.	No recorded connection.
Rosencrantz and Guildenstern are the names of two schoolmates of Hamlet's in the play. Two Danish students named Rosencrantz and Guildenstern studied at the Padua University, along with Roger Manners, Fifth Earl of Rutland. Manners also spent time in Elsinor, the scene of *Hamlet*. [75]	Roger Manners, the Earl of Rutland, married Mary's niece, Elizabeth (Philip's daughter).	No recorded connection.
Dr. John Caius appears in *The Merry Wives of Windsor* as a foul-mouthed, irascible, excitable Frenchman. Some scholars see this Dr. John Caius as the same man who was founder of Caius College at Cambridge and who had a temperament similar to the character in the play. He died in 1573, twenty-four years before *Merry Wives* was written.	Henry VIII's son, the young King Edward VI, died in the arms of Mary's father, Henry Sidney. One of King Edward's doctors was Dr. John Caius of Cambridge, indicating that Mary's father knew him well.	No recorded connection.
Many scholars agree with the statement "That Shakespeare was an ardent admirer of Essex seems almost certain." [76]	This Earl of Essex (Robert Devereux) was an intimate family friend and Mary's step-cousin. When Mary's brother Philip died, Essex inherited Philip's "best sword" and married his widow. There is an extant letter that Mary wrote to Essex. Essex was the stepson, protégé, and chief heir of Mary's uncle, Robert Dudley.	No recorded connection.

Source	Mary Sidney	Shakespeare
In *The Merry Wives of Windsor*, it is thought that the incident involving the three German horse thieves and their Duke is an insider joke for Elizabeth's courtiers regarding Count Mompelgard, a German nobleman who was obsessively intent on being inducted as a Knight of the Order of the Garter. In *Twelfth Night*, "Scholars have suggested that the Malvolio plot may reflect an incident at Queen Elizabeth's court in which the Comptroller of the Household, Sir William Knollys, interrupted a noisy late-night party dressed in only his nightshirt and a pair of spectacles, with a copy of the Italian pornographic writer Aretino's work in his hand."[77]	This was Mary's world, her peers and friends—the royal court and all its gossip.	No recorded connection.
In *The Merry Wives of Windsor*, there are clear and obvious references to the Knights of the Garter and its investiture ceremonies.	Mary's father, husband, two sons, and younger brother Robert were all invested as Knights of the Garter. Her brother Philip was knighted (not as K. G.) specifically so he could stand in as proxy for his close friend John Casimir, Duke of Bavaria, when Casimir was invested as a Knight of the Garter. Women were allowed to watch the ceremony from the shrine in the Great Hall of Windsor Castle.	No recorded connection.
The translation of Richard Robinson's *Gesta Romanorum* was used as a source for *The Merchant of Venice* (and possibly for *Pericles* and *The Comedy of Errors*).	Mary's father, Henry Sidney, and her brother Philip were generous patrons of Richard Robinson. Robinson was also the scribe of one of the *Arcadia* manuscripts.[78]	No recorded connection.

Source	Mary Sidney	Shakespeare
The central assertion of *The Chemical Theatre* by Charles Nicholl is that "the symbols and themes of Renaissance alchemy are woven into the language and structure of Shakespeare's great tragedy, *King Lear*."[79] The author also points out the many images and references to alchemy that appear in the plays and sonnets.	Mary had her own chemical/alchemy laboratory, as mentioned earlier. Aubrey said of Mary Sidney, "Her Honour's genius lay as much towards chemistry as poetry."[80] Mary's family, as well as her lab assistant Adrian Gilbert, was well acquainted with the famous alchemist and astrologer John Dee. "Dee had long been associated with Sidney's family, and probably began tutoring Sidney in alchemy and related magical pursuits in the early 1570s."[81] Giordano Bruno was the other most prominent alchemist and "magician" in Europe. He dedicated his two most important works to Philip Sidney.[82]	No recorded connection.
"The wording of Berowne's famous monologue in praise of love from *Love's Labor's Lost* mirrors a similar speech from Bruno's *The Expulsion of the Triumphant Beast*."[83]	Bruno dedicated *The Expulsion of the Triumphant Beast* to Mary's brother Philip.[84] Also see above.	No recorded connection.
Many plays are set in Europe, specifically Verona, Padua, Milan, Mantua, Venice, Vienna, and Bohemia. Scholars say some details about these places are amazingly accurate, while other details indicate the author wasn't really there but used second-hand descriptions.	Mary's older brother Philip spent more than three years in Europe and specifically stayed in Verona, Padua, Venice (which entailed going through Milan and Mantua), and Vienna, among other cities, including Prague (Bohemia), Hungary, and Cracow.[85] Philip "was certainly the most widely travelled of the major Elizabethan writers."[86] Mary's younger brother Robert Sidney also traveled extensively in Europe, visiting Prague, many cities in Germany, the Netherlands, and other places.[87] In her later years, Mary herself traveled extensively in northern Europe.	No record of having left England. No recorded connection with travelers.

Source	Mary Sidney	Shakespeare
Scholars have commented on the references, images, and dialects in the plays that seem to come directly from the areas of Kent (in southeast England) and Wales. Author Gilbert Slater noted, "Next to Kent, with London and Windsor, it is Wales that supplies the most local colour to the Shakespeare plays." [88] Frederick J. Harries produced an entire book on the influence of Wales in the plays (*Shakespeare and the Welsh*) and came to his own surprising conclusion that "it seems reasonably proved that he [Shakespeare] had Welsh blood in his veins, and it may have been from the lips of a Welsh grandmother that he obtained his first knowledge of Welsh tradition and folklore, which ... exerted no small influence upon his dramatic and lyrical genius." [89] The characters Fluellen in *Henry V* and Evans in *Merry Wives of Windsor* both speak with Welsh accents that are written directly into the dialogue in the plays.	Regarding Kent, Mary grew up in Kent at the Sidney family estate called Penshurst (which is now open to the public). Regarding London and Windsor, Mary had several homes in London and is documented as having spent time in Windsor by extant letters from her dated from Windsor. Regarding Wales, Mary was born on the border of Wales and spent summers in Ludlow Castle on the Welsh border. Her father, and later her husband, was Lord President of the Council of the Marches (border counties) of Wales. Her husband (whose father preferred to speak Welsh rather than English) was the Earl of the Welsh county of Pembrokeshire and owned the town of Cardiff in southern Wales, an estate that Mary administered. Her sister-in-law, Barbara Gamage, was Welsh and spent months at a time in Mary's home.	It has not been claimed that Shakespeare had Welsh ancestry (except in Harries' fantasy), nor that he ever spent time in Wales.
Harold Bloom wonders, "Shakespeare seems to have gone home again, to Stratford, in late 1610 or early 1611 [based on Stratford records], but then to have returned intermittently to London until sometime in 1613. After that, in the nearly three years before his death [1613 to 1616], he was in Stratford, writing nothing. The rest was silence, but why?" [90]	"In 1613, she [Mary Sidney] went abroad for almost three years. She was recorded at Flushing and Antwerp in 1614, and visited Stuttgart before returning to England in October 1616." [91]	No documented evidence regarding literary involvement during this time.

Source	Mary Sidney	Shakespeare
The use of falconry images in the Shakespearean plays has long been noted. The interesting thing is that there is only one scene that is actually about falconry. It is clear the author was so familiar with this sport that falconry images appear in political statements, love banter, jealousy, and other places.	In Mary's version of Psalm 83, she develops an extended metaphor from falconry to stress the hunting of God's people by their enemies. She also uses technical terms from falconry in Psalm 91.[92] Mary is known to have owned a book about hunting with hawks and falcons (a book written by a woman). Falconry was a common pastime among noblewomen.[93]	No recorded connection.
"'Shakespeare worked like a historical scholar, and made his histories by collating authorities, cross-checking and (in a word) Research.' There is no way of escaping from this conclusion. . . . Wilson found it necessary to suppose the existence of an intermediary, a dramatist 'soaked in the history of England,' who wrote Shakespeare's original, and so may be said to have done his research for him. This view is partly to be attributed to the difficulty we have in believing that Shakespeare worked on his material like a scholar-chronicler."[94] (See Chapter 11 for details.)	The Dudley genealogy (Mary's mother) includes the families of Neville, Beauchamp, Percy, Mortimer, and Hastings; the Herbert genealogy goes back to a bastard son of King Henry I.[95] The Kings Edward IV, Henry VII, Henry VIII, the Earls of Pembroke, Warwick, Northumberland, Westmorland, Salisbury, Kent, and others are in Mary's direct lineage. Every one of these families appears in the history plays, as well as Mary's family homesteads and homelands such as Baynards Castle, Ludlow, Shrewsbury, Kenilworth, Kent, Ampthill, and Wales, including Pembrokeshire and Milford Haven.[96]	No recorded connection.
Richard Grafton's 1569 edition of *A Chronicle at Large* is a source for the *Henry VI* plays and *King John*.	Mary's parents owned the 1548 edition of this work,[97] and then bought another one in 1573/74, which would be the 1569 edition, for which they paid 21 shillings.[98]	No recorded connection.
Lord Berners' translation of Jean Froissart's *The Chronicles of England* was used as a source for *Richard II*.	The Sidney family paid 27 shillings for a copy of this book in 1573/74.[99]	No recorded connection.

Just the Beginning

These are just the documented instances that I have found so far of Mary Sidney's direct connections to so many of the source books. We can assume her large private library held many more—unfortunately, her grandson auctioned off the entire collection years after her death. But this work is just the beginning—as researchers look more closely at Mary Sidney, I am confident many more connections will be found.

The Sources and How *They Were Changed*

"Fool," said my Muse
to me, "Look in thy
heart, and write."

Philip Sidney, Sonnet 1,
Astrophil and Stella

ONLY THREE PLAYS in the canon are original stories—and those three lean heavily on plot points, concepts, philosophies, even direct lines taken from other sources. The rest of the plays are based on a variety of sources established by and generally agreed upon by generations of scholars.

How did the author develop the original material? Do any patterns develop?

As You Like It

In the primary original source, three men are killed in the wrestling match; Celia/Aliena is kidnapped by outlaws whose purpose is to hand her over to her lecherous father as an incestuous gift; blood is shed when she is rescued; and her father is killed in a battle at the story's end. In contrast, there's not a hint of incest in *As You Like It*, and no one dies. Anne Barton in *The Riverside Shakespeare* describes it:

The incest, bloodshed, and father's death is removed.

> There are no outlaws either, only banished courtiers suffi-
> ciently tender-hearted to worry about preying upon the deer
> in the forest, let alone upon other human beings; and the
> usurping duke, Celia's father, never reaches the fatal battle-
> field [as in the original] because an old religious man meets
> and peaceably converts him on the way.[1]

115

David Bevington states:

> The conversion of Duke Frederick by a hermit instead
> of his being overthrown and killed is a characteristically
> Shakespearean softening touch. Shakespeare's added
> characters are virtually all foils to the conventional
> pastoral vision he found in his source.[2]

Titus Andronicus

The love of a mother and a father for their children is added.

The chapbook[3] on which *Titus* is thought to have been based does not include Titus's sacrifice of Tamora's son. In the Shakespearean version, the sacrifice of her son gives Tamora a stronger motive to persecute Titus, making her less monstrous because she is a broken-hearted mother. It also makes Titus partially responsible for the griefs which then befall him.

The chapbook shows nothing of Aaron's love for his child; in the play, this is the only hint of a redeeming quality we see in the otherwise hard-hearted Aaron.

The Taming of the Shrew

The misogyny is removed and Katarina's spirit unbroken.

The wife-taming plot in the Shakespearean version of *The Taming of the Shrew* differs markedly from the ballad considered to be its primary source, "A Merry Jest of a Shrewd and Curst Wife Lapped in Morel's Skin for Her Good Behavior." In the ballad, the husband confines his wife inside the skin of a dead horse named Morel. As Anne Barton explains in *The Riverside Shakespeare*:

> Verbal similarities indicate that Shakespeare knew this
> particular ballad; certainly he knew others like it, in which
> the approved remedy for a domineering wife was physical
> violence, the more ingenious and excruciating the better. By
> comparison with the husband who binds his erring spouse,
> beats her, bleeds her into a state of debility, or (in the case
> of the ballad mentioned above) incarcerates her inside the
> salted skin of a dead horse Morel, Petruchio—although no
> Romeo—is almost a model of intelligence and humanity. His
> aim, moreover, is not the crude one of the traditional wife-
> tamer, out to pulverize the woman's will as well as, in most
> cases, her body. What Petruchio wants, and ends up with,

is a Katherina of unbroken spirit and gaiety who has suffered only minor physical discomfort and who has learned the value of self control and of caring about someone other than herself.[4]

David Bevington also notes that "Shakespeare avoids the misogynistic extremes of this story despite the similarity of the narrative."[5]

Much Ado About Nothing

Although there are a number of sources for the plot of Hero and Claudio (some of which include slaying and poison), the plot of Beatrice—one of the brightest and wittiest characters in the canon—is original. Thus the scenes of the indissoluble bond between the women is also added. Beatrice finds herself in Act IV three times wishing "that I were a man."

The story of Beatrice and Benedick is added, and thus the close bond of women is also added.

No source has been found for Dogberry, the illiterate constable, one of two illiterate characters in the canon (both male). It is documented, however, that the constable in Wiltshire, the town where Mary Sidney lived, was illiterate.[6]

Measure for Measure

There are several source stories, each built on the previous. In the first, the husband is a murderer; in the second, a young man has sex with a number of women; in the third, the brother rapes a young virgin. In all three, the Isabella character has sex with Angelo to expiate the sins of the violent men, and in all the sources (written by men), all characters believe she did the right thing to sacrifice herself sexually for the crimes committed by a dissolute man.

The woman does not sacrifice herself sexually for a man who committed an immoral act. She chooses to stay true to her monastic ideals rather than marry.

But in the Shakespearean play, the stakes are raised—Isabella's brother has done nothing worse than consensually sleep with his beloved Juliet just before they are to be married, and she's pregnant. Isabella is a novice just entering a convent. The Shakespearean version is the only one in which Isabella does not have sex with Angelo in exchange for her brother's life—she is willing to let her brother die rather than compromise her values. Nor does she respond to either of the Duke's offers of marriage in the final scene.

The Comedy of Errors

The women are more virtuous, even the courtesan. A sister is added and thus the scenes of the bond between women.

In the Shakespearean version, the author "plays down the role of the courtesan, dignifies the part of the wife, invents the sympathetic role of Luciana her sister."[7] Plautus, in his original story, uses a detached ironic tone and a casual depiction of courtesans and parasites, but these are replaced in the Shakespearean play "by a thematic emphasis on patience and loyalty in marriage."[8]

The Two Gentlemen of Verona

The woman remains faithful to her man and does not die for love of a different man.

In the Shakespearean version, Sylvia does *not* fall in love with the disguised Julia ("Sebastian") and die of unrequited love—Sylvia is a much pluckier spirit, remains loyal to Valentine, and follows him into banishment (after escaping from the tower in which her father kept her locked).

Twelfth Night

The woman does not take a lover or get pregnant before marriage.

In the source story, Olivia takes Sebastian as her lover and after a one-night stand (in which she gets pregnant), he abandons her. Orsino throws Viola in jail. In the Shakespearean *Twelfth Night*, the playwright "eschews the pregnancy, the desertion, the imprisonment, and all of [Barnabe] Riche's stern moralizing [in the original] about the bestiality of lust."[9]

Othello

A murder becomes a love story. Private and close scenes between women are added.

In the original story, Othello has Iago bludgeon Desdemona to death with a sand-filled stocking, then together they make the ceiling collapse on her so it looks like she was brained with a rafter. But in the Shakespearean version, Othello suffocates Desdemona with a pillow, thus avoiding the appalling butchery of the original. "Most important," says Bevington, "Shakespeare transforms a sensational murder story into a moving tragedy of love."[10] "Speak of one that loved not wisely but too well," says Othello.

Both Othello and Iago are held accountable for the crimes they have committed, unlike in the source story.

The playwright also adds the intimate scene between Emilia and Desdemona as she prepares for bed.

The Winter's Tale

In the original story, Pandosto/Leontes is incestuously in love with his daughter. His wife actually gave him cause for jealousy and has died. Pandosto/Leontes kills himself in a melancholic fit after his daughter marries a young man.

In the Shakespearean version, all signs of incest are removed. Leontes is more irrationally jealous and his wife more virtuous. The enterprising and dynamic character of Paulina is added, as well as the fifteen-year secret kept by the two women. "Leontes' purgative sorrow is more intense and also more restorative than in the source."[11]

Incest is removed. Leontes' jealousy is increased. The Queen is more virtuous, and the brilliant Paulina is added. The fifteen-year secret between the two women is added.

Coriolanus

In the Shakespearean version of this historical piece, Volumnia's role is magnified into a strong and capable matriarch in her son's life and in the lives of the Roman people. "Shakespeare therefore makes Volumnia more fierce than she is in Plutarch, and emphasizes the powerlessness of Virgilia's pacific spirit and her inability to affect the course of her husband's life, or even her son's."[12]

The playwright makes the men in the mob more cowardly in war than they were in Plutarch's source.

The woman's role is greater, stronger, and fiercer—and the men more cowardly. The unpleasant result of weakness in a woman is emphasized.

Macbeth

Historically, Duncan was an ineffectual king and Banquo did conspire against him. In the play, Duncan becomes a well-beloved ruler, and Banquo (ancestor of King James) evolved into a more honorable man with a forceful ghost.

In the source material Macbeth hears the prophecies from a witch; the playwright changed the witch to the more intriguing trinity of Wyrd Sisters, the three Anglo-Saxon Fates or goddesses of destiny. Bevington points out that "Lady Macbeth's role is considerably enhanced, and her sleepwalking scene is original."[13]

The original witch was changed into three goddesses of destiny, the Wyrd Sisters. Lady Macbeth is given a larger and more powerful role.

Pericles

The woman's challenge is greater in the play, and the man she marries more dignified.

In other plays, this author consistently removed any incest that may have appeared in the source material. Act I of Pericles includes incest, but Act I is not believed to have been written by "Shakespeare" (for other reasons).

"Shakespeare has given a more sordid impression of the brothel in which Marina must dwell and has dignified the character of Lysimachus so as to render him worthy of marrying Marina." [14]

The Merry Wives of Windsor

The women are more virtuous and clever—rather than commit adultery, they make a fool of the man.

This play doesn't have a single direct source, but in similar stories, the wives do commit adultery. In the Shakespearean version, "Falstaff is tricked by a pair of wives who may be merry but are also fiercely chaste. It is the would-be lover [Falstaff] who is cleverly deceived, not the husband." [15]

Antony and Cleopatra

Cleopatra is more sympathetic. Two woman have been added, creating scenes of the bond between women. Antony is less of a lush.

Regarding one of the sources, Mary Sidney's translation, *Antonie,* Tina Krontiris says, "[Mary Sidney's] play interrogates conventional definitions of masculine and feminine virtue, opposes the established association of overt female sexuality with loose morals, and reveals the psychological and sexual complexes of those holding political power. . . . *Antonie* offers a sympathetic view of the adulterous lovers, and especially of Cleopatra, the woman who up to that time had been presented to the English public as a seductress." [16]

John Wilders, in the Arden edition of the play, states that the portrayal of Cleopatra in Mary Sidney's play, "unlike Plutarch, is consistently sympathetic," and that in the Shakespearean play, the playwright "may have been influenced by [*Antonie*] when he created the resolute, idealizing Cleopatra of the final scene." [17]

The characters of Iras and Charmian are developed from mere hints in the Plutarch source. And the playwright plays down Antony's bacchanalian nature.

The History Plays

The women in the history plays—from Mistress Quickly who appears in both parts of Henry IV and also Henry V (as well as in *The Merry Wives of Windsor*) to the daunting Queen Margaret, who appears in all three parts of Henry VI and also Richard III—are active participants who vigorously comment on unfolding events, reveal the impact of these events on their families and themselves, and often oppose the historical progress.

The playwright consistently adds scenes of powerful women to the historical record.

KING JOHN: The incredible queens Eleanor and Constance as forceful and unwavering mothers are much more important in this play than alluded to in the sources. The scene of Constance's grief is invented by the author, as well as Blanche's exasperation as her new husband leaves for war.

RICHARD II: The author adds three women to the Shakespearean play and invents three scenes that were not in any of the historical sources:

Queen Isabel and the famous garden scene.
Duchess of York as a protective mother.
Duchess of Gloucester mourning for her husband.

HENRY IV, PART 1: The author adds two women not included in the historical narrative, the witty wives of devoted husbands, Mortimer and Hotspur. And we are introduced to Mistress Quickly who runs the tavern.

HENRY VI, PART 2: Young Queen Margaret starts to feel her own power.

HENRY VI, PART 3: The playwright invents the scene where the formidable Queen Margaret, remorseless defender of her son's right to the throne, takes down the most powerful man in the land, Richard, Duke of York.

RICHARD III: The longest scene in this play, invented by the author, is that of three commanding and passionate women on stage: the Duchess of York, Queen Elizabeth, and Queen Margaret. The playwright includes Margaret in this play, the fourth she appears in, even though historically she was back in France.

A Pattern?

This playwright consistently ennobles and strengthens the female characters and makes them more virtuous than their original counterparts. All references to incest are eliminated. Women are often added where they didn't appear in the source material, and scenes of women's emotional, intimate bonds with each other are invented. There is an undeviating pattern of faithful, dedicated wives with an emphasis on loyalty in marriage, even though a surprising number of these wives have irrationally jealous husbands. In the history plays, women who are barely mentioned or ignored in the historical record are given strong voices and powerful statements.

This playwright, unlike any other dramatist of the time, displays a reverence for the wit, intelligence, maternity, capacity, and strength of women.

The Plays
and Mary's Life

11

Every writer, by the way he uses the language, reveals something of his spirit, his habits, his capacities, his bias .... creative writing is communication through revelation—it is the self escaping into the open. No writer long remains incognito.

E.B. White
1899–1985

WRITERS, RESEARCHERS, SHAKESPEAREANS, OXFORDIANS, Marlovians—everyone wants to find parallels in the plays to a particular author's life. I hesitate to do this because one can make a case for just about any play to reflect just about any author. But—as an exercise in possibilities—we'll take a look at some intriguing (and documented) events in Mary's life and how they might connect to just a few of the Shakespearean plays. After all, if she *is* the author of the plays, one would *expect* to find some reflections.

As Betsy Lerner states in *The Forest for the Trees: An Editor's Advice to Writers,* "Writing what you know is a given. Writing what you know is unavoidable. All people write what they know, for God's sake. It's the air you breathe."

Titus Andronicus

In Chapter 2 I talked of Mary Sidney's heartbreaking and agonizing year when her little girl Katherine died, her father died, her mother died, and her beloved brother Philip was killed at war. These deaths in such a close-knit family were devastating.

Because she was a woman, Mary was not allowed to participate in her brother Philip's elaborate state funeral nor to contribute to the publications of elegies that were collected. Even the joyful promise of the pregnancy of her young sister-in-law Frances, Philip's widow, was destroyed when the baby miscarried. The year was 1586. Mary was barely 25 years old.

"Her love for her brother passes even her own understanding. . . . there is no doubt that the deepest emotional commitment of her life was to her brother, both before and also after his death."[1] Mary went into deep mourning and seclusion for two years.

Did Mary Sidney, as a writer, use writing as solace and create *Titus Andronicus,* a violent, heart-wrenching, horrifying play that contains more tragedy than anyone could imagine living through?

John Klaus makes the following point in his article, "Politics, Heresy, and Martyrdom in Shakespeare's Sonnet 124 and *Titus Andronicus*": "The suggestiveness of plot, character, and allusion rather than any set of allegorical correspondences indicates that Shakespeare's mind in composing *Titus Andronicus* was engaged by the bloody history of Europe's and especially England's religious conflicts."[2] It was in one of these religious conflicts that Mary's brother Philip was killed.

The play contains an astonishing collection of anguished cries:

There greet in silence, as the dead are wont,
And sleep in peace, slain in your country's wars.
1.i.93–94

He lives in fame, that died in virtue's cause.
1.i.390

Sorrow concealed, like an oven stopp'd,
Doth burn the heart to cinders where it is.
2.iii.36–37

If I do dream, would all my wealth
    would wake me.
If I do wake, some planet strike me down,
That I may slumber in eternal sleep!
2.iii.13–15

For these, tribunes, in the dust I write
My heart's deep languor and my soul's sad tears.
3.i.11–12

Therefore I tell my sorrows to the stones; . . .
When I do weep, they humbly at my feet
Receive my tears and seem to weep with me.
3.i.37, 41–42

When will this fearful slumber have an end?
3.i.53

Titus, prepare thy agèd eyes to weep;
Or, if not so, thy noble heart to break;
I bring consuming sorrow to thine age.
3.i.59–61

Will it consume me? Let me see it then.
3.i.62

My grief was at the height before thou cam'st,
And now, like the Nile, it disdaineth bounds.
3.i.71–72

It was my dear, and he that wounded her
Hath hurt me more
    than had he killed me dead.
3.i.92–93

O, what a sympathy of woe is this.
3.i.149

Is not my sorrow deep, having no bottom?
Then be my passions bottomless with them.
3.i.217–18

If there were reasons for these miseries,
Then into limits could I bind my woes.
3.i.220–21

These miseries are more than may be borne.
3.i.244

I have not another tear to shed.
3.i.267

. . . when my heart, all mad with misery,
Beats in this hollow prison of my flesh.
3.ii.9–10

Wound it with sighing, girl, kill it with groans,
Or get some little knife between thy teeth
And just against thy heart make thou a hole,
That all the tears that thy poor eyes let fall
May run into that sink and, soaking in,
Drown the lamenting fool in sea-salt tears.
3.ii.15–20

She says she drinks no other drink but tears,
Brewed with her sorrow, mashed upon her cheeks.
3.ii.37–38

O heavens, can you hear a good man groan
And not relent or not compassion him?
4.i.123–24

Yet wrung with wrongs more than our backs can bear.
4.iii.49

                . . . let him tell the tale,
While I stand by and weep to hear him speak.
5.iii.93–94

O, take this warm kiss on thy pale cold lips,
These sorrowful drops upon thy bloodstained face.
5.iii.152–53

I cannot speak to him for weeping;
My tears will choke me, if I ope my mouth.
5.iii.173–74

Many a time he danc'd thee on his knee,
Sung thee asleep, his loving breast thy pillow;
Many a story hath he told to thee
And bid thee bear his pretty tales in mind,
And talk of them when he was dead and gone.
5.iii.161–65

Bid him farewell; commit him to the grave;
Do him that kindness, and take leave of him.
5.iii.169–70

Titus Andronicus is one of the first Shakespearean plays known to have existed. Because of what scholars refer to as its relatively amateur style, it is often considered to be the first play written by its author. Ben Jonson made a reference to the play that would date it to about 1588.[3] The first theater troupe to stage *Titus* in 1589 or 1590 was the Earl of Pembroke's Men, the acting company sponsored by Mary and her husband.[4]

Titus Andronicus was published anonymously in 1594. In 1658, Edward Ravenscroft, an English dramatist, wrote in the preface to his version of the play, "I have been told by some anciently conversant with the Stage that it was not Originally his [William Shakespeare's], but brought by a private Author to be Acted, and he only gave some Master-touches to one or two of the Principal Parts or Characters."[5]

In 1588, just before the play was staged by Pembroke's Men, Mary Sidney was twenty-seven years old, had buried two sisters, been married for twelve years, birthed four children, buried her daughter, father, mother, and brother, and was the Lady of the House of four large estates.

William Shakespeare was twenty-four years old and had very recently been named, along with his parents, in a legal action against a neighbor in Stratford, which suggests he was still living at home.

All's Well That Ends Well

All's Well That Ends Well is particularly interesting in regard to documented people and events in Mary's life.

a) This play is considered by most scholars to have been written around 1604. In it a Countess has a womanizing, profligate, arrogant, unmarried son, Bertram.

> In early 1604, Mary Sidney was a Countess with a womanizing, profligate, arrogant, unmarried son, William Herbert.

b) In the play, the husband of the Countess has died, and the son is heir to his father's estate.

> Mary's husband had recently died (1601), and her son was heir to his father's estate.

c) In the play, the doctor who lived in her house has more recently died.

> The doctor who lived in Mary's house, Dr. Moffett, had more recently died (early 1604). A new physician, Dr. Matthew Lister, had come to live at her estate.

d) In the play, the deceased doctor left a daughter, Helena, who wants to marry the Countess's son, Bertram. The Countess thinks this is a splendid idea.

> Mary herself fell passionately in love with the handsome young doctor in her house. She was with him for the rest of her life, although they never married "for marriage out of one's degree was a debasing of the blood which blemished successive generations."[6]

e) The King promises Helena, the doctor's daughter, she can marry whomever she likes if she can cure the King's fatal illness. Helena cures the King and chooses to marry Bertram. Bertram is horrified at the idea of a high-born aristrocrat such as himself marrying the daughter of a person of such an exceedingly inferior class as a doctor. (At the time, a doctor was of a lower class than lawyers and soldiers and was not even considered as respectable as the "gentleman" class.) When the King insists he marry Helena, Bertram cries out to him:

> *But follows it, my lord, to bring me down*
> *Must answer for your raising? I know her well:*
> *She had her breeding at my father's charge.*
> *A poor physician's daughter my wife! Disdain* [Rather than marry her,
> *Rather corrupt me ever!* let my disdain for her
> ruin me forever in your eyes!]
>
> 2.iii.113–117

As M. C. Bradbrook says of Helena, "she is only the daughter of a poor gentleman belonging to the least dignified of the professions."[7]

f) The King lectures Bertram on the source of true nobility— the assessment of human worth by merit *earned* versus merit *inherited*, that which is outside of class distinctions—and wholeheartedly approves the union, much to Bertram's dismay.

> *She is young, wise, fair;*
> *In these to nature she's immediate heir,*
> *And these breed honor. That is honor's scorn*
> *Which challenges itself as honor's born*
> *And is not like the sire. Honors thrive*
> *When rather from our acts we them derive*
> *Than our foregoers. . . .*
> *If thou can like this creature as a maid,*
> *I canst create the rest. Virtue and she*
> *Is her own dower; honor and wealth from me.*
>
> 2.iii.131–144

The Countess in the play berates her son's behavior when she discovers how ill he has treated Helena.

> *There's nothing here that is too good for him*
> *But only she, and she deserves a lord*
> *That twenty such rude boys might tend upon*
> *And call her, hourly, mistress.*
>
> 3.ii.79–82

g) Bertram swears eternal love and service to a young virgin, Diana, if she will sleep with him. But after he sleeps with her (he *thinks* it's her), he immediately dumps her.

William Herbert had recently created a scandal at court by sleeping with one of Queen Elizabeth's maids-of-honor, getting her pregnant, and abandoning her without remorse. The Queen threw him in prison.

All's Well That Ends Well was written at the beginning of Mary's love affair with the young doctor; he was ten years younger than Mary. About this same time, she had a disagreement with her oldest son, William (who was only nine years younger than the doctor), that separated them for the next decade.[8] Was the disagreement about Mary's romantic relationship with Dr. Lister, a relationship that embarrassed William as being shameful or degrading?

Dr. Matthew Lister. He was eventually knighted, years after Mary's death.

In this play, is Mary as the Countess trying to justify her liaison with the young doctor? In the original source,[9] there is no Countess at all, just a dead Count; the King does *not* approve of the marriage between Bertram and Helena, although he reluctantly agrees to it because of his bargain; and this author made Betram into a more reprehensible scoundrel than he was in the source.

So why would William Shakespeare have chosen this story as the source material for a play? (Or Oxford, Marlowe, Bacon, or Neville—other possible candidates for authorship—for that matter?) Why would he add a Countess to the story? Especially a Countess who encourages her son to marry such a virtuous young woman regardless of propriety? Why would he change the original story to show a Countess who believes it to be perfectly appropriate, even commendatory, that her high-born son should marry the daughter of a doctor, and whose advice is supported by the King? The men in the royal court well knew that noblemen and women ended up in jail or banishment from court for marrying outside of their social class.

Yet Mary Sidney was, at the time of this play's conception, a widowed Countess desperately in love with a handsome young doctor, a situation that could only have upset her spoiled, arrogant, womanizing son.

There is no record that this play was ever performed or printed in either Shakespeare's or Mary Sidney's lifetime, and many scholars consider it to be an unfinished draft. Statistically, it is still the least-performed of all the plays.

Love's Labor's Lost

Love's Labor's Lost, probably written around 1594, is one of the few plays that has an original plot. It explores the concept of an "academy" of aristrocratic scholars. David Bevington says, "Certain historical facts about Henri of Navarre may well have provided Shakespeare a model for the play's action, especially the visit of Catherine de' Medici with her daughter [Marguerite de Valois] . . . to Henri's court in 1578 and a similar visit in 1586. Published accounts of these visits were not available when Shakespeare wrote his play, but he may well have heard the gossip." [10]

Richard David, editor of the Arden edition of *Love's Labor's Lost*, is more definite about Shakespeare: "It is, however, extremely unlikely that Shakespeare had any direct knowledge of Navarre's academy." [11]

Henri of Navarre became one of Philip Sidney's closest friends after his visit to Navarre in 1572. They stayed in touch for the rest of Philip's life. As Gary Waller explains, "When Sidney visited France in the 1570s he met a number of the members of the palace academy centered on Marguerite de Navarre. . . . The developments at Wilton in the 1580s, then, were an attempt on the part of the Sidneys to instigate a revival of English aristrocratic culture. For her own part, in providing Wilton's hospitality and its unique atmosphere of these crucial years of Elizabethan literature, the Countess [Mary Sidney] was also re-creating in her own, perhaps typically English, way a pattern of patronage by noble women that had flourished in Italy and France for a century or more." [12]

Even after Philip's death, the Sidney family stayed close to the French court. Henri's secretary, Ségur, visited Mary at her Wilton and Ramsbury estates in 1583. [13] Mary's younger brother Robert was chosen to go to Europe in 1593 as ambassador to Henri of Navarre.

A.H. Upham states that "the versatile career of the Countess of Pembroke was modeled considerably on that of Margaret of Navarre, the 'amiable mother of the Renaissance' in France." [14] Margaret Hannay agrees, "Before [Mary Sidney] Pembroke, no woman had achieved such a prominent public literary identity in England, although she may well have looked to France and Marguerite de Navarre as a role model." [15]

"There is every reason that Sidney's sister should have been familiar with the character of Margaret and the significance of her patronage of French letters; every reason too that she should have admired and imitated such a personality."[16] John Aubrey, not long after Mary's death, wrote, "We are now to consider it [Wilton House] within, where it will appear to have been an academy as well as palace."[17]

But the Navarre academy was not the only topical allusion in this play. "Many literary quarrels in England of the 1590s have been adduced as possible sources for Shakespeare's play [*Love's Labor's Lost*], especially the controversy between Thomas Nashe and Gabriel Harvey...."[18] Intriguingly, both Mary's and Philip's names were involved in the decade-long Nashe-Harvey battle in print. "Whether the countess herself took any part in this quarrel, Harvey apparently wanted his readers—particularly Nashe—to think that she did," says Hannay. "If Mary Sidney was angry with Nashe, she would have had cause, quite apart from his quarrel with Harvey."[19]

A number of references to people and events in the play have compelling connections to Mary. "It is possible that Shakespeare drew Holofernes [a 'pompous, conceited, ignorant village schoolmaster'] on the model of some well-known learned men of his day, like John Florio or Gabriel Harvey."[20] Mary knew Florio and Harvey very well and had reason to mock both of them. She was not pleased with Florio because "the countess's literary judgment was attacked by John Florio in his dedication of Book II of Montaigne's *Essays*...."[21] And Harvey, as mentioned above, had dragged her into a public literary quarrel.

In *The Poems of Robert Sidney*, the editor P. J. Croft includes an essay describing the influence of the work of Robert Sidney (Mary's younger brother) on the play *Love's Labor's Lost*. But the editor can't explain how Shakespeare would have read Robert's poetry, since it was never published and the handwritten poems were circulated only within his family or, at most, to a select few who visited the family. "If a formal manuscript were presented, it seems that the Countess followed Robert's wishes in keeping it closely to herself."[22] This notebook of poems, only recently discovered, was inscribed "For the Countess of Pembroke."

The Tragic Plays

The earlier Shakespearean plays include *The Comedy of Errors, The Two Gentlemen of Verona, The Taming of the Shrew, Romeo and Juliet, As You Like It, Twelfth Night, A Midsummer Night's Dream,* and all but one of the English history plays. Just after the turn of the century, the plays took a turn from light comedy and romance into the darker tragedies. After 1601 we get *All's Well That Ends Well, Hamlet, Othello, Macbeth, King Lear, Measure for Measure, Timon of Athens.* Dr. Charles G. Bell of St. John's College in Santa Fe calls it "The Tragic Divide." Most scholars believe the author must have gone through personally difficult and trying times during this period.

What was Mary Sidney doing in those early years of the seventeenth century? Her husband died in 1601 and with him she lost much of her power, wealth, and influence. Many of those who had flocked around her disappeared, mirroring what happens to Timon in *Timon of Athens.* Essex, husband of her niece, had his head smit off for trying to overthrow the Queen. Mary's son was thrown in the Fleet prison for impregnating a young woman and was, as usual, embarrassingly unrepentant. Dr. Moffett, the estate physician and a member of her literary circle, died in 1604 and was buried at Wilton House. His replacement arrived, Dr. Matthew Lister, with whom she fell boldly in love (bold because it was socially unacceptable), but then she thought he was in love with her own niece, who was really having an affair with Mary's oldest son. The citizens of Cardiff rose against her, trying to pull down parts of her castle and beating her servants. She spent years in two hostile lawsuits, with no help from her oldest son in whose hereditary interests she was working.

It was around this time that her older son William stopped speaking to her for the next ten years. Her younger son Philip was ingratiating himself with King James through "intimacies" with the king. This son also secretly arranged a marriage for himself. And in 1606 her 23-year-old daughter died. This was indeed a difficult and disappointing time of Mary's life.

The English History Plays

There are ten English history plays that cover periods of time from 1199 (the opening of *King John*) to 1533 (the end of *Henry VIII*). One might think history plays were a popular genre and that's why this author wrote so many. But they weren't. There is only one known English history play written before the Shakespearean set, an anonymous one (attributed to Richard Tarleton) called *Famous Victories of Henry V*. David Bevington says Shakespeare "was an important innovator in the new genre of the history play" and that "the English history play as a recognizable form came into being with [the Shakespearean play] *Henry VI*."[23] Why would an unknown upstart writer begin a body of work with an unproven form of drama? Especially a form that entails such zealous historical research? It's intriguing that Margaret Hannay notes, "By importing Garnier's topical use of Roman history, [Mary Sidney Herbert, the Countess of] Pembroke paved the way for explicitly political history plays in English, including those of Shakespeare and Daniel."[24]

The history plays in particular indicate an intimate knowledge of life in the royal court and among noblemen. It's true that if William Shakespeare were the author, he might have picked up a lot of insider knowledge while hanging around court—once he became a famous writer. But these plays were some of the earliest written, as early as 1589, so many of them were complete before Shakespeare had time to become well known and allowed at court.

Curious about Mary Sidney's connections with the history plays, I procured copies of her genealogy from the Bodleian Library in Oxford, England. I entered Mary's lineage from her papers into a genealogy program, researched every family member and every historical person in the ten English history plays, and condensed a huge amount of data into a list.

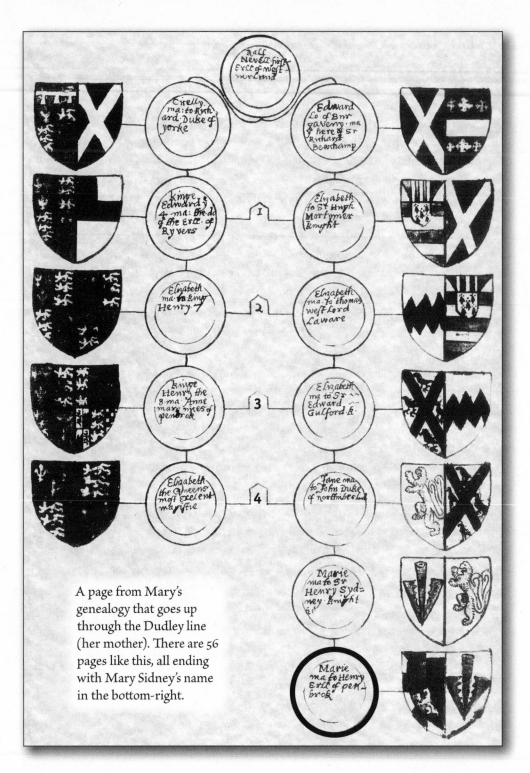

A page from Mary's genealogy that goes up through the Dudley line (her mother). There are 56 pages like this, all ending with Mary Sidney's name in the bottom-right.

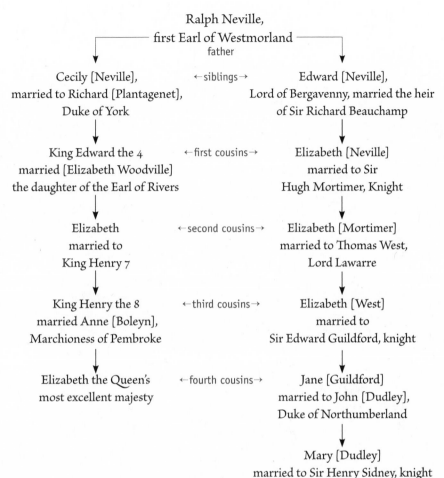

Ralph Neville,
first Earl of Westmorland
father

Cecily [Neville],   ←siblings→   Edward [Neville],
married to Richard [Plantagenet],   Lord of Bergavenny, married the heir
Duke of York   of Sir Richard Beauchamp

King Edward the 4   ←first cousins→   Elizabeth [Neville]
married [Elizabeth Woodville]   married to Sir
the daughter of the Earl of Rivers   Hugh Mortimer, Knight

Elizabeth   ←second cousins→   Elizabeth [Mortimer]
married to   married to Thomas West,
King Henry 7   Lord Lawarre

King Henry the 8   ←third cousins→   Elizabeth [West]
married Anne [Boleyn],   married to
Marchioness of Pembroke   Sir Edward Guildford, knight

Elizabeth the Queen's   ←fourth cousins→   Jane [Guildford]
most excellent majesty   married to John [Dudley],
                                  Duke of Northumberland

Mary [Dudley]
married to Sir Henry Sidney, knight

Mary [Sidney] married to Henry [Herbert],
Earl of Pembroke

Above is a clarification of the page, shown
opposite, of Mary Sidney's genealogy.
Every person in the left-hand column
(straight above) appears in one or more
of the history plays.

This chart makes it easy to see
how Mary is related to anyone else.
For instance, you see above that Queen
Elizabeth is Mary's fourth cousin
(horizontal), twice removed (vertical).

Below is a list of Mary Sidney's relatives who appear in two of the history plays (the rest of the plays are in Appendix F). The code for the relationship is simple: "1C 2R" means that person is her first cousin (1C), 2 times removed (2R), or two generations ago, as shown on the previous page. "3G Grandmother" means that person is the great-great-great grandmother of Mary Sidney. The farther back in time the history play took place, the more removed the relatives are, of course.

King John

Character	Relation to Mary Sidney
King John	11G Grandfather
Queen Eleanor	12G Grandmother
Prince Henry, afterward Henry III	10G Grandfather
Arthur Plantagenet	1C 12R
Constance of Brittany	12G Aunt
William Marshall, 1st Earl of Pembroke	12G Uncle
Geoffrey FitzPeirs, 4th Earl of Essex	10G Grandfather
William Longsword, 3d Earl of Salisbury	12G Uncle
Roger Lord Bigot, 2d Earl of Norfolk	11G Grandfather
Hubert de Burgh	--
Philip, King of France	--
Lewis, the Dauphin	*married to Mary's 1C 12R*
Blanche of Castile	1C 12R
Cardinal Pandulph	--

mentioned in the play:
Richard the Lionheart	12G Uncle
Geoffrey Plantagenet, 3d son of Henry II	12G Uncle

Richard II

Character	Relation to Mary Sidney
King Richard II	1C 7R
Queen Isabel	*(by marriage)*
John of Gaunt, Duke of Lancaster	6G Grandfather
Eleanor de Bohun, Duchess of Gloucester	7G Aunt
Edmund of Langley, 1st Duke of York	7G Uncle
Duchess of York, mother of Aumerle	7G Aunt
Edward of Norwich, Duke of Aumerle	1C 7R
Henry Bolingbroke, Duke of Hereford, afterward King Henry IV	6G Uncle (half)
Thomas Mowbray, 1st Duke of Norfolk	5G Grandfather
Thomas Holland, Duke of Surrey	2C 5R
John Montacute, 3d Earl of Salisbury	*his son married Mary's 2C 5R*
Thomas Lord Berkeley	6G Grandfather
Sir Henry Green	4G Uncle

Character	Relation to Mary Sidney
Sir John Bushy	--
Sir William (or John) Bagot	--
Henry Percy, 1st Earl of Northumberland	7G Uncle
Henry Percy, called Hotspur	1C 7R
William Lord Ross	*married to 1C 7R*
William, 5th Baron Willoughby de Ersby	6G Uncle
Walter Lord Fitzwater	*very distantly related*
Thomas Marke, Bishop of Carlisle	--
William de Colchester, Abbot of Westminster	--
Thomas Holland, Lord Marshall	2C 5R
Sir Stephen Scroop (Scrope)	*unclear*
Sir Piers of Exton	--

As you can see, a large number of the noblemen and women in these plays are directly related to Mary Sidney. The aristocracy was a fairly large group: In Queen Elizabeth's time, there was 1 duke, 2 marquises, 23 earls, 3 viscounts, and 50 barons, and this group did not include the many untitled aristocrats such as Mary's father, Henry Sidney, and her brother Philip. Each day 133 court officials and their servants were entitled to dine in the Great Hall.

Holinshed wrote in 1587 about the court of King Richard II, who reigned from 1377 to 1399: "He kept the greatest port and maintained the most plentiful house that ever any king in England did either before his time or since. For there resorted daily to his court above ten thousand persons that had meat and drink there allowed them."[25]

Ten thousand is probably an exaggeration, but it clearly indicates that the royal courts about which these plays are written include many more people than are mentioned in the plays. The point is that it's interesting to note which historical persons this playwright chose to include. It's also interesting to note how the historical characters have been changed between the source material and the plays.

For instance, in *Richard II*, Henry Percy, the 1st Earl of Northumberland, is much more prominent in the play than in the historical source material. Yet the playwright "omits the blackest of all Northumberland's acts, his perjury at Conway."[26] This Northumberland was not only Mary's 7G Uncle, but her grandfather also held a Northumberland title as Duke (as shown on pages 134–35).

Also in *Richard II*, "The character and behavior of Richard's uncle, John of Gaunt, Duke of Lancaster, constitute one of the most marked departures from Holinshed, and one of the greatest things in the play. … The Gaunt of Shakespeare is a father and patriot of grandiose stature, a prophet whose dying speech on England attracted the attention of the anthologist (for *England's Parnassus*) as early as 1600. Where did Shakespeare get this utterly unhistorical Duke of Lancaster?"[27] John of Gaunt, Duke of Lancaster, is Mary's 6G Grandfather.

In *Henry IV, Part 1*, Sir Walter Blunt was dressed in armor to look like King Henry IV, as were several other men on the battlefield. Mistaking him for the king, Douglas kills him, as well as the other similarly dressed men. The playwright emphasizes Blunt's role; he is "a good deal more important in the play than is the simple standard-bearer we know from Holinshed."[28] Sir Walter Blunt was Mary's 7G Grandfather.

In *Henry IV, Part 2* the playwright attributes the historical cold-blooded treachery of Westmorland to Bedford, brother of the king. The Earl of Westmorland was Mary's 5G Grandfather.

How it would have joyed brave Talbot to think that after he had lain two hundred years in his tomb, he should triumph again on the stage, and have his bones new embalmed with the tears of ten thousand spectators at least, who, in the Tragedian that represents his person, imagine they behold him fresh bleeding?

Thomas Nashe
Pierce Pennilesse, 1592

Historically, Orleans and Rouen were not recovered by the English, as is portrayed in *Henry V*. "Shakespeare's intention is to suggest that France is lost through England's political divisions at home, not through any failure on the part of Lord Talbot. Shakespeare exalts Talbot's might and chivalry (hence the [invented] scene with the Countess of Auvergne) …."[29] Lord Talbot and his son are Mary's 4G Grandfather and 3G Grandfather.

The Welsh Captain Fluellen, invented by Shakespeare, is thought to be based on Davy Gam; Gam's daughter became the mother of William Herbert, 1st Earl of Pembroke in the Herbert house.

The murder in *Henry VI, Part 3*, of Richard, 3d Duke of York is much more emotional and powerful than stated in the original historical source. York was Mary's 5G Uncle.

In *Henry VIII* there is a clear and elaborate reference to the Field of the Cloth of Gold, the meeting place where Henry VIII met the King of France, an event at which Mary's father was present.

The significance of these associations is yet to be determined, but it is intriguing to consider how much of the historical material was Mary Sidney's birthright.

Part Five

The Women

I grant I am a woman; but withal
A woman that Lord Brutus took to wife:
I grant I am a woman; but withal
A woman well-reputed, Cato's daughter.
Think you I am no stronger than my sex,
Being so father'd and so husbanded?
Tell me your counsels, I will not disclose 'em:
I have made strong proof of my constancy,
Giving myself a voluntary wound
Here, in the thigh: can I bear that with patience.
And not my husband's secrets?

Portia in *Julius Caesar*, 2.i.293–303

Methinks a woman of this valiant spirit
Should, if a coward heard her speak these words,
Infuse his breast with magnanimity
And make him, naked, foil a man at arms.

Prince Edward, speaking of Queen Margaret, his mother,
as she leads them into battle in *Henry VI, Part 3*, 5.iv.39–42

12 Do You Not Know *I Am a Woman?*

Rosalind in *As You Like It*

THE WOMEN OF THE SHAKESPEAREAN PLAYS defy their fathers to marry the men they choose, defy their husbands when they feel it necessary, disguise themselves as men to accomplish what needs to be done, and regularly make fools of foolish men. They show themselves to be women of strength, intelligence, resilience, and independence in an Elizabethan/Jacobean male-dominated society where women were still considered property.

What is particularly interesting in the plays is the underlying thread of strength, wit, and intelligence in the female characters, even the minor ones, that underpins both plot and narrative of the plays and gives the collective group of women a power not often recognized.

The creative ways in which these women gain their power is not merely a series of coincidences, but a pattern created by the author.

God made him, and therefore let him pass for a man.
Portia in *The Merchant of Venice*, 1.ii.54

Froward Females

In the Spring 1998 issue of *Shakespeare* magazine sponsored by Cambridge University Press and Georgetown University, the foreword to a series of articles about "Shakespeare's Froward Females" included these statements:

> It is interesting, amazing really, that within this context [of the Elizabethan and Jacobean cultures] we see in Shakespeare's plays a number of women who defy male domination. They choose to avoid the time-honored path to marriage, they choose to find their own path to marriage, or they choose to follow their own consciences rather than obey a husband or father or male authority figure . . . . They know what society expects of them, they know what particular men expect of them, but they choose another course and—for a time at least—they are successful.[1]

In a different article in the same magazine:

> Shakespeare's women have the reputation of being unruly, and indeed many of them have minds of their own. They may defy authority, get what they want, and sometimes dominate the action. But what they think, what they want, and what they do can only be successful if they operate within limits acceptable to the admittedly changing social expectations of their time.[2]

The author of the plays was singular among writers of the day, creating complex female characters who defied and defined the mores. Anne Barton states in *The Riverside Shakespeare:*

> Shakespeare's sympathy with and almost uncanny under-standing of women characters is one of the distinguishing features of his comedy, as opposed to that of most of his contemporaries. His heroines not only tend to overshadow their male counterparts, as Rosalind overshadows Orlando, Julia Proteus, or Viola Orsino: they adumbrate and urge throughout the play values which, with their help, will triumph in the new, more enlightened society of the end.[3]

In the book *Seven Shakespeares,* Gilbert Slater shows a reflection of Mary Sidney's position as a lady governing several estates and as a woman by birth and marriage involved in a politically powerful family, as he sees it in *Coriolanus*:

> All the political wisdom displayed by the Patricians in the play was concentrated in the person of Volumnia. Shakespeare's attitude in this play was, I think, that of a lady accustomed, in the absence of her lord on State business, to manage his estates, thus mastering the principles of government in a relatively small field, and accustomed also to discuss State affairs confidentially with relatives in Elizabeth's service.[4]

Professor Juliet Dusinberre concludes her thought-provoking book, *Shakespeare and the Nature of Women,* with this:

> Shakespeare saw men and women as equal in a world which declared them unequal. He did not divide human nature into the masculine and the feminine, but observed in the individual woman or man an infinite variety of union between opposing impulses. To talk about Shakespeare's women is to talk about his men, because he refused to separate their worlds physically, intellectually, or spiritually. Where in every other field understanding of Shakespeare's art grows, reactions to his women continually recycle, because critics are still immersed in preconceptions which Shakespeare discarded about the nature of women.[5]

At a time when contemporaries created few memorable parts for women, the author of these plays opened a window into the complexity of human experience—as often through the eyes of the quiet and unassuming women as through the vital, outspoken ones.

On the following pages are more than fifty of the female characters in the plays with brief descriptions of their courageous acts—some bold, some subtle. There are several engaging patterns in their actions that are worth further discussion.

Woman	Play	Description
Hero	*Much Ado About Nothing*	She is a virtuous woman unjustly accused of gross infidelity by her fiancé and thus also spurned by her own father and Don Pedro.
Hermione	*The Winter's Tale*	She is a virtuous wife unjustly accused of infidelity by a jealous husband. With her waiting woman, she hides herself for fifteen years, until exonerated.
Mrs. Ford	*The Merry Wives of Windsor*	She is a virtuous wife unjustly accused by a jealous husband, whom she brings around with humor and a good nature. She also humiliates a lecherous and sleazy knight.
Desdemona	*Othello*	She is a virtuous wife unjustly accused of gross infidelity by her husband. She defies her father and society to marry the man of her choice.
Juliet	*Romeo and Juliet*	She defies her father to marry the man of her choice.
Lavinia	*Titus Andronicus*	She defies her father to marry the man of her choice.
Anne Page	*The Merry Wives of Windsor*	She defies her father and mother to marry the man of her choice.
Hermia	*A Midsummer Night's Dream*	She defies her father to marry the man of her choice.
Sylvia	*The Two Gentlemen of Verona*	She defies her father to marry the man of her choice. Her father throws her in jail, she escapes, and is captured by outlaws.
Bianca	*The Taming of the Shrew*	She defies her father to marry the man of her choice.
Perdita	*The Winter's Tale*	She defies her lover's father to marry the man of her choice.
Imogen	*Cymbeline*	She defies her father and wicked stepmother to marry the man of her choice. She dresses as a man, runs away, and later joins the Roman army.
Jessica	*The Merchant of Venice*	She defies her father to marry the man of her choice. She dresses as a man and runs away.

Woman	Play	Description
Portia	*The Merchant of Venice*	She dresses as a man (a judge) and wins an eminent court case. She is the head of a large estate. She manipulates and shames her new husband for his fickleness.
Nerissa	*The Merchant of Venice*	She dresses as a man (a law clerk) to appear in court. She manipulates and shames her new husband for his fickleness.
Rosalind	*As You Like It*	She dresses as a man, runs away into the forest, buys property, arranges the forest society, and marries the man of her choice.
Viola	*Twelfth Night*	She dresses as a man, takes a job, and marries the man of her choice.
Joan of Arc	*1 Henry VI*	She dresses as a man and leads armies into battle. In this play she possibly has lovers.
Julia	*The Two Gentlemen of Verona*	She dresses as a man and runs away. She is a steadfast woman scorned by an inconstant lover.
Helena	*A Midsummer Night's Dream*	She is a steadfast woman scorned by an inconstant lover.
Celia	*As You Like It*	She runs away from her father to be true to herself and to her girlfriend. She marries the man of her choice.
Cordelia	*King Lear*	She defies her father to be true to herself.
Olivia	*Twelfth Night*	She runs an estate and marries the man of her choice.
Beatrice	*Much Ado About Nothing*	She is a brilliant woman who wittily chooses not to marry (but eventually does marry the man of her choice). Against several men, she is true to her female cousin.
Helena	*All's Well That Ends Well*	With her medical knowledge, she cures a king of a fatal disease that his male doctors have been unable to treat. She travels from Paris to Florence as a pilgrim. She manipulates events to marry the man of her choice.

Woman	Play	Description
Isabella	*Measure for Measure*	She is a noble, virtuous woman who manipulates a powerful leader. She dupes a man with the bed-trick. There is no indication that she chooses to accept the twice-offered marriage proposal from the Duke.
Diana	*All's Well That Ends Well*	She conspires to hoodwink a profligate man and plays the bed-trick on him.
Maria	*Twelfth Night*	She devises a plot to make a fool of a man.
Mrs. Page	*The Merry Wives of Windsor*	She is a middle-aged woman, wise and witty, who humiliates a sleazy knight. She defies her husband's preference of a marriage choice for her daughter.
Mistress Quickly	*The Merry Wives of Windsor*	She takes advantage of all the men and makes buffoons of them.
Princess of France & her ladies Rosaline, Maria, and Katharine	*Love's Labor's Lost*	The Princess is the political emissary for her country. These self-possessed women baffle and torment the men. They consign the men to a year of meditation and celibacy before they will consider marrying them.
Regan and Goneril	*King Lear*	Indomitable, power-hungry sisters who defy their father and husbands. Each takes a lover.
Queen Margaret	*1, 2, 3 Henry VI and Richard III*	She rules her husband, leads an army into battle for the sake of her son, murders the usurper, takes a lover, and prophesies truths.
Queen Elizabeth (Grey)	*3 Henry VI and Richard III*	She refuses the sexual advances of the King until he marries her and then manipulates life at court for the betterment of her family. She scorns Richard III and refuses him her daughter.
Constance of Bretagne	*King John*	She goes into battle for the sake of her son. Her intense grief over the death of her son is scorned by the men.
Eleanor of Aquitaine	*King John*	Almost 80 years old, she marches off to battle in France.

Woman	Play	Description
Volumnia	*Coriolanus*	She rules the country while her son is away. She saves Rome from destruction by controlling her son, a powerful man.
Cleopatra	*Antony and Cleopatra*	She is a powerful ruler of her country. She loves whom she pleases.
Fulvia	*Julius Caesar*	She leads a Roman army into war and is first on the field.
Tamora, Queen of the Goths	*Titus Andronicus*	She leads an army, fights for her sons, murders when necessary, loves whom she pleases.
Queen Katherine of Aragon	*Henry VIII*	She is a virtuous, steadfast woman who perseveres with grace through her husband's perfidy.
Lady Macbeth	*Macbeth*	She has the strength and mettle "of a man" to do what needs to be done to have power. Wishes she could be a man so she would have the capability to be cruel.
Portia and Calpurnia	*Julius Caesar*	Their quiet wisdom and family values are ignored by their husbands. Portia commits suicide by holding hot coals in her mouth to avoid the shame of her husband's defeat.
Adriana and her sister Luciana	*The Comedy of Errors*	They debate "obedience" to a husband vs. "servitude."
Katharina	*The Taming of the Shrew*	A complex woman who defies men and their marriage plans for her until "wooed" by one of her own mettle.
Mistress Quickly	*1, 2 Henry IV, Henry V*	She runs a business, a tavern.
Paulina	*The Winter's Tale*	Strong and undaunted, she stands up to powerful men, including the King. She keeps a secret with another woman for fifteen years, until the oracle is proven true.
Charmian	*Antony and Cleopatra*	Her loyalty is so strong that she commits suicide with Cleopatra.

Another way of looking at them

Below is the same list of women, just organized differently.

Women who defy their fathers to marry the men they choose

Desdemona in *Othello*.
Juliet in *Romeo and Juliet*.
Anne Page in *The Merry Wives of Windsor*.
Hermia in *A Midsummer Night's Dream*.
Sylvia in *The Two Gentlemen of Verona*.
Bianca in *The Taming of the Shrew*.
Perdita in *The Winter's Tale* (defies her lover's father).
Imogen in *Cymbeline*.
Jessica in *The Merchant of Venice*.

Women who dress as men

Imogen in *Cymbeline*, to run away from her father
and stepmother and later to join the Roman army.
Jessica in *The Merchant of Venice*, to run away from her father.
Portia in *The Merchant of Venice*, as a judge to win a court case.
Nerissa in *The Merchant of Venice*, to act as law clerk in court.
Rosalind in *As You Like It*, to run away from her uncle
into the forest where she buys property.
Viola in *Twelfth Night*, to take a job.
Joan of Arc in *1 Henry VI*, to lead battles.
Julia in *The Two Gentlemen of Verona*, to run away
from her father and follow her lover.

Steadfast women who are scorned by inconstant lovers

Helena in *A Midsummer Night's Dream*.
Queen Katherine of Aragon in *Henry VIII*.
Julia in *The Two Gentlemen of Verona*.
Helena in *All's Well That Ends Well*.

Virtuous women who are unjustly accused of infidelity by jealous husbands (or fiancé)

Desdemona in *Othello*.
Hero in *Much Ado About Nothing*.
Hermione in *The Winter's Tale*.
Mrs. Ford in *The Merry Wives of Windsor*.
Imogen in *Cymbeline*.

Women who make fools of men or expose them

Maria in *Twelfth Night*.
Mrs. Page in *The Merry Wives of Windsor*.
Mrs. Ford in *The Merry Wives of Windsor*.

Mrs. Quickly in *The Merry Wives of Windsor*.
Princess of France and her ladies in *Love's Labor's Lost*.
Diana and Helena in *All's Well That Ends Well*.
Isabella and Marianna in *Measure for Measure*.
Paulina and Hermione in *The Winter's Tale*.
Portia and Nerissa in *The Merchant of Venice*.

Leaders of armies

Tamora, Queen of the Goths in *Titus Andronicus*.
Queen Margaret in 3 *Henry VI* and *Richard III*.
Constance of Bretagne in *King John*.
Eleanor of Castile, almost 80 years old, in *King John*.
Cleopatra in *Antony and Cleopatra*.
Fulvia in *Julius Caesar*.

Female Relationships

It's thought-provoking to take a look at the close female-female relationships this author has created, especially when compared to the male-male relationships as described on page 152.

Paulina and Hermione in *The Winter's Tale*.

Hermia and Helena in *A Midsummer Night's Dream*.

Rosalind and Celia in *As You Like It*.

Desdemona and Emilia in *Othello*.

Beatrice and Hero in *Much Ado About Nothing*.

Queen Margaret, Queen Elizabeth, Queen Ann,
 and the Duchess of York in *Richard III*.

Maria and Olivia in *Twelfth Night*.

Adriana and Luciana (sisters) in *The Comedy of Errors*.

Julia and Silvia in *The Two Gentlemen of Verona*.

The Princess of France, Rosaline, Maria, and Katherine
 in *Love's Labor's Lost*.

Portia and Nerissa in *The Merchant of Venice*.

Mistress Ford and Mistress Page in *The Merry Wives of Windsor*.

Juliet and her Nurse in *Romeo and Juliet*.

Cleopatra with Charmian and Iras in *Antony and Cleopatra*.

Volumnia, Virgilia, and Valeria in *Coriolanus*.

Questionable Men

It's curious that so many books and articles have been written about what "William Shakespeare" thought of women, but few about what Shakespeare thought of men. When their qualities are listed, it's remarkable how many of these men are complete cads, scalawags, or outright villians.

Of course, there are several wicked and evil women in the plays: Regan and Goneril, Lady Macbeth, Tamora, Queen Margaret—all remorseless (well, Lady Macbeth had some remorse). And there are some wonderful men in the plays—Kent, Albany, France, and Edgar in *King Lear*; Horatio in *Hamlet*; Adam, Orlando, and Duke Senior in *As You Like It*; Antigonus in *The Winter's Tale*; Ferdinand and Gonzalo in *The Tempest*; the King's sons in *Cymbeline*; the good-natured Sir Hugh Evans in *The Merry Wives of Windsor*. The professional Fools in all plays tend to be witty and kind-hearted.

But consider the top names in the canon: Richard III, Othello, Iago, Macbeth, Romeo, Hamlet, Claudius—murderers all (not to mention their cadres of hired killers).

The list of characters below is not complete, nor does it include most of the history plays. Parentheses indicate the man is also in another category.

I would there were no age between sixteen and three-and-twenty, or that youth would sleep out the rest; for there is nothing in the between but getting wenches with child, wronging the ancientry, stealing, fighting—Hark you now! Would any but these boiled brains of nineteen and two-and-twenty hunt this weather?

Old Shepherd in *The Winter's Tale*, 3.iii.58–64

Murderers

Titus in *Titus Andronicus*.
Demetrius in *Titus Andronicus*.
Chiron in *Titus Andronicus*.
Aaron the Moor in *Titus Andronicus*.
Romeo in *Romeo and Juliet*.
Tybalt in *Romeo and Juliet*.
Hamlet in *Hamlet*.
Claudius in *Hamlet*.
Laertes in *Hamlet*.
Brutus and Cassius in *Julius Caesar*.
Othello in *Othello*.
Iago in *Othello*.
Edmund in *King Lear*.
Macbeth in *Macbeth*.
Richard III in *Richard III*.
Achilles in *Troilus and Cressida*.

Overbeating fathers

Capulet in *Romeo and Juliet*.
Mr. Page in *The Merry Wives of Windsor*.
Egeus (encouraged by Theseus)
    in *A Midsummer Night's Dream*.
Shylock in *The Merchant of Venice*.
Portia's father in *The Merchant of Venice*.
Baptista Minola in *The Taming
    of the Shrew*.
Duke of Milan in *Two Gentlemen*.
King Lear in *King Lear*.
King Cymbeline in *Cymbeline*.
Prospero in *The Tempest*.
Duke Frederick in *As You Like It*.

Insanely jealous husbands

(Othello in *Othello*.)
Posthumous in *Cymbeline*.
Leontes in *The Winter's Tale*.
Mr. Frank Ford in *The Merry Wives
    of Windsor*.

Pompous and pedantic men

Don Adriano de Armado in
    Love's Labor's Lost.
Holofernes in *Love's Labor's Lost*.
Sir Nathanial in *Love's Labor's Lost*.
Robert Shallow in *The Merry Wives
    of Windsor*.
Malvolio in *Twelfth Night*.
Lucio in *Measure for Measure*.
Polonius in *Hamlet*.

Drunkards

Sir John Falstaff in *Henry IV Parts 1
    and 2, The Merry Wives of Windsor*.
Sir Toby Belch in *Twelfth Night*.
Sir Andrew Aguecheek in *Twelfth Night*.
Christopher Sly in *Taming of the Shrew*.

Cowards, liars, hypocrites, extortionists

Parolles in *All's Well That Ends Well*.
Angelo in *Measure for Measure*.
Bertram in *All's Well That Ends Well*.
Cloten in *Cymbeline;* attempted rape.

Sir Eglamour in *Two Gentlemen*.
Proteus in *Two Gentlemen;*
    attempted rape.
Iachimo in *Cymbeline*.
(Sir John Falstaff in *Henry IV Parts
    1 and 2, Merry Wives of Windsor*.)

Men who get women pregnant out of wedlock

Gloucester in *King Lear*.
Richard the Lionheart in *King John*.
Claudio in *Measure for Measure*.
Launcelot Gobbo in *Merchant of Venice*.
(Aaron in *Titus Andronicus*.)
(Lucio in *Measure for Measure*.)
(Bertram, sort of, in *All's Well
    That Ends Well*.)

Fickle men

Demetrius in *A Midsummer Night's Dream*.
Bassanio (a golddigger) in *The Merchant
    of Venice*.
Claudio in *Much Ado About Nothing*.
Don Pedro in *Much Ado About Nothing*.
Leonato in *Much Ado About Nothing*.
Cassio in *Othello*.
(Proteus in *Two Gentlemen*.)
(Romeo in *Romeo and Juliet*.)

Cruel men (besides the murderers)

Antonio the Merchant in *The Merchant
    of Venice*.
Don John in *Much Ado About Nothing*.
Duke of Cornwall in *King Lear*.
Thersites in *Troilus and Cressida*.
(Chiron and Demetrius in *Titus
    Andronicus;* rape and mutilation.)
(Titus in *Titus Andronicus;* cannibalism.)
(Launcelot Gobbo in *The Merchant
    of Venice*.)

Obnoxious, loudmouthed, or hot-headed

Gratiano in *The Merchant of Venice*.
Dr. Caius in *The Merry Wives of Windsor*.
Oswald in *King Lear*.

Men who usurp or kill their brothers, or attempt to
Duke Frederick in *As You Like It*.
Oliver in *As You Like It*.
Sebastian in *The Tempest*.
Antonio in *The Tempest*.
(Claudius in *Hamlet*.)
(Richard III in *Richard III*.)
(Don John in *Much Ado About Nothing*.)
Hamlet senior, as Ghost in *Hamlet*.

Dimwits
Abraham Slender in *Merry Wives* .
(Christopher Sly in *Taming of the Shrew*.)
Gremio and Hortensio in *Shrew*.
Thurio and Launce in *The Two Gentlemen of Verona*.
Anthony Dull in *Love's Labor's Lost*.
The six rude mechanicals in *A Midsummer Night's Dream*.
Dogberry and Verges in *Much Ado*.
Silvius in *As You Like It*.
Sir Andrew Aguecheek in *Twelfth Night*.
Ajax in *Troilus and Cressida*.
Elbow, Froth, and Pompey in *Measure for Measure*.
Borachio and Conrade in *Much Ado*.
(Prince Cloten in *Cymbeline*.)
Trinculo and Stephano in *The Tempest*.

Male Relationships

It's a bit alarming to look at the male-male relationships in the plays. There are some heartwarming master/servant relationships (Lear/Kent, Hamlet/Horatio), the brothers Guiderius and Arviragus, or the odd relationship between Antonio and Bassanio or Sebastian and Antonio, but many men betray or murder their best friends.

Henry V executes three of his friends and spurns another.

Richard III has his friends murdered.

Macbeth has his best friend murdered.

Romeo inadvertently causes the murder of his best friend.

Leontes accuses his best friend of adultery with his wife and plots his murder.

Hamlet has his two schoolfriends murdered.

Othello is destroyed by his trusted friend Iago.

Tullus Aufidius betrays Coriolanus.

Proteus tries to steal his best friend's girlfriend and attempts to rape her.

Iachimo lies to his friend Posthumus about sleeping with his wife.

And yet in the literary criticism written about the Shakespearean canon, the normalcy of all these "men acting badly" tends to be unquestioned and the prevailing complexity of the women unexamined.

13 The Imagery in the Plays

From women's eyes this
doctrine I derive:
They are the books, the
arts, the academes
That show, contain, and
nourish all the world.

Berowne, *Love's Labor's Lost*,
4.iii.324–27

In her enlightening and highly respected *Shakespeare's Imagery and What It Tells Us*, Caroline Spurgeon gathers every image from every play and sonnet to categorize them in a variety of ways. She demonstrates that *mere references* to law, religion, war, etc., are quite different from *images*: "The imagery [the playwright] instinctively uses is thus a revelation, largely unconscious, given at a moment of heightened feeling, of the furniture of his mind, the channels of his thought, the qualities of things, the objects and incidents he observes and remembers, and perhaps most significant of all, those which he does not observe or remember."[1]

Following are some of the results Spurgeon discovered after charting her voluminous data.

Kitchen and living room

"Shakespeare has an unusually large number [of images] drawn from the daily work and occupations of women in a kitchen and living room: washing glass and knives, breaking glass and cracking china, scouring, wiping, dusting, sweeping, removing spots and stains, preparing food, knitting, patching, lining, turning and remaking clothes . . . steeping, scouring, wringing, sponging, wiping and hanging out in the sun to dry . . . ."[2]

> *O gentle son,*
> *Upon the heat and flame of thy distemper*
> *Sprinkle cool patience!*
>
> Gertrude in *Hamlet*, 3.iv.126–27

Cooking

"His interest in and acute observation of cooking operations are very marked all through his work. . . . we see how extraordinarily close is his knowledge of different kinds of cooking—the kneading, baking, boiling, mincing, broiling, stewing, frying, stuffing, larding, basting and distilling . . . ."[3] For instance, in *Henry VIII*, the noblemen, discussing their hatred of Cardinal Wolsey, use an analogy of what happens when milk boils on a stove:

> *Know you not*
> *The fire that mounts the liquor till it run o'er*
> *In seeming to augment it wastes it?*
>
> Norfolk in *Henry VIII*, 1.i.143–45

Hamlet creates a cooking metaphor while raging against his mother:

enseamed = greasy
stewed = steamed in a
slow, moist heat

> *Nay, but to live*
> *In the rank sweat of an enseamed bed,*
> *Stew'd in corruption, honeying and making love*
> *Over the nasty sty!*
>
> Hamlet in *Hamlet*, 3.iv.93–95

"That which, next to an orchard and garden, has registered itself most clearly and continuously upon his mind is the picture of a busy kitchen, and the women's work forever going on in it."[4] In *Troilus and Cressida* no less than twelve different processes of cooking are alluded to or described.[5] Pandarus tells Troilus, "He that will have a cake out of the wheat must tarry [wait for] the grinding" and the bolting (sifting) and the leavening:

> *Ay, to the leavening; but here's yet in the word*
> *"hereafter" the kneading, the making of the cake, the heating*
> *of the oven and the baking; nay, you must stay the cooling too,*
> *or you may chance burn your lips.*
>
> Pandarus in *Troilus and Cressida*, 1.i.14–28

Sewing and mending

"Shakespeare also noticed the women's sewing and mending which he saw going on round him, and there is clear evidence of his observation of and interest in needlework in the many images he draws from it and things pertaining to it, such as a bodkin [a thick, blunt needle], a silken thread, a twist of rotten silk . . . mending, ripping up an old garment, facing, lining . . . basting . . . showing a knowledge of trimming a garment, and the way a needlewoman would set about preparing it, which is somewhat unusual."[6]

> *Sleep that knits up the raveled sleave of care . . .*
>
> Macbeth in *Macbeth*, 2.ii.41

raveled = tangled
sleave = skein of soft floss silk used for weaving

> *Deep clerks she dumbs; and with her needle composes*
> *Nature's own shape, of bud, bird, branch, or berry,*
> *That even her art sisters the natural roses;*
> *Her inkle, silk, twin with the rubied cherry . . . .*
>
> Gower in *Pericles*, Act 5 Prologue

deep clerk = a well-versed scholar
inkle = linen thread

> *. . . thou idle*
> *immaterial skein of sleave-silk, thou green sarcenet flap*
> *for a sore eye, thou tassel of a prodigal's purse, thou?*
>
> Thersites in *Troilus and Cressida*, 5.i.30–32

sleave-silk = floss silk that is unwoven and thus worthless
sarcanet = a soft silk cloth
tassel = ornamental bunch of silk threads

> *No, girl, I'll knit it up in silken strings*
> *With twenty odd-conceited true-love knots.*
>
> Julia in *The Two Gentlemen of Verona*, 2.vii.45–46

odd-conceited = strangely devised
true-love knots = a specific intertwined stitch that symbolizes eternal love

> *Nay, mock not, mock not. The body of your discourse*
> *is sometime guarded with fragments, and the guards*
> *are but slightly basted on neither . . . .*
>
> Benedick in *Much Ado About Nothing*, 1.i.273–76

guarded = decorated
fragments = poor rags
guards = decorations
basted = sewn on lightly and temporarily

Babies and children

"Shakespeare's interest in and observation of children and child nature from babyhood are remarkable."[7]

> As looks the mother on her lowly babe
> When death doth close his tender dying eyes,
> See, see the pining malady of France!
>
> Joan la Pucelle in 1 *Henry VI*, 3.iii.47–49

> Ah, my poor princes! Ah, my tender babes!
> My unblown flowers, new-appearing sweets!
> If yet your gentle souls fly in the air
> And be not fixed in doom perpetual,
> Hover about me with your airy wings
> And hear your mother's lamentation!
>
> Queen Elizabeth (Grey) in *Richard III*, 4.iv.9–14

> We do not know
> How he may soften at the sight o' the child:
> The silence often of pure innocence
> Persuades when speaking fails.
>
> Paulina in *The Winter's Tale*, 2.ii.39–42

Showing King Leontes his new-born daughter, Paulina describes how the baby girl looks so much like him:

> Although the print be little, the whole matter
> And copy of the father—eye, nose, lip,
> The trick of's frown, his forehead, nay, the valley,
> The pretty dimples of his chin and cheek,
> His smiles,
> The very mold and frame of hand, nail, finger.
>
> Paulina in *The Winter's Tale*, 2.iii.99–103

Lawn bowling

"Of all the games and exercises Shakespeare mentions—tennis, football, bowls, fencing, tilting, wrestling—there can be no doubt that bowls [lawn bowling] was the one he himself played and loved best. He has . . . more than thrice as many as from any other game . . . . Although we know the game of bowls was popular in Shakespeare's day . . . yet this image cannot be classed as a commonplace of Elizabethan writers. . . . So that Shakespeare's interest in it is unusual and is a personal characteristic."[8]

At the reference to bowling in *The Winter's Tale* (4.iv.330), Hardin Craig points out that bowling was "a game played mainly by the aristocracy."[9] There is a topographical painting by Leonard Knyff, painted about 1700, of Mary's Wilton estate that shows an enlarged inset of the bowling green.[10] The painting is hanging and can be viewed at Wilton House.

> *Well, forward, forward! Thus the bowl should run,*
> *And not unluckily against the bias.*
> Petruchio in *The Taming of the Shrew*, 4.v.24–25

bowl = small wooden ball
bias = an off-center weight inside the ball that makes it roll in an oblique or curving path

> *'Twill make me think the world is full of rubs,*
> *And that my fortune runs against the bias.*
> Queen Isabel in *Richard II*, 3.iv.4–5

rub = an obstacle or impediment that diverts the ball from its course

> *Nay, sometimes,*
> *Like to a bowl upon a subtle ground,*
> *I have tumbled past the throw . . . .*
> Menenius in *Coriolanus*, 5.ii.22–24

subtle ground = deceptively irregular
past the throw = overshot the mark

Animal sports

"Shakespeare's attitude as seen in his images [of animal sports] is unique among the dramatists of his time, for he shows a sympathy with and understanding of the animal's point of view and sufferings which no one else in his age approaches."[11]

> *To the which place a poor sequestered stag,*
> *That from the hunter's aim had ta'en a hurt,*
> *Did come to languish. And indeed, my lord,*
> *The wretched animal heaved forth such groans*

That their discharge did stretch his leathern coat
Almost to bursting, and the big round tears
Coursed one another down his innocent nose
In piteous chase. And thus the hairy fool,
Much markèd of the melancholy Jaques,
Stood on th'extremest verge of the swift brook,
Augmenting it with tears.

First Lord in *As You Like It*, 2.i.33–43

War images

"Next come his war images, and in this selection of them I find nothing which indicates any direct knowledge of war or of fighting."[12] "Bacon, compared with Shakespeare, has very few 'war' images, but he definitely asserts that he strongly approves of war, and believes it to be as necessary to a State as healthy exercise to a man's body. Shakespeare hates war and condemns it . . . he constantly symbolizes it by and associates it with loud and hideous noises, with groans of dying men, with 'braying trumpets and loud churlish drums, clamours of hell.'"[13]

. . . this day hath made
Much work for tears in many an English mother,
Whose sons lie scattered on the bleeding ground.
Many a widow's husband groveling lies,
Coldly embracing the discolored earth . . . .

French Herald in *King John*, 2.i.302–306

Now for the bare-picked bone of majesty
Doth doggèd war bristle his angry crest,
And snarleth in the gentle eyes of peace.

The Bastard in *King John*, 4.iii.148–150

. . . all those legs and arms and heads, chopped off in a
battle, shall join together at the Latter Day and cry all,
"We died at such a place"—some swearing, some crying
for a surgeon, some upon their wives left poor behind
them, some upon the debts they owe, some upon their
children rawly left. I am afeard there are few die well
that die in a battle . . . .

Michael Williams, soldier, in *King Henry V*, 4.i.136–142

> *What would you have me do? Go to the wars,*
> *would you, where a man may serve seven years*
> *for the loss of a leg and have not money enough*
> *in the end to buy him a wooden one?*
>
> Bolt in *Pericles*, 4.vi.171–74

The war imagery in the plays is particularly intriguing. The few mentions of tactical maneuvers are copied from the historical sources. Armed conflicts in the plays are merely described in the stage directions as "Alarums. They Fight." This author describes battle scenes in the form of human interactions, of connections and dissensions, of emotionally charged confrontations between individuals.

In *Henry IV, Part 1*, Prince Hal saves his father, Henry IV, in a battle. The author's stage directions state only that "They fight. Douglas flieth." The point of the scene is not the fight, but the relationship between father and son.

In *Henry V*, the King wanders among the soldiers at night to philosophize on life and death and the responsibilities of kingship.

In *Henry VI, Part 3*, a young man drags a soldier he has killed onto the stage to steal his goods, only to discover it is his own father; an older man drags a soldier he has killed onto the stage to steal his goods, only to discover it is his only son. The father cries:

> *These arms of mine shall be thy winding-sheet;*
> *My heart, sweet boy, shall be thy sepulcher,*
> *For from my heart thine image ne'er shall go;*
> *My sighing breast shall be thy funeral bell . . .*
> *I'll bear thee hence and let them fight that will,*
> *For I have murdered where I should not kill.*
>
> Father in *Henry VI, Part 1*, 2.v.114–22

Says Henry VI upon seeing these events:

> *O piteous spectacle! O bloody times!*
> *Whiles lions war and battle for their dens,*
> *Poor harmless lambs abide their enmity.*
> *Weep, wretched man, I'll aid thee tear for tear;*
> *And let our hearts and eyes, like civil war,*
> *Be blind with tears, and break o'ercharged with grief.*
>
> Henry VI in *Henry VI, Part 1*, 2.v.73–78

Also in *Henry VI, Part 3*, Queen Margaret has Clifford murder young Rutland, son of Richard, Duke of York. When her men have captured York, she taunts him mercilessly with the murder of his son, then gives him a handkerchief steeped in Rutland's blood to wipe away his tears. It is a highly emotional exposé of the humanity and inhumanity of war, not a technical account of a particular battle.

This playwright is concerned about the human relationships during wartime, not martial strategies. There is nothing in the plays that indicates the writer was ever in a battle or witnessed one, but clearly condemns and vilifies war. As the herald said in *King John*, "This day hath made much work for tears in many an English mother."

Part Six

The Antagonist

I hate ingratitude more in a man than
lying, vainness, babbling, drunkenness,
or any taint of vice . . . .
Viola in *Twelfth Night*, 3.iv.355–57

Ingratitude! thou marble-hearted fiend,
More hideous when thou show'st thee in a child
Than the sea-monster.
King Lear in *King Lear*, 1.iv.257–59

Documented Data

- Mary Sidney's oldest son, William Herbert, became the wealthiest and most powerful man in England, second only to King James.

- William Herbert successfully changed the power structure at court by acting as bawd (pimp) for the King. As Lord Chamberlain from 1615 until his death in 1630, William controlled the printing of all plays, books, and other documents in England.

- Mary Sidney's younger son, Philip Herbert, gained his title and power in the royal court through "intimacies" with King James.

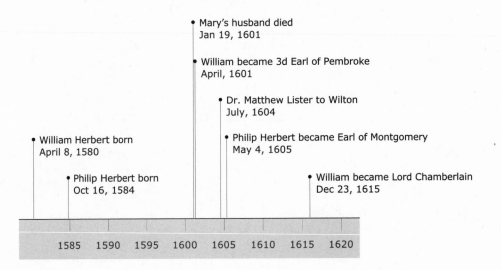

Mary's husband died
Jan 19, 1601

William became 3d Earl of Pembroke
April, 1601

Dr. Matthew Lister to Wilton
July, 1604

William Herbert born
April 8, 1580

Philip Herbert became Earl of Montgomery
May 4, 1605

Philip Herbert born
Oct 16, 1584

William became Lord Chamberlain
Dec 23, 1615

1585   1590   1595   1600   1605   1610   1615   1620

14 The Incomparable Brethren at Court

It is the essence of a
gentleman's character
to bear the visible mark
of no profession
whatsoever.

Samuel Johnson
1709–1784

UP TO THIS POINT the focus has been on Mary Sidney Herbert; her
background and literary circle; her connections with the source
materials; and the similarities between her life, the sonnets, and the
plays. But if Mary Sidney is truly the author of the Shakespearean
works, why didn't she publish the plays under her own name?

What if William Herbert, Mary's oldest son, had discovered that his
mother was writing stage plays for the public theater—bawdy, licentious, and politically insurgent works? It is difficult today to understand why the publication of his mother's creative writings would have
created problems for William.

A brief look at what life was like in the royal court in the late 1500s
and early 1600s will provide a better understanding of the situation
and his dilemma.

Getting Ahead at Court

First, it's important to understand that courtiers did not get "jobs"—
they received preferments, grants, or offices. The Queen or King would
reward a person with one of these "favors." A preferment rarely
entailed actually working for a living—generally, one merely reaped
the rewards. For instance, you might be granted the import duty on
currants, silk, or sweet wine, which would mean you'd get all of the

duty fees. Of course, you'd hire a tradesman to actually do the *job* of collecting and recording the duty fees and that person would send you the money regularly.

Being granted a monopoly on the manufacture of such things as starch for collars, on gold and silver thread, or on clay for making tobacco pipes (which was owned for a time by Archie Armstrong, the King's fool) meant that everyone involved in that trade had to buy a license from you.

Two creative courtiers had lighthouses erected on the coast and charged a penny a ton on all ships that passed by. A courtier might receive lands out of the royal holdings, the dowry for a daughter's marriage, or a flat-out payment of cash (in 1611 Mary's younger son Philip received £6,000 from the King simply as royal "benevolence"). A title, such as "Earl of Pembroke," gave you the right to collect rents and other fees from every person in that particular shire (county), such as Pembrokeshire.

Don't Get on the Wrong Side

But, "Not everybody prospered at court. Some made the wrong alliances and secured powerful enemies. Some bankrupted themselves trying to keep up with the senseless extravagance of the court, and had to retire at last, impoverished. Some incurred the dire fate of the King's active displeasure. There was, for instance, the luckless soul who was so intent upon begging a suit [making his request heard] that he neglected to admire the King's handsome new saddle. When his friends asked the King why he had not granted the man's petition, James snorted, 'Shall a King give heed to a dirty paper, when a beggar noteth not his gilt stirrups?'"[1] It was a world of favors and volatile royal opinion.

As an example, Sir Walter Raleigh incurred the Queen's disfavor by impregnating one of her maids-of-honor, then marrying her secretly without the Queen's permission. Even though he had honorably married her, Raleigh and his new wife were both imprisoned in the Tower for several months and were not readmitted to court for many years. "Now that the Queen was no longer his friend, he [Raleigh] found himself 'like a fish cast on dry land, gasping for breath, with lame legs and lamer lungs.'"[2]

There is a well-known story about an argument on a tennis court (probably at Greenwich Palace) between Philip Sidney (Mary's older brother) and Edward de Vere, the Earl of Oxford. Philip was playing tennis with friends when the ever-arrogant Earl of Oxford arrived and wanted the tennis court. Oxford, "born great, greater by alliance, and superlative in the prince's [Queen's] favour," imperiously ordered Philip Sidney and his friends to leave. "On Sidney's calm refusal, Oxford grew heated, and 'commands them to depart the court. To this Sir Philip temperately answers that if his lordship had been pleased to express desire in milder characters, perchance he might have led out those that he should now find would not be driven out with any scourge of fury. This answer, like a bellows blowing up the sparks of excess already kindled, made my lord [Oxford] scornfully call Sir Philip by the name of puppy.'"[3] The argument became "loud and shrill" on both sides until Sidney and his friends abruptly left the tennis court.

Actually, Philip hadn't been knighted (Sir) at the time of the quarrel. He was technically an untitled commoner, born into the gentleman class.

When Philip complained to Queen Elizabeth about being treated so badly, the Queen lectured Philip on "the difference in degree between earls and gentlemen; the respect inferiors owed to their superiors; and the necessity in princes [Kings or Queens] to maintain their own creations [those they invested with a rank or title], as degrees descending between the people's licentiousness and the anointed sovereignty of crowns."[4] Essentially the Queen was reminding Philip that there is an order in the universe and Philip was of a lower order (an untitled gentleman) than the Earl of Oxford and therefore "inferior" to Oxford and so rightfully must abase himself before his "superior."

Queen Elizabeth seems to have had a relentless dislike of Philip, as I mentioned in Chapter 2. Since blood relations are so important in the English social system, the queen's dislike of Philip extended to his family: "The queen's suspicion [of the growing popularity of Philip] seems to have extended to Robert [Philip's younger brother], with dismal effects on the younger brother's prospects. . . . All his requests for advancement were denied, his military achievements scorned or ignored, his personal initiative discouraged, and his aspirations frustrated. Although his ambitions were more personal and far less grandiose than Philip's, Elizabeth took no chances where Robert was concerned. She never raised him to the position at the court for which his inheritance and service qualified him." [5] Here is a clear case of the reputation of one family member destroying the court opportunities for another member.

A further example was when the Queen finally learned that her "favorite," Robert Dudley, the Earl of Leicester (Mary and Philip's uncle, their mother's brother), had secretly married the Queen's cousin. Not only was the Queen furious with Dudley, but her sense of betrayal stretched to Mary's mother, the Queen's trusted lady-in-waiting. Court life as Dudley's sister finally became too difficult and so she retired to Penshurst, another victim of the system of preferment and rank. Mary's mother was treated with disdain even though she had risked her life contracting smallpox while nursing the Queen through the disease years earlier. She was so disfigured from the pustules that she rarely appeared again in public, and never without a veil. Yet even that sort of sacrifice didn't guarantee a place in court if a family member fell out of favor.

In 1601, William Herbert, 21 years old, had been at court for several years when he saw what happened to John Donne, the poet, who "did little better [at advancement at court]. An early mistake of marrying above his station without his patron's . . . permission removed him for years from the usual paths of advancement." [6] What was Donne's sin? Marrying above his station and without permission, for which he was thrown into the Fleet prison for several weeks, dismissed from his post as private secretary to the Lord Keeper of the Great Seal, and forced into church work because King James eventually declared that Donne could not be employed outside the church. "In his 'Satire 5,' Donne created a relentless downward spiral of depression as he described the vicissitudes and degradation of preferment-hunting at the royal court." [7]

Growing up, Mary's oldest son William Herbert would have been painfully attuned to these tacit threats toward his family and perfectly aware that status and advancement at court was dependent not only on a person's own reputation, but on the unsullied reputation of every other member of the family.

William Herbert's Troubles

Around 1601 William had his own troubles at court. He openly resented the time spent with his dying father at Wilton House, worried that his enemies at court were "taking this advantage of my absence when I could make no answer for myself." When his father died, William seemed to express no grief ("Old Earl of Pembroke dead" was all his letter stated), more concerned to obtain "certain small offices that his father had held."[8]

Just a week after his father's death in 1601, it was discovered that William's mistress, Mary Fitton, was "proud with child." This Mary, who also was a maid-of-honor to the Queen and two years older than William, would dress in men's clothes to meet him away from court. Although he admitted paternity, William refused to marry her and Queen Elizabeth threw him into the Fleet prison for several months. Mary Fitton's baby boy was born dead. "His reason for refusing to marry Mary Fitton is not known, but he probably intended to make a more advantageous match, as he later did with Mary Talbot, daughter of the Earl of Shrewsbury." (Mary Fitton was of a lower rank, her father being untitled.)

William was released from the Fleet prison, but Queen Elizabeth banished him first to Baynards Castle in London and then to the country, to Wilton House, where he complained, "I have not yet been a day in the country, and I am as weary of it as if I had been prisoner there seven year." He asked permission to leave England "that the change of the climate may purge me of melancholy," but the Queen refused. William even had the gall to try to salvage his own reputation by asking the Queen to grant a patent to Mary Fitton's father as appeasement. "He was oblivious to the impropriety of asking the queen for a grant to pacify the Fittons, thereby requesting that she pay for his irresponsibility, and he never considered paying Fitton out of his own vast wealth."[9] William was not released from his disgrace and allowed back at court until Queen Elizabeth died in March of 1603.

The court of her successor King James grew to be even more divided and decadent than that of Queen Elizabeth—a hotbed of factions, favoritism, and intrigue. "In a court where men and women 'loved but from the teeth outwards,' the competition for favor and position was relentless and brutal.... In this desperate place, lone individuals had no chance, and faction was the means by which people sought to protect themselves from their enemies and further their own interests."[10]

And one had to keep an eye on one's own family. For instance, "The Earl of Suffolk [Thomas Howard] had become an object of suspicion on account of his daughter's scandalous behavior and would never again be as powerful as he had been."[11] Note that it's not the Earl of Suffolk himself who did anything scandalous, but his daughter—yet her behavior irreparably damaged his own reputation and power.[12]

William's Struggle for Rewards

History shows that as soon as William Herbert arrived at King James' royal court as a young man of 23, he immediately began working toward advancement. "The state papers and parliamentary records show [for William] an immensely detailed and patient building up of political power over the first decade of James's reign [1603–1613] ...."[13]

William's career started off well enough. King James awarded him the lucrative keepership of various lands and offices in the tin-mining districts. He was also appointed Lord Lieutenant of Cornwall and governor of Portsmouth.[14]

But in 1607 the favored positions of both William and his younger brother Philip were jeopardized when the King fell in love with the minor Scottish courtier, Robert Carr. Over the next few years both brothers were involved in violent and acrimonious public quarrels with other courtiers, and proposals were put before the Commons to exclude all Scots from court. "By 1611 the ambitions of the various factions at court were becoming more polarized."[15]

William Herbert was prepared to go to great lengths to protect his position in court and advance himself. He particularly desired the job of Lord Chamberlain, the person in charge of the public theater, printing, and the court entertainments, a position held at the time by the King's favorite, Robert Carr. Carr was the Earl of Somerset and well entrenched in the opposing Howard faction.

Having been passed over for several significant posts during the years, William at last recognized a window of opportunity through which he could change the power structure at court and gain for himself the position he coveted. "In 1614, seemingly resigned to a minor political role, Pembroke held one of the most significant factional supper meetings in British politics at Baynards Castle. Pembroke, [Archbishop] Abbott, [Sir Ralph] Winwood, and Sir Thomas Lake decided to provide James with a new favorite to supplant Carr. The bait was Sir George Villiers, a Lancashire knight—handsome, sparkling, and superficial."[16]

The plan was that George Villiers would catch the eye of King James, topple Carr, the King's current favorite on the Howard side, with the result that William and his faction would then be in power.[17] They coached George how to walk, talk, primp, curl his hair, tie his ribbons, and sweeten his breath to entice King James.[18] Ben Jonson wrote a masque specifically for the occasion, *The Golden Age Restored,*[19] that included a dance to be performed by George to show off his dancing legs to the King.

It worked. King James fell madly in love, George Villiers eventually became the Duke of Buckingham, and in 1615 William Herbert became the Lord Chamberlain with the specific condition that the position be passed on to his brother Philip when William died.

Thus Mary's son, William Herbert, the 3d Earl of Pembroke, went on to become the wealthiest and most powerful man in England, second only to the King. In 1615, "His pension of £3,600 was supplemented by additional perquisites that brought it to nearly £5,000, one of the highest incomes of any royal official."[20] William was responsible for court activities; access of suitors and embassies to the king; the master of the revels, the court plays and musicians; and had direct supervision of almost two thousand people in the court system. In 1617 he became Chancellor of Oxford University.[21] Thus, "In matters of political preferment at Oxford, Pembroke predictably sought to exercise the power and influence invested in the Chancellorship directly to his own benefit."[22] Nor did he forget those who did him favors: In 1619 Ben

George Villiers and his famous dancing legs.

Jonson was given an honorary degree from Oxford at the behest of William Herbert.[23] From 1618 to 1625 William served as the Grand Master of the Freemasons.[24]

Even William's marriage to Mary Talbot, daughter of the Earl of Shrewsbury, was arranged to further his wealth and status. "Both [William Herbert and Mary Wroth, his cousin and lover] married for family aggrandizement: Pembroke to acquire money and lands, marrying a woman of apparently little physical attractiveness or social grace—who eventually went, or more likely was conveniently declared, insane, largely for the financial benefit of her husband's family."[25]

Maintaining the Reputation

Reputation, reputation, reputation! O, I have lost my reputation! I have lost the immortal part of myself, and what remains is bestial. My reputation, Iago, my reputation!

Cassio in *Othello*, 2.iii.256–259

William's machinations into power and his preoccupation with appearances was noted at the time. William Herbert, 3d Earl of Pembroke, was "Characterized by 'Justice, Religion, and Piety,' of 'a lofty mind,' delights in 'Magnanimity . . . Courteous and affable to his friends but Cannot bear Injury or Cross in his *reputation*.' He is 'bountiful to his friends . . . but because of his regard for honor and *reputation*,' he 'shall be very dainty in the choice out of jealousy and suspicion.'"[26] [emphasis added]

Fully understanding how to manipulate the court system to achieve his goals and maintain his power, William did just that. "Clarendon likewise distinguished Pembroke from the bulk of Stuart nobles and statesmen in that he had 'fame and *reputation* with all men, being the most universally beloved and esteemed of any of that age, and despite having a great office in the Court, he made the Court itself better esteemed, and more reverenced in the country.'"[27] William had a lot to protect in his position at court, but Clarendon does go on to acknowledge that he also had his particular vices, such as indulging in excesses of all pleasures and being "immoderately given up to women."[28] [emphasis added]

In this world of the royal court, one can see that if Mary Sidney had been known to be writing "inappropriate" literary work, such as plays for the public theater, there would have been a scandal easily capable of impeding, or more likely, destroying William's career at court.

Margaret Hannay explains, "The lives of these aristocratic women, although less restricted in many ways than those of women in the lower classes, were still tightly constrained by an emphasis on the virtues of chastity, silence, and obedience." [29]

Cerasano and Wynne-Davies agree: "As a female author/translator, not to mention a member of the nobility, Mary Sidney would have opened her *reputation* to considerable risk by involving herself in public theater." [30] [emphasis added] Any question of his mother's reputation would have been valuable material for William's enemies.

Consider what other professional scholars have to say about women and writing in the early 1600s:

> In a world in which privilege was attached to coterie circulation and published words were associated with promiscuity, the female writer could become a "fallen" woman in a double sense: branded as a harlot or a member of the non-elite. [31]

> The English Renaissance lady lived quashed in a double bind. If her family was rich and powerful enough, she was encouraged to develop her mind, learn languages, absorb the best of ancient wisdom. . . . If her mind made use of what it had been given and created some lines of verse, the lady was thought charming. If by some chance she was taken seriously, she walked thump against a wall that would effectively stop even the most passionately creative soul. The wall was called *reputation.* [32] [emphasis added]

> Wisdom, discretion, a wise and religious heart, humility: in the name of these virtues, women were prevented from asserting their own intellectual competence in any secular and most religious spheres. To do so was to risk the charge, perhaps even by their own consciences, of being foolish, indiscrete, vain, and even irreligious, all attributes of "loose" women. No wonder educated women were on the defensive to show that their learning had accomplished no permanent damage to their character! [33]

> Constrained by the norms of acceptable feminine behavior,
> women were specifically discouraged from tapping into the
> newly popular channel of print; to do so threatened the
> cornerstone of their moral and social well-being.[34]

> When their work was published, it was often anonymous;
> if it was known to be by a woman, it was usually restricted
> to manuscripts in the family circle . . . .[35]

Mary Sidney, of course, did write and even publish "appropriate" works
that were within the sphere of acceptance, yet pushing the boundaries.
But writing for the public theater?

> If [Mary Sidney, Countess of] Pembroke had boldly written
> more secular works, then her *reputation* might well have
> been soiled.[36] [emphasis added]

> Women were not able to write works for production in a
> public theatre, but they were allowed to write plays for
> performance within their own homes, the parts being read,
> and perhaps acted, by members of their family and close
> friends.[37] (These were called "closet dramas," such as Mary's
> acknowledged and published work, *Antonie*.)

> If female courtiers [women at the royal court] could arouse
> suspicion regarding their sexual and moral virtue because of
> their speech, female writers were even more suspect, and the
> majority of women who published their works felt the need
> to justify their boldness. They often claimed that their works
> were really private, but that some external force had
> compelled their publication. For writers of religious works it
> was divine inspiration, of advice manuals their duty as
> mothers, of political pieces the special gravity of the situation.
> Poets and playwrights stressed pressures by male friends or
> the desire to correct pirated versions of their work published
> without their consent. Even women's works published
> posthumously, often by their husbands or other male
> relatives, included such justifications and claims that the
> author had been a paragon of female modesty whose writing

had been done only out of duty to God or her children and had never interfered with her household or marital duties.[38]

Mary Sidney was already testing the limits by presenting herself at court "as a woman of culture, and not as a wife and mother."[39] But writing bawdy and often politically subversive plays for the public theater was over the edge—even more so during the reign of the misogynist King James.

Lord Chamberlain Above All

Why did William Herbert want the position of Lord Chamberlain so desperately? "Once he became Lord Chamberlain, he was responsible for overseeing all the court's entertainment *as well as having final control of licensing the public theater.*"[40] [emphasis added] This would, of course, include making sure his mother's work would never be published under her own name.

In E.E. Willoughby's classic book on the printing of the First Folio of the Shakespeare plays, he notes that "no new edition of the plays of Shakespeare had appeared since 1615."[41] The year 1615 is the year William Herbert became Lord Chamberlain.

Did William Herbert spend most of his career at court maneuvering for the position of Lord Chamberlain out of fear that his mother would expose herself as an author of popular, licentious, politically explosive plays for the public theater? Only as Lord Chamberlain would he have absolute control over their publication.

Philip Herbert at Court

William Herbert wasn't Mary's only child at the royal court—her younger son, Philip, was there as well. He gained his power at court, however, through a very different process from that of his older brother William.

Being a younger son, Philip had no chance at a hereditary title. As Lawrence and Jeanne Stone explain in *An Open Elite?*, "A third distinctive feature of the English landed elite was the fact that their younger sons were downwardly mobile, with few career options . . . unless they should have the good fortune to marry an heiress. Because there were no special legal privileges or hereditary titles attached to them, younger sons had to make their own way in the world."[42]

Nor did younger sons of the nobility have a history of accomplishing much: "They certainly had the opportunity of making large fortunes and buying their way back into the society into which they had been born, perhaps indeed at a higher level, but few of them seem to have made it."[43]

Perhaps it was this automatic strike against Philip that made him so different from his older brother: "Aubrey described William as 'a good scholar' who 'delighted in poetry'. In contrast, he insisted that Philip 'did not delight in books, or poetry', preferring outdoor pursuits to the company of scholars and poets. Clarendon confirmed this view, representing William as endowed with 'a good proportion of learning', while Philip 'pretended to no other qualifications than to understand horses and dogs very well.'"[44]

As Philip's second wife later remarked, "He was no Scholar at all to speak of for he was not past three or four months at the University of Oxford being taken away from thence by his friends, presently after his father's death . . . to follow the court, as judging himself fit for that kind of life when he was not passing 15 or 16 years old." She also complained that he was "extremely choleric [ill-tempered] by nature."[45]

But Philip had other gifts. "As Clarendon remarked, Philip 'had the good fortune, by the comeliness of his person, his skill, and indefatigable industry in hunting, to be the first who drew the King's eyes towards him with affection.'"[46]

Wilder and handsomer than William, "Philip Herbert was even more successful than his elder brother in catching the royal eye. Before James's coronation, he was appointed as a Gentleman of Queen Anne's bedchamber and made a Knight of the Bath. Gossip about the King's favour for Philip grew when late in 1603 he received, along with [two others], a grant for the transport of cloth, rumoured to be worth not less than £10,000."[47]

"By the time of the coronation in July he [Philip] was familiar enough with the king to be able to get away with kissing him on the lips rather than the hand at the ceremony, and he had great influence with the king from the earliest days of the reign." [48]

Philip was just 19 years old.

Philip's Reward

On the first New Year's night of King James's court, 1603–1604, "Philip Herbert was exploiting to the full the effects which his physical charms were having upon the King. When he [Philip] was asked for an interpretation of his device [heraldic design], 'a fair horse colt in a fair green field,' Philip explained that it signified 'a colt of Bucephalus's race and had this virtue of his sire that none could mount him but one as great at least as Alexander.' Delighted by such innuendoes, James 'made himself merry with threatening to send this colt to the stable.'" [49]

In 1604, Philip married Susan de Vere, a match arranged by the lovers themselves. She was the youngest daughter of Edward de Vere, the Earl of Oxford; they arranged their marriage six months after the Earl died. On their first morning after the wedding, with great glee, "the King in his shirt and nightgown gave them a Reveille Matin [morning reveille] before they were up and spent a good time in or upon the bed, choose which you will." [50]

Philip's relationship with the King progressed: "Robert Cecil's letters of 1605 are filled with references to Philip's intimacy with James." [51] Finally, the pay-off: "In May, 1605, King James granted Philip Herbert an earldom in his own right, even though he was a younger son." [52]

Alvin Kernan in *Shakespeare, the King's Playwright,* is more explicit: "Later James took up with [William] Herbert's younger brother, the even more handsome Philip, who as a result of this intimacy was made Earl of Montgomery in 1605." [53]

An earldom wasn't the only honor King James heaped upon Philip Herbert. He also presented the handsome young man with lands worth £1,200 a year in rents and tithes. The King "paid out of the royal purse the debts which the loose-living and extravagant young man had accumulated," created him a Knight of the Garter, the highest order of knighthood in England, and outright gave him £6,000 as a gift.[54]

Although William and Philip received their awards through different means, "By July 1616, when the Earl of Pembroke, as Lord Chamberlain, presided over the arrangements for the King's summer progress, the Herbert brothers were widely recognized as being among James's most intimate advisers and friends."[55]

With both of her surviving children clawing their way up the factious court ladder, how could Mary Sidney, as their mother, engage publicly in any potentially subversive literary activity?

A Bawd, a Whore, and a Matron

When King James died in 1625 at the age of 59, it was in the arms of William Herbert, just as the young King Edward VI (son of Henry VIII) died in the arms of William's grandfather (Mary's father).

So Mary's sons became two of the wealthiest and most powerful men in the English court, and the self-proclaimed poet laureate Ben Jonson had a part in their success with his masque for George Villiers, the King's bait. Several years later, right before Mary died, a collection of the Shakespearean plays went to press in a book now called the First Folio, as discussed at length in Chapter 16. The First Folio is dedicated to Mary Sidney's two sons, and Ben Jonson wrote a eulogy praising the author of the plays.

One of the most intriguing features of Jonson's poem is his own introduction to it. He complains that some people might pretend to praise a person, while actually trying to ruin him. He says this is how a bawd (pimp) or a whore might treat an older gentlewoman:

> *Or crafty malice, might pretend this praise,*
> *And think to ruin, where it seemed to raise.*
>
> *These are, as some infamous Bawd, or Whore,*
> *Should praise a Matron. What could hurt her more?*

There has been no reasonable clarification as to why Ben Jonson mentions a bawd, a whore, and a matron in the introduction to the eulogy to "The AUTHOR." Jonson was a careful writer who enjoyed clear and specific language and symbolism; it would be unlike him to use these words thoughtlessly. What do a bawd, a whore, and a matron have to do with William Shakespeare?

An explanation might be that Jonson was a key player in William Herbert's plot to change the power structure in King James' court by providing the King with a new lover. In this plot, William essentially acted as a bawd/pimp. And Jonson was well aware (as everyone at court seemed to be) that Mary's younger son, Philip Herbert, acted as whore in exchange for the title Earl of Montgomery and other favors. If Mary Sidney was the author of these plays, how could Jonson have made it any clearer?

> This is the way a bawd (such as Mary's older son) or whore
> (such as Mary's younger son) might pretend to praise an older
> gentlewoman (Mary herself) while really planning to subvert
> or undermine her. What could hurt her more?

The entire poem, published in 1623, is filled with other odd references. For instance, Jonson compares Shakespeare to Lyly, Kyd, and Marlowe, three writers he had previously disparaged. Lyly wrote letters that complained of failure and neglect, he hadn't written anything since 1590, and had died in 1606; Kyd had been imprisoned and tortured for atheism and died in poverty in 1594; Marlowe was murdered in 1593. What is Jonson saying?

The following two pages include a paraphrase of the introduction. The full poem and a paraphrase are in Appendix C for those who might like to study the many odd ambiguities it includes.

To the memory of my beloved,
The AUTHOR
MR. WILLIAM SHAKESPEARE:
And
what he hath left us.

1. To draw no envy (Shakespeare) on thy name,

2. Am I thus ample to thy Book, and Fame:

3. While I confess thy writings to be such,

4. As neither Man, nor Muse, can praise too much.

5. 'Tis true, and all men's suffrage. But these ways

6. Were not the paths I meant unto thy praise:

7. For seeliest Ignorance on these may light,

8. Which, when it sounds at best, but echoes right;

9. Or blind Affection, which doth ne'er advance

10. The truth, but gropes, and urgeth all by chance;

11. *Or crafty Malice, might pretend this praise,*

12. *And think to ruin, where it seem'd to raise.*

13. *These are, as some infamous Bawd, or Whore,*

14. *Should praise a Matron. What could hurt her more?*

15. But thou art proof against them, and indeed

16. Above th'ill fortune of them, or the need.

17. I, therefore will begin. Soul of the Age!

[paraphrase]

1. To avoid attracting malice and spite (Shakespeare) to your *name*,

2. Is why I am consequently so unrestrained in the matter of your written works and your reputation.

3. At the same time that I acknowledge that your writings to be the kind

4. That neither Man nor Muse can commend more than they deserve.

5. It's true, and all men can attest to this. But this kind of praise

6. Is not the course of action I had in mind with which to honor you.

7. Because people, who have been intentionally blinded and thus uninformed, may read these lines,

8. Which, though at the time their ignorance believes these lines to be good, it turns out the lines are only imitations of what is true.

9. Or you might be praised with "blind affection"—people who have never actually seen you in person but love your works—which never gets any closer to or promotes

10. The truth, but only searches for it uncertainly and stimulates or incites what it does by accident (but not by honesty).

11. *Or with cunning ill will, some people might use this praise as a pretext to elevate someone*

12. *But actually intend to undermine the power of a person in a place (such as this eulogy) where it gives the appearance of putting someone in a higher position.*

13. *These are the sorts of tricks with which some notorious pimp or whore*

14. *Might praise a respectable elderly lady. What could actually hurt her more?*

15. But you are impervious to these tricks and, to be sure,

16. You are far above the unfortunate destiny they plan for you, or the necessity of it.

17. I, accordingly, will lay the true foundation: Soul of the Age!

To seel is to sew a hawk's eyelids closed for training, or to close a person's eyes to prevent him or her from seeing or discovering something.

On to the Plays

More information about Ben Jonson, his poem, and his important contribution to the printed collection of Shakespearean works is in Chapter 16, "The Publication of the First Folio." But first, let's look at the publication of the plays themselves during Mary Sidney's and William Shakespeare's lifetimes.

Part Seven

The Publication

Thus doing, your name shall flourish
  in the printers' shops.
Thus doing, you shall be of kin
  to many a poetical preface.
Thus doing, you shall be most fair,
  most rich, most wise, most all;
  you shall dwell upon superlatives.

Philip Sidney,
The Defense of Poesy
published 1595

Plays in print during Shakespeare's lifetime

Queen Elizabeth died in March, 1603. Shakespeare died in April, 1616. Mary Sidney died in September, 1621.

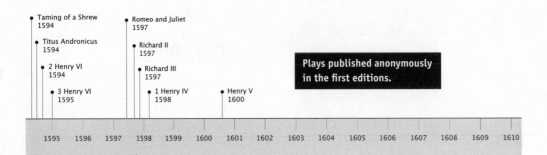

- Taming of a Shrew
  1594
- Titus Andronicus
  1594
- 2 Henry VI
  1594
- 3 Henry VI
  1595
- Romeo and Juliet
  1597
- Richard II
  1597
- Richard III
  1597
- 1 Henry IV
  1598
- Henry V
  1600

Plays published anonymously in the first editions.

| 1595 | 1596 | 1597 | 1598 | 1599 | 1600 | 1601 | 1602 | 1603 | 1604 | 1605 | 1606 | 1607 | 1608 | 1609 | 1610 |

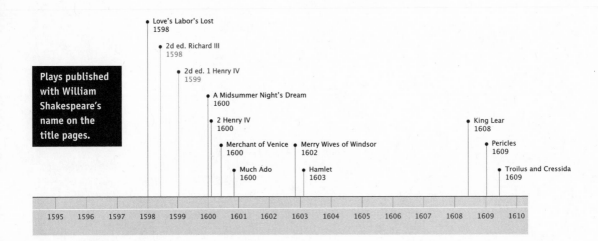

Plays published with William Shakespeare's name on the title pages.

- Love's Labor's Lost
  1598
- 2d ed. Richard III
  1598
- 2d ed. 1 Henry IV
  1599
- A Midsummer Night's Dream
  1600
- 2 Henry IV
  1600
- Merchant of Venice
  1600
- Much Ado
  1600
- Merry Wives of Windsor
  1602
- Hamlet
  1603
- King Lear
  1608
- Pericles
  1609
- Troilus and Cressida
  1609

| 1595 | 1596 | 1597 | 1598 | 1599 | 1600 | 1601 | 1602 | 1603 | 1604 | 1605 | 1606 | 1607 | 1608 | 1609 | 1610 |

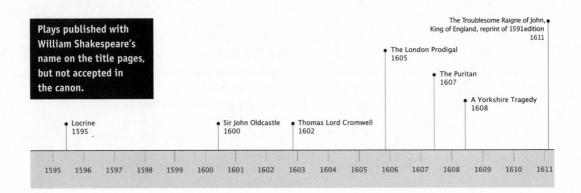

Plays published with William Shakespeare's name on the title pages, but not accepted in the canon.

- The Troublesome Raigne of John, King of England, reprint of 1591 edition
  1611
- The London Prodigal
  1605
- The Puritan
  1607
- A Yorkshire Tragedy
  1608
- Locrine
  1595
- Sir John Oldcastle
  1600
- Thomas Lord Cromwell
  1602

| 1595 | 1596 | 1597 | 1598 | 1599 | 1600 | 1601 | 1602 | 1603 | 1604 | 1605 | 1606 | 1607 | 1608 | 1609 | 1610 | 1611 |

15 The Publication of *the Plays*

AS IT IS IN LONDON TODAY, the theater was a vibrant and thriving enterprise during the English Renaissance. There were from five to nine theaters open at all times, holding from 1,500 to 3,000 people apiece. Plays were staged every day except Sunday—often sold out.

Between 1610 and 1620, when the population of London is estimated to have been about 200,000, the attendance of theatergoers *daily* "finally settled down to a range of 8,000 or less to just over 10,000."[1] In 1595, the Admiral's Men and the Lord Chamberlain's Men "together averaged about 2,500 paying customers a day, or 15,000 a week."[2]

There were more than a thousand professional players (actors) in town,[3] just over fifty professional dramatists,[4] and slightly more than 200 amateur play writers.[5]

In competition with theater performances were bearbaiting, bullbaiting, and cockfighting, with the most important matches held on Sundays. Rich and poor, commoners and nobility attended the theaters and the baitings. Queen Elizabeth was so fond of bearbaiting that for a time she had the theaters closed down two extra days a week so they wouldn't compete with the bears.[6]

Because theater was so popular, the acting companies constantly needed new material. "The urban audience included a substantial

In bearbaiting, a bear was tied to a stake and set upon by a pack of mastiff dogs. The bear usually killed or maimed a couple of dogs, and when the dogs would hang back, new dogs were introduced until the bear was beaten or had maimed all of the dogs. Rarely was the bear killed by the dogs. Bullbaiting was similar.

number of repeat visitors who required a continuously varied menu of dramatic entertainments. The typical life span of a new script . . . was about two weeks, with double admission prices on opening day. The very factor that made the new playhouses so lucrative—their sheer size—made a steady supply of new plays an economic imperative."[7]

Sir Peter Hall estimates that 800 new plays were performed between the mid-1580s and 1616, but admits that we do not know the half of it.[8] Gerald Bentley reports that we know the titles of about 1,500 plays from 1590 to 1642. We know nothing at all regarding the authorship of 370 others.[9] And in addition, "there probably were written as many as 500 plays of which we know not even the titles." [10]

It boils down to this conservative estimate: During the publication of the Shakespearean plays that spanned about 25 years (1590–1615), approximately 1,500 plays were written and produced—that's more than one new play every week. Although the only playwright of this time whom most people can name is "Shakespeare," there were actually fewer plays from this writer than from almost any other popular dramatist—only 37 of those 1,500 plays, as compared to 200 for Thomas Heywood, 69 for John Fletcher, and 64 for Thomas Dekker.[11] Henry Chettle had a hand in 52 plays in 5 years.[12]

The Anonymous Author

A careful look at the publication history of the Shakespearean plays shows a number of interesting things.

In the first printed collection of plays, called the First Folio (discussed at length in the following chapter), there are 36 plays, all of which are believed to be written by the same author. (Research indicates that one of the very early plays and several of the very late plays include additions from other authors.)

In the second edition of the Third Folio (the third printing of the Folio in 1664) and in the Fourth Folio (1685), seven plays attributed to Shakespeare were added: *Locrine, The Life of Sir John Oldcastle, The Puritan, A Yorkshire Tragedy, The London Prodigal, Thomas Lord Cromwell,* and *Pericles.* All of these were in print with Shakespeare's name or intials during his lifetime, as shown on page 182. Today, the only one of these seven that has been accepted as (mainly) authored by

Shakespeare is *Pericles*. So that makes a total of 37 plays that comprise the canon.

There are a number of apocryphal plays that have been attributed to Shakespeare for one reason or another,[13] including *The Two Noble Kinsmen*, *Edward III*, and *Cardenio*. But we're going to concern ourselves in this chapter with just the accepted 37 of the canon, plus the plays attributed to Shakespeare while he was alive.

The first eight Shakespearean plays that appeared in print were published anonymously:

> *Titus Andronicus* (1594)
>
> *The Taming of a Shrew* (1594)
>
> *Henry VI, Part 2* (1594, 1600)
>
> *Henry VI, Part 3* (1595, 1600)
>
> *Romeo and Juliet* (1597, 1599)
>
> The first edition of *Henry IV, Part 1* (1598)
>
> The first edition of *Richard the Second* (1597)
>
> The first edition of *Richard the Third* (1597)

Scholars are not in agreement over whether the anonymous printed version of *The Taming of a Shrew* is a source play for *The Taming of **the** Shrew* by someone else or a "bad quarto" of a Shakespearean play.

Provocatively, the title pages of *Titus Andronicus*, *The Taming of a Shrew*, and *Henry VI, Part 3*, while listing no author, all state they had been played by the Earl of Pembroke's Men, the acting company sponsored by Mary Sidney and her husband. Scholars believe *Henry VI, Part 2* was also played by Pembroke's Men,[14] documenting that at least three (and probably four) of the early, anonymous Shakespearean plays were played by the acting company sponsored by Mary.

The first play printed with Shakespeare's name on it, *Love's Labor's Lost*, does not appear until 1598. Its title page does not state, "By William Shakespeare"—it says, "Newly corrected and augmented By W. Shakespere."

Three of the previously anonymous plays were reprinted:

> The 1598 reprint (and succeeding ones) of *Richard III* states, "Newly augmented by W. Shakespeare."
>
> The 1599 reprint of *Henry IV, Part 1* states, "Newly corrected by W. Shakespeare." But regarding the notation that it is

newly corrected, Oscar James Campbell writes, "This statement is not true, for there are only very small differences between the texts of the two quartos."[15]

The 1598 reprint of *Richard II* states, "By William Shakespeare."

A ninth play, *Henry V*, was printed anonymously in 1600 and reprinted anonymously in 1602.

The next ten plays that were printed before Shakespeare's death, as shown on page 182, had Shakespeare's name on the title pages. So out of approximately 1,500 plays that were produced during the 25 years of Shakespearean authorship, 37 plays are indisputedly in the Shakespearean canon.

Of these 37 plays, only 12 appeared bearing William Shakespeare's name while he was alive—12 out of 1,500 plays over a period of 25 years.

Pirates Ahead

Some of these plays that went into print individually were reproduced by means of what experts call "memorial reconstruction."[16]

"According to the theory of memorial reconstruction, an actor (or actors) reconstructed the entire play from memory; evidence suggests that attempts at memorial reconstruction were usually made by actors who had had minor roles in the play."[17] Berryman believes that *Henry VI, Part 2* was "constructed probably from memory by a minor actor with Pembroke's Men . . . ."[18]

The printed works attributed to Shakespeare were all unauthorized publications. Shakespeare's works were by far the most frequently pirated (after "Anonymous"). Other authors were pirated, such as Francis Beaumont, John Fletcher, Robert Greene, Christopher Marlowe, and George Peele, but not more than two printings each.[19] As Diana Price explains, "Shakspere was a shrewd businessman, yet the flow of unauthorized editions went unchecked. Although copyright laws existed to serve licensing procedures and the stationers rather than to protect the author, it is not as though writers, even those who had less business savvy than Shakspere, had to tolerate unauthorized publications."[20] She describes the actions taken by Thomas Lodge, Samuel Daniel, George Chapman, Nicholas Breton, and Thomas

Heywood when pirated editions of their work were published. "These writers protested, even if their protests came to naught. Shakspere did nothing."[21]

In Shakespeare's time, the only people who would have known a play's authorship would have been those very closely involved with the theater. And even of that small and closeknit group, no one personally mentions William Shakespeare as a *writer* of plays, although he was known to be an actor and a shareholder. Nor did anyone in this close-knit group record paying him for writing a play.

This documented event tells us something of Shakespeare's reputation: In early 1601 the followers of the Earl of Essex went to the Globe playhouse and asked the Lord Chamberlain's Men to perform *Richard II*, hoping to incite the citizens of London to revolt with Essex against the Queen. (The Lord Chamberlain's Men complained because the play was so old, having first been seen about four years previously.) Scholars make much of Essex's choice of a play, as if to prove Shakespeare himself was so incredibly popular. But not once in the records of the court trial of Essex is it mentioned that this play was *written by William Shakespeare* or that they requested *a play by William Shakespeare*—they requested *Richard II*. When examinations were made regarding the presentation of the play, one of the Lord Chamberlain actors was called to the stand, but never the playwright.[22]

Clearly the play itself was well known, even among the aristocracy, but not the author. Names of dramatists appear to have been no more well known to the general public at that time than screenwriters are today.

And Who Wrote These?

Have you ever heard of *Locrine, Sir John Oldcastle, A Yorkshire Tragedy,* or *The London Prodigal?* These plays, among others, appeared in print while Shakespeare was alive, his name is on the title pages,[23] and they appear in several of the Folios of Shakespearean plays.

Scholars have created the mythology that Shakespeare's name appears on so many other plays because he was so popular as a dramatist. Supposedly, having his name on the written play would sell more copies of the play or make more people show up at the theater.

But *The Tragedy of Locrine*, included in the Third Folio of Shakespeare's works in 1664, was published "by W. S." in 1595, three years *before* the first play appeared with his name on it. Interestingly, the title page of *Locrine* states that the play was "Newly set forth, overseen, and corrected by W.S." This attribution is remarkably similar to the title pages of two other plays that I recently mentioned:

> 1598: *Love's Labor's Lost* states, "Newly corrected and augmented By W. Shakespere." (Oddly, the 1631 reprint is anonymous.)

> 1599: The reprint of *Henry IV, Part 1* states, "Newly corrected by W. Shakespeare."

Perhaps a more likely reason Shakespeare's name appears on the title pages of those other plays is that the man named William Shakespeare also sold those other plays to printers, in addition to the twelve known Shakespearean plays. Diana Price, in her book *Shakespeare's Unorthodox Biography*, sets forth a clear argument that William Shakespeare was a play broker.

"Never blotted out a line"

Writers would create a draft of a play, which was called the "foul papers." This draft was copied, often by a professional scribe, into a neat and clean version which was called the "fair papers." This is particularly interesting in light of comments about the manuscripts of the Shakespearean plays—it was recorded twice (after his death) that Shakespeare wrote so easily and fluidly that the players received manuscripts from him with not a single line blotted out. Ben Jonson mentioned that the players told him this, and it's also mentioned by the actors who wrote an introduction in the First Folio.[24]

Few scholars believe even Shakespeare could write these complex, lengthy, and finely crafted plays so perfectly with no drafts at all, so it's a bit of a puzzlement why this bit of information has come down through history with so much certainty. Is it possible the acting companies never saw blotted lines because Shakespeare actually gave them, not his own "perfect" foul papers, but the fair papers from another author?

Documented Data

- Nine of these plays were originally published anonymously.

- At least the first four published plays were performed by Pembroke's Men, the acting company sponsored by Mary Sidney, the Countess of Pembroke.

- The first several plays with Shakespeare's name on them claimed to be "newly corrected" by Shakespeare, but weren't.

- Several of the plays were sold to printers by a bit actor.

- Several of the plays that were originally published anonymously were reprinted later with Shakespeare's name on the title pages. Scholars tell us all the printed plays were pirated—it was not Shakespeare who took them to press. Why, then, would a pirate assign a *reprint* to Shakespeare? Unless that pirate were Shakespeare himself?

- In extant legal documents, William Shakespeare signed his name as Shakp, Shakspe, Shaksper, Shakspere, and Shakspear.[25] Yet on all but two printings of every play that bears his name over a thirty-year period, the plays were attributed to "Shakespeare."[26]

Was William Shakespeare the bit actor who intercepted these manuscripts and realized he could safely take credit for them in the playhouse? Did William Shakespeare take credit for the manuscripts and surreptitiously sell them to the printers? Was he, as Diana Price outlines, a play broker?

We'll look next at the huge task of printing the entire collected works, known today as the First Folio.

Documented Data

- The first printed collection of Shakespearean plays is called the First Folio. It went to press five years after William Shakespeare died, and printing was completed two years later.

- There is no record of who paid for this large and expensive undertaking.

- The book is dedicated to Mary Sidney's two sons.

- Not a scrap of an original manuscript has ever been found.

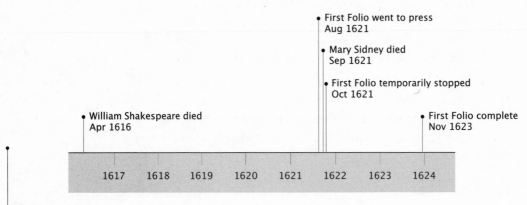

First Folio went to press
Aug 1621

Mary Sidney died
Sep 1621

First Folio temporarily stopped
Oct 1621

First Folio complete
Nov 1623

William Shakespeare died
Apr 1616

| 1617 | 1618 | 1619 | 1620 | 1621 | 1622 | 1623 | 1624 |

Queen Elizabeth died
1603

16 The Publication of the First Folio

IN 1623, THE PUBLICATION OF THE ENTIRE COLLECTION OF PLAYS was completed in what we now call the "First Folio." Examining the publication history of this important book offers some interesting reflections on the possible author of the works.

The term "First Folio" is actually rather generic—it means this was the first time the plays were printed on large sizes of paper which were folded in half, called folios, as opposed to the smaller-sized pages that were folded in quarters, called quartos. Shakespeare's First Folio is a book about 13 inches tall, 8.5 inches wide, and 2 inches thick.

The First Folio was dedicated to Mary Sidney's two sons: William Herbert, the third Earl of Pembroke, and Philip Herbert, the first Earl of Montgomery. No other personal or professional connection between Shakespeare and Mary's sons has ever been found. In fact, *The Reader's Encyclopedia of Shakespeare* muses that "[Philip] Herbert was a generous patron of the arts, but he was habitually in debt, a fact which makes his selection as a dedicatee of such an expensive volume as the folio somewhat unusual."[1]

By the time the dedication was written, William Shakespeare had been dead for seven years. The dedication is not from him—it's from two actors in the King's Men (the acting company of which Shakespeare was a member) named John Heminges and Henry Condell. They are assumed to be the editors of the First Folio. The famous portrait of Shakespeare in the First Folio was engraved by Martin Droeshout who was only 15 years old when Shakespeare died and never knew him.

The Missing Manuscripts

A writer's original draft was called the "foul papers." When a draft was completed, the foul papers were neatly rewritten, often by a professional scribe, into the "fair papers" that would be sent to the print shop or playhouse. A "prompt book" was the authoritative playhouse copy of the entire script, sometimes broken down into acts, scenes, and stage directions. From the prompt book, each actor's part was written on a long paper scroll, or roll, from which comes our present terminology of an actor's "role."

Not one scrap of paper from any of the original handwritten Shakespearean manuscripts has ever been found. Not one piece—no plot outline, no foul papers, no fair papers. Thirty-seven lengthy plays spanning a publishing period of more than twenty-five years (1594 to 1619, with *Othello* going to press in 1622), and not one word in anyone's handwriting.

Shakespearean scholars insist this is not a big deal, that once a play was in print, the original handwritten manuscripts were useless and the paper recycled—cooks would use it to wrap fish or line baking pans, or bookbinders would use it to attach hard-bound covers.

Some people will even tell you there are no original manuscripts of anyone else's plays either. But in *Dramatic Documents from the Elizabethan Playhouses,* W.W. Greg describes in great detail the original handwritten plots, actor's parts, prompt books, and manuscript plays from that era that are in museums and collections, and he doesn't even include the extant pages from early dramas, masques (performances by masked players, usually at court or in great houses), court entertainments, closet dramas, or academic plays. Greg's oversized companion book, *Reproductions & Transcripts,* provides reproductions of many of the documents. There are handwritten manuscripts for plays by a number of Shakespeare's contemporaries, such as Munday, Massinger, Heywood, Suckling, Daborne, Fletcher, Beaumont, and others—many of which went to press.

Paul Werstine, in "Plays in Manuscript," complains that Greg's work was too limited, that he did not record the extensive holdings of the Folger Shakespeare Library in Washington, D.C., the Huntington Library in San Marino, California, or Alnwick Castle, north of Newcastle, England.[2]

And just recently—within the past twenty-five years—dramatic manuscripts from the Elizabethan and Tudor eras have been found at the Warwickshire Record Office, Arbury Hall in Nuneaton, and Castle Ashby.[3]

But even Werstine's more far-reaching scope has yet to find one page of a manuscript of a Shakespearean play or sonnet.

There are a great number of manuscript documents of other written work, besides plays, that also went to press. Bentley tells us that "Between 1594 and 1601 Greville wrote three tragedies, *Antonie and Cleopatra, Mustapha,* and *Alaham.* The first he himself destroyed; *the other two are extant in both manuscript and print.*"[4] [emphasis added]

H.R. Woudhuysen in *Sir Philip Sidney and the Circulation of Manuscripts* tells us "There are three such manuscripts of *Astrophil and Stella* and eleven of the *Old Arcadia* or parts of it. . . . One manuscript of the *New Arcadia* survives, two of *A Defence of Poetry,* and a dozen or so private miscellanies contain poems in texts not copied from the early prints."[5] All of these works went to press, yet we still have the manuscripts. Woudhuysen also states that "Copies of individual shorter poems presented to specific patrons or friends also sometimes survive entirely in the author's hand."[6]

An "authorial" (handwritten by the author) manuscript by John Donne, "The Gunpowder Plot Sermon," was recently discovered to add to the sixteen other *manuscripts* of Donne's *printed* collection of sermons.

There are even extant preliminary *drafts* of works by various authors. "There are plenty of examples of Bacon's working drafts of his philosophical and scientific works, especially in Latin; Camden's autograph preliminary version of Edward Herbert, Lord Cherbury's prose works are preserved in the National Library of Wales. Autograph notes for *Of the lawes of ecclesiasticall politie* and a draft of one of Hooker's sermons are at Trinity College Dublin. . . . Several notebooks and sets of memorandums in Sir Walter Raleigh's hand are extant."[7]

Why are the manuscripts of these writers still available? Often it is because an author had a sense of his own importance and knew the manuscript would one day be valuable. It is difficult to imagine that the man named William Shakespeare, the most profound genius in literary history, did not understand and appreciate the value of his own work and thus simply tossed in the rubbish bin the original manuscripts for every play he wrote over a period of twenty-five years.

The First Folio itself belies the traditional theory that, as most experts insist, there are no Shakespearean manuscripts because they were always destroyed as soon as a play was printed. As Charlton Hinman explains, "Some of the plays in the Folio apparently do reproduce Shakespeare's own 'foul papers' . . . and a number were set into type from combinations, part manuscript and part printed, or materials variously related to Shakespeare's original papers."[8]

Eighteen of the plays in the Folio had been printed in the previous thirty years, most of them in several editions, before the First Folio was compiled. Of these eighteen plays previously in print, scholars believe that the editors of the First Folio used original manuscripts or even foul papers (drafts) for five of the plays, and the prompt books for three others.[9] Each of these eight plays had been in print between 1594 and 1609, yet the original manuscripts or at least prompt books were still available in 1622. This indicates it was *not* common practice to destroy the manuscript after a play went to press.

Publishing Literary Works

Woudhuysen states that it was the posthumous publication of Philip Sidney's work that paved the way for writers like Shakespeare to print their own works:

> [Philip] Sidney's sudden availability in print [beginning in the 1590s] also had an important influence on the production of literature. It is too simple to suggest that writers thought that if his work could be exposed to the public view their own could be as well, but there may be an element of truth in this. . . . Sidney became a standard author, as Daniel . . . Spenser,

Drayton, Jonson, Shakespeare, and eventually Greville were all to do within the next few years. In this way, it could be argued that the 1598 folio [of Philip's literary works] served as a model for later writers and promoted the idea of a predominantly print-based literary culture.[10]

Philip had died in 1586—*it was Mary Sidney who published Philip's writing in the form and style appropriate to the work, thus establishing a permanent place for him in the literary world.*

Ben Jonson, in 1616, set a precedent for considering plays as enduring intellectual achievements by publishing his plays in *The Works of Benjamin Jonson*. Rosalind Miles states, "By his insistence that plays were worthy of the kind of formal treatment and attention that had previously been reserved for other literary productions, Jonson made an incalculable contribution to the raising of the drama's status in England."[11]

It has often been said by Shakespeareans, as a way to explain Shakespeare's odd reluctance to produce an authoritative collection of his own work while he was alive, that everyone laughed when Jonson published his plays. This aspersion is used to explain away the anomaly of William Shakespeare taking no care for any of his work to be printed, but this is simply not true.

Jonson's own Folio "was ushered into the world with the support of laudatory verses from many of Jonson's friends," including John Selden, George Chapman, Francis Beaumont, Edward Hayward, and Abraham Holland. The portrait engraved for the book was "printed and sold separately, which gives some indication of Jonson's popularity and the public interest in him at this time."[12] David Riggs assures us that Jonson was "a man who outshone even Shakespeare and Donne in the eyes of his contemporaries."[13]

The derogatory comment that Shakespeareans refer to is this, by an anonymous wit: "Pray tell me Ben, where doth the mystery lurk, What others call a play you call a work." Not only was this the only statement recorded in this vein, but it was answered, anonymously: "Ben's plays are works, when others' works are plays."[14]

Printing the First Folio

The entire collection of Shakespearean plays, half of them never printed before and several never performed on stage, was first taken to the press in August of 1621.[15] William Shakespeare had been dead for five years. Did Mary Sidney begin the printing process?

The First Folio went to press without being licensed[16]—not an extremely rare occurrence, but it is unusual. "Before a play could be printed, it had to be licensed. The licensing agent responsible for printed matter was a panel of London clergymen . . . operating under the authority of the Privy Council, the Bishop of London, the Archbishop of Canterbury, *and the Lord Chamberlain.*"[17] [emphasis added]

Who was the Lord Chamberlain in 1621? Mary's oldest son, William Herbert. "Once he became Lord Chamberlain . . . he was responsible for overseeing all the court's entertainment as well as having final control of licensing the public theater."[18]

Is it possible Mary Sidney had to circumvent licensing a book that would have threatened the reputation of the Lord Chamberlain?

The title page of the First Folio falsely states, "Published According to the True Original Copies." The first four plays in the Folio[19] were printed from copies made by a professional scribe; the others are cobbled together from a variety of sources. "If the editors had planned to continue this practice [of using fair copies] throughout the volume, however, they abandoned it after the fourth play and turned instead to a variety of sorts of copy."[20]

Did Mary provide the printer with these first four plays, planning to supply the others as the project progressed? We know that in July of 1621 she entertained King James at Houghton House, but she was back in her London home on Aldersgate Street in August of 1621. Did she come into London for the specific purpose of finally publishing her own work?

Several documented events intersect here: The printer began production of the book in August, 1621.[21] Mary Sidney died in late September. Production of the book stopped in October.

Her funeral was held at St. Paul's in London; her tomb is believed to be under the choir steps of Salisbury Cathedral, near her Wilton home. The parish records of Salisbury Cathedral state only that she was buried, but John Chamberlain (a gentleman and scholar in the court of King James) gossiped in a letter from London, "The old Countess of Pembroke died here some ten days since of the smallpox, and on Wednesday night was carrred with a great store of coaches [probably no less than a hundred] and torchlight toward Wilton where she is to be buried."[22] No will was found.

Printing eventually resumed for the First Folio and the project was completed in November, 1623—seven years after William Shakespeare died and two years after the death of Mary Sidney.

In *Who Wrote Shakespeare?*, John Michell remarks on the finished book:

> The editors of the First Folio hinted by two or three phrases that the author was the man buried at Stratford-upon-Avon, but they never openly stated it. There were no biographical notes on the great dramatist, nor any indications of where and when the plays were written. On the question of how they acquired authentic copies and the rights to plays previously published, the editors were secretive and mendacious. The originals from which they worked have never been seen since.[23]

The traditional explanation of the publication of the First Folio contradicts standard scholarship that once a play was bought by the acting company, it was owned by the acting company.

> [It] does not tell us why the King's Men [the company in which William Shakespeare was an actor] would let two of their members appropriate so valuable a property and dispose of it on their own—for there is no suggestion that the company itself had any hand in publishing the plays. It does not tell us how two actors would have raised the small fortune such a publishing venture would have called for or why anyone putting up the funds would have left the immensely important task of editing the thirty-six plays and preparing them for the printer to two undistinguished stage-players with no experience to fit them for the work,

one of them to turn grocer. If we seek answers to the crucial questions the First Folio raises, I think we shall be forced to accept the indications that those primarily responsible for the publication were the Herbert brothers . . . .[24]

The Herbert brothers, of course, are Mary's sons.

If Mary Sidney were the author, where are *her* manuscripts of these plays? Is it possible that her son William Herbert destroyed any manuscripts he came across, as he is known to have destroyed documents about his illegitimate children? (It's intriguing that she supposedly had no will.) It's also possible that manuscripts are yet to be found; perhaps we've been looking in the wrong places. If Mary Sidney were the author, would she have hidden the manuscripts from her son? With extensive libraries, several estates, and the ability to travel freely, where might a brilliant woman safely leave her writing?

Ben Jonson's Poem to "the AUTHOR"

Ben Jonson, self-proclaimed poet laureate of England.

Ben Jonson wrote a poem for the First Folio that is rather puzzling. In 1618 (two years after William Shakespeare died) Jonson specifically told the poet Sir William Drummond that Shakespeare "wanted art," meaning he lacked study in the art and craft of writing. Yet in the First Folio poem Jonson praises the author for the study of the craft of writing and the meticulous fine-tuning. "This well-known poem is not merely a conventional tribute. The deep sincerity of Jonson's admiration and his true love for the dead Shakespeare are everywhere apparent. He salutes Shakespeare as 'Soul of the Age!' He places him above all contemporary poets; he is the one genius with which Britain may rival the classical writers of old, and Jonson envisages him transported to heaven to reign as a 'star of poets' to inspire his successors." [25]

David Riggs, a biographer of Jonson, is more critical: "Much of what Jonson has to say in this poem is strikingly at odds with his previous references to Shakespeare. . . . Heretofore, [Ben Jonson] had always championed the cause of art and had repeatedly chastised the popular playwrights of his day for relying on their own raw talent; now Jonson turned the tables and praised Shakespeare for the very qualities he had derided in the past. . . . But his willingness to grant that Shakespeare actually satisfied this criterion comes as a surprise and has even prompted critics to question his sincerity." [26]

For all of Jonson's acclamation in the First Folio in 1623, on Shake-speare's death in 1616, Jonson had never written a word.

Nor did he acknowledge Shakespeare later as one of the great writers. In his prose piece *Timber, or Discoveries* (printed in 1641 but written earlier), Jonson recommends, "And as it is fit to read the best authors to youth first, so let them be of the openest and clearest. As Livy before Sallust, *Sidney* before Donne; and beware of letting them taste Gower or Chaucer at first . . . ." He also recommends that students read Edmund Spenser. [emphasis added]

But no Shakespeare.

Ben Jonson had long been closely associated with Mary and her Wilton Circle, her sons, and her younger brother Robert. In 1616 (the year William Shakespeare died) Jonson had written a poem about Mary's childhood home, Penshurst, where Robert continued to live as an adult. "Sir Robert Sidney . . . despite his own insoluble financial difficulties, offered Jonson both patronage and hospitality at his country house Penshurst in Kent, which Jonson came to love dearly." [27]

One reason for his love is that the Sidneys and Herberts treated Jonson with warmth and respect, seating and conversing with him at the same supper table and serving him the same beer and bread—treatment he was not accorded in other noble households. William Herbert gave Ben Jonson £20 every New Year's Day to buy books. When Ben copied out sonnets written by Lady Mary Wroth (Mary Sidney's niece, Robert's daughter), he claimed that he became "a better lover and much better poet." [28]

He wrote numerous poems and epigrams to and about members of the family. "Jonson consistently portrays the Sidneys and the Herberts as members of a self-contained aristocratic community that is answerable only to its own ancestral traditions." [29]

Understanding how the generally cantankerous Ben Jonson admired and respected the Sidney and Herbert families, is it possible, after Mary Sidney died and the First Folio was on the press, that William Herbert confided to Ben Jonson that his mother was the author of these plays? Was Jonson the editor?

It might explain why Jonson, who had previously spoken poorly of William Shakespeare, in this eulogy calls "the AUTHOR" the Star of Poets and the Sweet Swan of Avon.

It is *assumed* that Heminges and Condell, two actors with the King's Men, were the editors of the First Folio. But in *The Reader's Encyclopedia of Shakespeare*, Oscar James Campbell observes, "The text was obviously edited by someone familar with the plays who would be responsible for eliminating profanity, making acting divisions, and other details. It is doubtful that Heminges and Condell would be qualified for this exacting work."[30]

David Riggs believes that Jonson may well have been one of the editors. He notes that whoever prepared the Folio "remade Shakespeare in Jonson's image," describing how the prefatory letters and poems in the book "transform Shakespeare into a specifically literary figure whose works have achieved the status of modern classics; the closest analogue to these tributes are the poems prefixed to Jonson's 1616 folio."[31] Riggs describes how the First Folio follows the same method of punctuation that Jonson used in his own *Works* instead of that used in the previously published editions of the Shakespearean plays. And, "The extensive use of parentheses, semicolons, and end-stopped lines in the 1623 folio [Shakespearean First Folio] owes more to Jonson's example than to Shakespeare's habits of composition."[32] Interestingly, a line in *Julius Caesar* that Jonson had derided as ridiculous appears in the First Folio as corrected and logical.[33]

The Possibility

If Mary Sidney began the printing process in 1621, is it possible that after she died, the printer contacted her son the Lord Chamberlain about the unfinished project—and payment?

As mentioned in Chapter 4, Mary Sidney and William Herbert had been estranged for at least ten years, beginning about 1604. The cause of the estrangement is not clear; was it her relationship with the lower-class doctor—or did William discover his mother was writing plays for the public theater? Up until this time, William Herbert might have been the only person aware that Mary Sidney was the author. But now, to finish the project and attribute the plays to William Shakespeare for posterity, Herbert would have needed help—did he at this point call on Ben Jonson? And why did Ben Jonson call the author of the plays the "Sweet Swan of Avon"?

17 The Sweet Swan *of Avon*

SPECIFICALLY WRITTEN FOR THE PUBLICATION of the First Folio, the poem by Ben Jonson calls the author of the plays his "Beloved" (in the title) and the "Sweet Swan of Avon":

> *Sweet Swan of Avon! what a sight it were*
> *To see thee in our waters yet appear,*
> *And make those flights upon the banks of Thames,*
> *That so did take Eliza [Queen Elizabeth] and our [King] James!*

Why would Ben Jonson call a great writer a "Sweet Swan"? No one has been documented referring to William Shakespeare as a swan.

A good writer uses symbols to enrich phrases and to capture all of the connotations of an image into a succinct impression. Ben Jonson was no exception; throughout his life he insisted on the importance of correct speech. He chided careless writers who used "such impropriety of phrase, such plenty of solecisms [grammatical mistakes], such dearth of sense, so bold prolepses, so racked metaphors."[1] To Jonson, literary sloppiness in speech was a sign of intellectual weakness.

So why a swan? A swan is sometimes called the Bird of Return. White swans are famous for their beauty—and for being mute all their lives until just before they die.

A cygnet is a baby swan. The "organ-pipe of frailty" is the long neck of the swan, through which her dying gasp creates a sort of song.

> 'Tis strange that Death should sing.
> I am the cygnet to this pale faint swan,
> Who chants a doleful hymn to his own death,
> And from the organ-pipe of frailty sings
> His soul and body to their lasting rest.

Prince Henry, to his dying father in
King John, 5.vii.20–24

The traditional interpretation of "Sweet Swan of Avon" in Jonson's poem is that he is referring to William Shakespeare who lived in the village of Stratford situated directly on the Avon River—which still doesn't explain the swan, or the swan making flights on the banks of the Thames river.

But was Jonson really referring to Shakespeare?

His entire eulogy to "the AUTHOR" is suspect in that he seemingly idolizes a man for whom he is on record as having disliked and whom he later ignored.[2]

Certainly, there are several rivers in England named Avon, and Ben Jonson never mentions Stratford in any reference to Shakespeare.

Mary Sidney, however, lived on an estate encompassing 14,000 acres at the time, or 22 square miles. The Wiltshire Avon ran through her property. A tributary of the Avon, called the Wylye, flows right past Wilton House (as does the River Nadder). And she is buried in Salisbury Cathedral, located directly on the Avon River.

Mary chose to be known by her maiden name, Sidney. We know that her brother, Philip Sidney, was referred to as a swan by his French friends because of his name: "So his French admirers made play with the similarity of sound between *Sidney* and *cygne* [French for swan] and made puns about swans."[3] A portrait of Philip printed in a French translation of *Arcadia* is topped with swans.[4]

Philip was immortalized by poets as a swan, as in this example by Du Bartas:

> And (World-mourn'd) Sidney, warbling to the Thames
> His Swan-like tunes, so courts her coy proud streams . . .[5]

Perhaps it was the French influence of *Sidney* vs. *cygne* that encouraged Mary to take the swan as her own personal emblem, or perhaps it was a memorial to Philip after his death. In 1592, Samuel Daniel, an important writer of the era and a close friend of hers, wrote of Mary in his sonnet sequence titled *Delia*, Sonnet 48. Delia, according to every Sidneian scholar, refers to Mary Sidney:[6]

> *But Avon, rich in fame, though poor in waters*
> *Shall have my song, where Delia hath her seat.*
> *Avon shall be my Thames, and she my song;*
> *I'll sound her name the river all along.*

Of this phrase in the sonnet, Margaret Hannay remarks, "In fact, Wilton [the house itself] is not far from the Avon, which runs through Salisbury, but a more plausible reference is to Mary Sidney's seat at Ivychurch, a few miles southeast of Wilton on the Avon."[7]

The writer Michael Drayton, a contemporary of Mary's who was honored with burial in Poets' Corner in Westminster Abbey, referred to Mary as a swan on the Thames in his poem "Shepherd's Garland":

> *The lofty subject of a heavenly tale,*
> *Thames' fairest Swan, our summer's Nightingale.*[8]

In a portrait of Mary when she was 57 years old (shown on the following page), she posed wearing a large, lace collar and wrist-cuffs embroidered with a motif of swans. Swan wings connect the bottom of the oval frame. The portrait is surrounded by two large, feather pens in ink wells (a female swan is called a "pen"). Was Mary's swan motif a poignant message of her anonymous writing? She is shown holding one of the books she wrote, *David's Psalms,* and the image is topped with a poet's laurel wreath above the Sidney spearhead. This is the image of a woman who wanted to be remembered as a writer and as a Sidney.

As I mentioned, Ben Jonson refers to the author of the First Folio as the "Sweet Swan of Avon." Five lines later, Jonson declares that the author is a constellation:

> *But stay, I see thee in the Hemisphere*
> *Advanc'd, and made a constellation there!*

The constellation Jonson refers to could easily be Cygnus, also known as the Bird of Return, the swan.

The Sidney family emblem, the spearhead (pheon) is right below the laurel wreath.

The inscription at the bottom refers to her as "Mary Sidney," her maiden name, and not Mary Herbert.

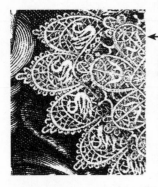

Knowing that this brilliant writer adopted the swan as her personal symbol, combined with the tangible Avon associations—contemporary poets called her a swan; the name she preferred to be known by is, in French, essentially "Swan"; the Avon River ran through her estate; she is buried on the Avon River—is it possible that Ben Jonson was referring to Mary Sidney as the *Sweet Swan of Avon*?

Part Eight

The Possibility

*All truths are easy to understand once they are discovered—
the trick is to discover them.*

Galileo, 1564–1642

It has become fashionable in recent literary criticism . . . to deny the relevance of the author . . . . Whatever justification our personal interest in Shakespeare may have, I can only say that I feel no need to apologize for it. Our curiosity is too natural and too common to be blushed at. Like millions of others, I am interested in who Shakespeare was as a simple matter of historical fact; and if the doctors of literature condemn our inquiry, we can appeal to the historian.

Joseph Sobran in *Alias Shakespeare*

Mary Sidney,
alias Shakespeare

18

And didst thou
  thirst for Fame
    (as all Men do)
Thou wouldst,
  by all means,
    let it come to light.

John Davies of Hereford,
Mary's secretary,
writing about her [1]

THE FOLLOWING IS A WHAT-IF STORY that involves the known facts about the lives of William Shakespeare and Mary Sidney. In the story, all of the statements are documented facts except for the italicized phrases, which are suggestions based on my research.

⬥

MARY SIDNEY, born into the aristocracy in 1561, is invited by Queen Elizabeth to be a maid-of-honor in the royal court after the death of both of her sisters; she is 13 years old. Her first experience at court is the 19-day extravaganza held at Kenilworth Castle, home of her uncle Robert Dudley, the Queen's favorite. Mary, at 13, is acknowledged for her intelligence and her beauty.

Robert Dudley arranges a politically motivated marriage for Mary, age 15, with a 43-year-old nobleman, the widowed Welsh Earl of Pembroke. Within a year after the wedding Mary leaves Elizabeth's court to preside over her own "court" at Wilton House, her husband's estate.

Mary's beloved older brother, Philip Sidney, spends most of his time at Wilton after returning from his European tour. Philip nurtures their mission to create great works of literature in the English language. He and Mary study, write, and develop a literary salon at Wilton House.

While Philip writes his sonnet sequence that will inspire the sonnet craze in England, Mary writes *seventeen "procreation" sonnets for Philip because he is nearing 30 years old, is the only heir to two powerful Earls, and is unmarried.*

Tragedy strikes: Mary's cherished and spirited three-year-old daughter dies the day Mary gives birth to her second son. Within the year Mary's father dies. Three months later her mother dies. Devastated, Mary herself takes ill and almost dies. Two months later Mary's beloved brother Philip dies while fighting a war for the Queen. Mary is barely 25 years old.

Mary *writes Sonnet 18 ("Shall I compare thee to a summer's day") as a goodbye letter to Philip,* but is not allowed to participate in the public eulogies at his funeral because she is a woman. She publishes several elegies to her brother in other works over the next few years.

She spends two years in mourning, *writes Titus Andronicus,* and at the end of this period literally marches triumphantly into London in a grand and brilliant procession. Mary takes the literary mantle from her brother—her mentor—and carries on his work. She is 26 years old.

While Mary Sidney marries, then births and buries her children and other close family members, William Shakespeare, 18 years old, takes a license to marry young Anne Whately of Temple Grafton. But the next day he is hauled off by two older men (friends of Ann Hathaway's dead father) to marry Ann Hathaway of Stratford—half-again as old as Shakespeare and three months pregnant. Ann gives birth to a girl, then two years later, twins (a boy and a girl). Shakespeare abandons his family to live in London.

"For almost two decades Mary Sidney and her household at Wilton become one of the most dynamic cultural influences in late Elizabethan England, and at the center of Wilton's life were her writings."[2]

Mary publishes her brother's works and zealously strives to keep his memory alive as a poet. While her children grow up, Mary writes.

Members of the Wilton Circle, however, do not know that Mary writes *plays for the public theater.* Mary publishes the works of her own that are considered "appropriate" for women—direct translations and religious works—to the critical acclaim of contemporaries.

Titus Andronicus is acted by Pembroke's Men, the troupe sponsored by Mary Sidney and her husband, and printed anonymously. *The Taming of a Shrew* and *Henry VI, part 3* are also acted by Pembroke's Men and printed anonymously.

Meanwhile, Shakespeare publishes two long, overwrought poems dedicated to the Earl of Southampton (*Venus and Adonis* and *The Rape of Lucrece*), and becomes a member of the Lord Chamberlain's Men, an acting company.

In 1592, Mary Sidney publishes a lengthy meditative work on life and death.

In 1596, Shakespeare's son Hamnet, 11 years old, dies in Stratford. There is no extant poem, sonnet, or note written by William Shakespeare about the death of his only son.

The following year, 1597, *Shakespeare,* a play broker, sells three plays to the printer. Shakespeare pays £60 cash for the deed to the second-largest house in Stratford (we don't know how much he paid for the house). He still spends most of his time in London. This year he also defaults on taxes of 5 shillings.

Shakespeare, *who has been claiming authorship of and selling Mary's plays, as well as plays by other writers,* now begins to attach his name to the printed works. He restores and remodels his large home. In 1599 he defaults on his taxes of 13 shillings 4 pence. In 1601 a shepherd's will claims Shakespeare and his wife still owe him 40 shillings (£2—in the prime of his popularity he doesn't pay back the money he borrowed from a shepherd).

In 1601, Mary's husband dies and with him most of her power and influence. Over the next several years she is abandoned by almost all who had previously sought her patronage. She is in court over jewel thieves and the murder of her servant. Her house and servants are attacked; she struggles to maintain control of her holdings for her ungrateful son. This same son, William Herbert, is imprisoned for impregnating a maid-of-honor to the Queen, whom he abandons (the baby dies). He turns against Mary when he discovers *she is writing dramatic productions for the public theater.* They don't speak for about ten years.

Around this time in 1601, William Herbert inherits his father's title and estates, *and Shakespeare makes a deal with Herbert (is it blackmail?)*. In 1602 Shakespeare pays £320 cash for 107 acres near Stratford and also buys a cottage. In 1604 he sues an apothecary in Stratford for 35 shillings. In 1605, Shakespeare pays £440 for a share in the lease of tithes in Stratford; at a yield of £60/year, it will be more than seven years before he starts making his investment back.

Besides running Wilton House with its 200 servants, Mary was also responsible for several other family estates: Baynards Castle in London; Cardiff Castle in Cardiff, Wales; Ludlow Castle in Wales; Ivychurch (near Wilton, on the Avon River); and Ramsbury, a smaller estate in northern Wiltshire. The family lived in Wales each summer.

Struggling after her husband's death, in 1604 Mary falls deeply in love with Dr. Matthew Lister, who is far beneath her social status. Interrupting their lifetime of devotion to each other, there is a period of profound emotional distress when she thinks her adored niece and goddaughter, Mary Wroth, is having an affair with Lister, but it turns out that isn't true—Wroth is actually having an affair with Mary's oldest son, Will Herbert, while both are married to other people.

Mary expresses these powerful and conflicting emotions *in the form of sonnets*.

Mary suffers a devastating loss in 1606 when her 23-year-old daughter dies of a recurring illness.

In 1607, Mary and Dr. Lister cross the Channel and travel to Spa in Belgium where they stay for a short time.

In 1608 Shakespeare sues John Addenbrooke in Stratford for £6.

Mary's son William is outraged by her affair with the lower-class doctor and for *writing plays for the public theater that threaten his career in the royal court*. In 1609, *he steals her sonnet collection and has it printed in Shakespeare's name*. The sonnets are dedicated from the publisher to Mr. W. H.

Shakespeare *discovers that* most of the sonnets published in his name are love poems to a man and *demands that William Herbert suppress the book*.

In 1613, Shakespeare buys a share in the Blackfriars gatehouse (£80 of it in cash). The elaborate arrangements of the deal effectively deprive Shakespeare's widow of her dower right to a share for life in this part of his estate.

Meanwhile, Mary's oldest son William Herbert has been constantly involved in machinations for advancement at court.

Mary's younger, wilder, and more handsome son, Philip Herbert, acts as whore to King James and in exchange is rewarded with his own earldom and cash gifts.

Around 1614, William Herbert plots to change the power structure at court to become Lord Chamberlain. In that position he can control the publication of his mother's plays. Included in the plan is William's friend Ben Jonson, as well as several noblemen and an archbishop. The scheme is successful in providing King James with a new boyfriend (George Villiers becomes the King's favorite lover and eventually the Duke of Buckingham), and William gets the job of Lord Chamberlain with the condition that when he dies, his younger brother takes over the position. William is extremely protective of his hard-won power and wealth.

Shakespeare retires to Stratford. He apparently stops writing plays.

Mary spends three years on the Continent with her lover, hosts a literary salon, entertains, dances, smokes, and continues to write.

William Herbert fathers two illegitimate children with his first cousin, Mary Wroth, shortly after Mary Wroth's husband dies in 1614. William covers up all references to this union and issue (an event discovered in 1935), to the extent of destroying pertinent documents.

No Shakespearean plays are published after 1615—William Herbert, as Lord Chamberlain, prevents any plays with Shakespeare's name on them from getting into print.[2]

Shakespeare's younger daughter, Susanna, is now 31 years old and still unmarried. She runs off and marries the village ne'er-do-well, Thomas Quiney, 23 years old. Because Thomas already has another woman pregnant, Susanna and Thomas marry in a hurry without a license and are excommunicated. Shakespeare immediately changes his will. The young woman Thomas impregnated and her baby both die in childbirth.

Shakespeare, in 1616, dies at the age of 52 (possibly on his birthday), one month after he changes his will. Susanna's rascal husband eventually abandons her, and all of their children die.

Mary builds Houghton House in England with her lover, Dr. Lister.

Five years after Shakespeare dies, Mary approaches her sixtieth birthday. *She takes the manuscripts of four plays to the printer and* publication begins on what is now called the First Folio, a collection of all the plays believed to be written by "William Shakespeare." The works are not licensed before printing begins, even though it's required by law—the license would need to come from the Lord Chamberlain, Mary's son, William Herbert.

Fair copies of four of the plays are taken to the printer. *Mary plans to bring fair copies of the others as the printing progresses.* She lives in London on Aldersgate Street at the time. But Mary dies in her London home, allegedly of smallpox, one month after printing of the First Folio begins, and one month before her 60th birthday. She is buried on an evening in a grand torchlight procession.

Her will is never found.[3]

The printer halts the printing of the collection of plays *and contacts the Lord Chamberlain. William confides in Ben Jonson, who was unaware of the true authorship of the plays until now. Jonson helps gather copies of the rest of the plays and acts as editor. William wants to perpetuate the attribution of his mother's plays to William Shakespeare.*

Jonson writes a poem titled "To the Memory of my Beloved, the AUTHOR" to include in the publication. In its introduction he complains how a pimp/bawd and a whore pretend to praise someone when they're really trying to ruin an old gentlewoman. Jonson calls the author the "Sweet Swan of Avon."

The printer continues production of the First Folio. The book is licensed the day before it comes off the press, seven years after Shakespeare has died. It is dedicated to the two Herbert brothers, the Earl of Pembroke and the Earl of Montgomery.

No one has ever found a single page of any original manuscript of the plays or the sonnets.

Consider the Question

Until a pertinent letter or an original manuscript of any play or sonnet is found that provides conclusive evidence of one author or another, the Authorship Question will remain alive as a vital inquiry. With rigorous documentation, the profile of contenders may become more realistic. Ironically, of the candidates brought forward, William Shakespeare presents some of the weakest documentation.

Mary Sidney Herbert, the Countess of Pembroke, may very well be the most logical and compelling choice for authorship of the plays and sonnets.

With her extensive education, knowledge of languages and music and law, leadership of the most important literary circle in English history, connections with the material known to be used as sources for the plays, involvement in the world about which the plays were written, documented evidence of her life reflected in the story of the sonnets, and as a forward-thinking, courageous woman working steadily despite strictures in a man's world—is it possible to imagine her in yet another role—unacknowledged author of the most influential literature written in English?

What could she have done, as a noble woman of the 16–17th centuries, when publishing the plays under her own name would have destroyed the careers of her two sons in the royal court? What recourse would there have been for her?

Mary Sidney Herbert, the Countess of Pembroke, is a literary enigma, a demonstrable force in Elizabethan literature, richly deserving modern recognition and further research in her own right—as well as a strong candidate for the curious Authorship Question.

*O*r I shall live your epitaph to make,
Or you survive when I in earth am rotten;
From hence your memory death cannot take,
Although in me each part will be forgotten.

Your name from hence immortal life shall have,
Though I, once gone, to all the world must die:
The earth can yield me but a common grave,
When you entombed in men's eyes shall lie.

Your monument shall be my gentle verse,
Which eyes not yet created shall o'er-read,
And tongues to be your being shall rehearse
When all the breathers of this world are dead;

    You still shall live—such virtue hath my pen—
    Where breath most breathes, even in the mouths of men.

SONNET 81

Part Nine

The Appendices

It is not the fashion to see the lady the epilogue; but it is no more unhandsome than to see the lord the prologue.

Rosalind in *As You Like It*, Epilogue.1–3

Appendix A
Old School

In 1924, Alexander Witherspoon wrote about the Wilton Circle in *The Influence of Robert Garnier on Elizabethan Drama*. In this book Witherspoon interprets Mary's importance to literature by stating that "from a pure sense of duty" to her brother to reform English drama, Mary "went about the task with the executive ability of a good housewife."[1]

Witherspoon claimed that Mary's intent with her group of writers was to combat the "uncouth and unlearned" plays on the popular stage, such as the Shakespearean ones. Unfortunately, there are scholars today who still parrot this unfounded presentation of Mary Sidney.

But Margaret Hannay, a modern biographer of Mary Sidney, retorts:

> Rather than portraying the countess as the leader of a campaign to destroy the native dramatic tradition, we can characterize her as among the first to bring the continental genre of historical tragedy to England, making her a precursor, certainly not an antagonist, of "the man Shakespeare" and of Jacobean political drama.[2]

Hannay also says:

> Nor can the countess possibly be combating Shakespeare in her *Antonius* for he had only recently begun his career by the time she completed her translation in 1590. . . . Given the Dudley/Sidney family's long tradition of support for the popular drama and the Earl of Pembroke's nominal sponsorship of a dramatic troupe during the early 1590s, it is more likely that the countess would have encouraged the work of the rising dramatist than opposed him.[3]

This view is supported by other scholars. "Mary Sidney could hardly have been attacking the 'popular melodrama' of Shakespeare, since he had written very little by 1590. On the contrary, she should be acknowledged as one of the earliest contributors to politicized historical drama."[4]

As mentioned earlier, Mary was involved with the theater all of her life, as was her entire family. She grew up watching and participating in theater; she and her husband sponsored an acting troupe; her uncle sponsored a troupe; she acted in plays at the royal court; two of the most famous comic actors, Will Kempe and Richard Tarleton, were both on her uncle Robert Dudley's staff; her brother Philip acted as godfather to Richard Tarleton's son.[5]

An Odd Irony

Considering the possibility that Mary Sidney wrote the works attributed to a man, it's predictably ironic to discover that several men have assumed that a man must have really written Mary Sidney's works.

Regarding her *Psalms* versification, Sir John Harington (1561–1612) suggested that Mary had surely needed her Bishop, Gervase Babington, to advise her because "it was more than a woman's skill to express the sense so right as she hath done in her verse, and more than the English or Latin translation could have given her."[6]

About the ballad, "The Doleful Lay of Clorinda," that Mary Sidney wrote for her brother Philip on his death, Margaret Hannay points out that "Spenser's statement that the countess [Mary Sidney] wrote 'The Doleful Lay of Clorinda' was generally accepted until Ernest de Selincourt suggested in 1912 that 'Spenser wrote it in her name '."[7] Since then, says Hannay, the debate has been tedious, and the discussion "often turns on assumptions about gender."[8]

These are not antiquated sexist statements. Consider a question from 1978: "J. Max Patrick has even gone so far as to suggest that the Countess did not write her best works, asking whether we 'could account for the high excellence of the poetry attributed to the Countess of Pembroke by giving the credit for it to others? . . . was she putting her name on work composed by [the male] members of the Wilton Circle such as Breton, Fraunce, Lok, Daniel, and Greville, or on her own work radically improved by them?'"[9]

To which Gary Waller appropriately responds, "What we know of Breton's, Fraunce's, and Lok's work suggest they might have benefitted more from the Countess than she from them!"[10]

Shortly before her death, in what became her final portrait, Mary chose to have herself shown holding one of her works, the *Psalms*. The portrait is framed by ink wells and pens and is crowned with a laurel wreath, the traditional symbol of a writer/poet. This deliberate visual statement graphically reinforces the literary focus of Mary Sidney's life.

Appendix B
The Other Candidates

THE CURRENT AUTHORSHIP CANDIDATES (besides Mary Sidney) are Sir Francis Bacon; Edward de Vere, the 17th Earl of Oxford; Christopher Marlowe; Sir Henry Neville; and William Shakespeare. In this appendix I'll briefly outline the primary arguments for them. Rather than run the risk of misrepresenting any candidate, following these brief descriptions are web site links with detailed information.

When perusing arguments for any authorship candidate, it is essential to be a discriminating reader. Phrases like "must have been," "surely," "we can believe that," "certainly," "it can be assumed," etc., are clues to undocumented statements.

You'll find in these arguments that proponents of every candidate (except Mary Sidney) try to find connections to Henry Wriothesley, the Earl of Southampton. Why? Because the two narrative poems, *Venus and Adonis* and *The Rape of Lucrece* (see Appendix D), were both dedicated to Southampton early in the writing career of the author, in 1593 and 1594. There is no record of a response to the dedications nor any evidence that Southampton acted as patron to William Shakespeare. Sixteen years later, in 1609, the sonnets were printed without the author's approval, and the publisher of the book dedicated it to "Mr. W.H." Shakespeareans long ago concocted an idea that "W.H." is actually backwards and it really refers to "H.W." as in Henry Wriothesley!

A couple of authorship candidates are favored by some because they traveled to Italy; a number of plays take place partially or completely in Italy.[1] It's not clear why this is perceived as such an important qualification when there are plays set in what is now Belgium, Bohemia,

Turkey, Syria, Egypt and other parts of North Africa, the Balkan Peninsula, Cyprus, Lebanon, Greece—and no one claims their candidate went to all of these places. Christopher Marlowe wrote *The Jew of Malta* and *Doctor Faustus,* and yet no one insists Marlowe traveled to the island of Malta or ever visited Wittenberg (the setting for *Doctor Faustus*) before writing the plays.

Sir Francis Bacon (1561–1626)

Sir Francis Bacon was educated and intellectual, a noted lawyer, and loved cryptology. He was gay, and Baconians believe he wrote the sonnets to a variety of men and women (although there is no documented evidence), including Mary Sidney's son, William Herbert, whom Bacon was trying to convince to have an heir. He was a "concealed poet" (meaning he wrote poetry secretly), had an extensive vocabulary, coined new words, and his ideas and opinions appear in the plays.

A document called the Northumberland Manuscript, which is believed to have been in Bacon's possession, includes the names of both Shakespeare and Bacon and the title of two plays, *Rychard the second* and *Rychard the third.* Bacon also kept a notebook called *Promus* in which he collected expressions, phrases, and sentences, some of which appear in the Shakespearean plays.

Baconians find an anagram in a word used in *As You Like It:* "Honorificabilitudinitatibus" can be rearranged into a Latin phrase, "Hi ludi, F. Baconis nati, tuiti orbi," which roughly means "These plays, born of F. Bacon, are preserved for the world." This word was also found in the Northumberland Manuscript. (The long word can be rearranged into many other sentences, including "I built thou a fabrication, Sidni.")

Many Baconians also believe Francis Bacon was a secret child of Queen Elizabeth and Robert Dudley, the Earl of Leicester.

Why keep his authorship a secret? Because Bacon was a Rosicrucian and one of the six rules imposed on members is anonymity for one hundred years (although that doesn't explain why his name is on his other works).

www.SirBacon.org
www.WhoWroteShakespeare.org.uk

Edward de Vere, the 17th Earl of Oxford (c. 1550–1604)

Generally, Oxfordians propose that the first seventeen sonnets were written to try to convince Henry Wriothesley, the Earl of Southampton, to marry Elizabeth Vere, Oxford's eldest daughter (they didn't marry). In Sonnet 76, they say, you can substitute "E vere" for "ever" and it indicates that Oxford is writing about himself. Anne Vavasor, Oxford's mistress, could be the dark lady.

Oxford traveled to France and Italy, he wrote poetry, and owned the lease to the Blackfriars theater. He was a ward and then son-in-law of Lord Burghley, who many believe is caricatured in *Hamlet*. Oxfordians compare Ophelia to Oxford's wife, Anne Cecil, and Hamlet himself to Oxford.

One problem with Oxford's candidacy is that at least nine new plays were published and produced on stage after his death in mid-1604; some have contemporaneous references to events of the time. These include *Macbeth, King Lear, Othello, Antony and Cleopatra, The Tempest.* Oxfordians must recreate an elaborate timeframe for when the plays were written. They claim the plays had all been written before 1604, but were parceled out to the playhouses over the years and other writers added the contemporary references.

In some minds, an issue against Oxford is that he was considered a rather despicable person in his time; very few scholars can refrain from using pejoratives whenever his name is mentioned. With Oxford's well-documented misogyny, it's difficult to claim that he thought highly enough of females to create the lengthy list of great women in the plays.

The Authorship Studies page listed below provides a concise explanation of the Oxfordian argument.

www.AuthorshipStudies.org/articles/oxford_shakespeare.cfm
www.Shakespeare-Oxford.com
www.Sobran.com/oxfordlibrary.shtml

Christopher Marlowe (1564–1593)

Christopher Marlowe, a commoner, wrote some of the greatest plays of his time—*Dr. Faustus, The Jew of Malta, Edward II* (for Pembroke's Men), *Tamberlaine, Dido Queen of Carthage,* and the narrative poem

Hero and Leander. He was an innovator in the field of drama written in blank verse.

At the heart of the Marlowe case is his murder at the Bull's Inn in Deptford on May 30, 1593. Marlovians believe his murder was faked because he was a member of Walsingham's spy ring, and that he fled to Italy or France and sent plays from there to England for the next twenty-five years.

Some Marlovians believe he wrote the sonnets about *his* affair with Henry Wriothesley, the Earl of Southampton (although there is no documented evidence or even hints of this affair). Others believe Lord Burghley commissioned Marlowe to write the first seventeen sonnets to persuade Southampton (on his seventeenth birthday) to marry Burghley's granddaughter, Elizabeth Vere. (Again, no evidence.)

Sonnet 74 references what they believe to be Marlowe's death, "The coward conquest of a wretch's knife." Sonnet 71 includes the phrase "suffer disgrace," implying that if a youth was associated with a homosexual, it could hurt the youth's reputation. They claim thirty-six sonnets are of exile [most people consider these to be about traveling], which goes along with Marlowe's staged death.

All the plays Marlowe wrote were published and attributed to him after his death. Why weren't the five or six Shakespearean plays that were written before his supposed death also attributed to him?

www.Marlowe-Society.org
www.MuchAdoAboutSomething.com

Sir Henry Neville (*c.* 1564–1615)

Sir Henry Neville's claim to authorship is that his life, proponents believe, meshes with the chronology of the Shakespearean plays. For instance, from 1601 to 1603 Neville was confined to the Tower (with conjugal visits) for his participation in the Essex rebellion, which might have been why the plays took a turn toward tragedy at that point.

Neville's name is also written on the Northumberland Manuscript that the Baconians believe belonged to Bacon.

But they consider their most important piece of evidence to be the Tower Notebook of 1602. In this notebook are handwritten extracts from historical sources, plus annotations in another hand, that contain parallels with the coronation scene in the Shakespearean play *Henry VIII*, ten years before the play is believed to have been written. Although the Tower Notebook is not written in Neville's hand, advocates think he probably hired a scribe for the purpose.

Proponents of Neville believe that the dedicatee of the sonnets, Mr. W.H., "was certainly Southampton [Henry Wriothesley], and indeed, positing another dedicatee makes little sense. Many, conceivably most, of the Sonnets were written by Neville to Southampton during their joint imprisonment in the Tower in 1601–03. . . . 'Mr. W.H.' must have been Neville's affectionate nickname for Southampton."[2] They also think Lord Burghley commissioned Neville to write the first seventeen sonnets to persuade Southampton to marry Burghley's granddaughter, Elizabeth Vere, although there is no documented evidence for either of these theories.

www.SirHenryNeville.com
www.HenryNeville.com

William Shakespeare (1564–1616)

The web site below is dedicated to the proposition that Shakespeare wrote Shakespeare. The web site author is vitriolic in his scorn of the Authorship Question while not holding traditional Shakespearean scholars (or himself) to the same standards he insists from others. His use of hyperbole (*always, never, everyone, no one*) and "surely," as in "Shakespeare surely did this" and "most certainly did that" are red flags for uneven scholarship. Watch carefully for references to Shakespeare's "friends" who talked about him when in reality these "friends" talked about the *work attributed* to Shakespeare, not the man.

www.ShakespeareAuthorship.com

Mary Sidney Herbert, the Countess of Pembroke (1561–1621)

The following web sites have information about Mary Sidney as the possible author of the Shakespearean works:

www.MarySidney.com
www.MarySidneySociety.com

Appendix C
Jonson's Eulogy

The full text of Ben Jonson's poem to the "AUTHOR" follows, with a corresponding line-by-line paraphrase on the facing page.

To the memory of my beloved,
The AUTHOR
Mr. William Shakespeare:
And what he hath left us.

1. To draw no envy (Shakespeare) on thy name,
2. Am I thus ample to thy Book, and Fame:
3. While I confess thy writings to be such,
4. As neither Man, nor Muse, can praise too much.
5. 'Tis true, and all men's suffrage. But these ways
6. Were not the paths I meant unto thy praise:
7. For seeliest Ignorance on these may light,
8. Which, when it sounds at best, but echoes right;
9. Or blind Affection, which doth ne'er advance
10. The truth, but gropes, and urgeth all by chance;
11. Or crafty Malice, might pretend this praise,
12. And think to ruin, where it seem'd to raise.
13. These are, as some infamous Bawd, or Whore,
14. Should praise a Matron. What could hurt her more?
15. But thou art proof against them, and indeed
16. Above th'ill fortune of them, or the need.
17. I, therefore will begin. Soul of the Age!
18. The applause! delight! the wonder of our Stage!

19. My Shakspeare rise; I will not lodge thee by
20. Chaucer, or Spenser, or bid Beaumont lie
21. A little further, to make thee a room:[1]
22. Thou art a Monument, without a tomb,
23. And are alive still, while thy Book doth live,
24. And we have wits to read, and praise to give.

[paraphrase]

1. To avoid attracting malice and spite (Shakespeare) to your "name,"

2. Is why I am consequently so unrestrained in the matter of your written works and your reputation.

3. At the same time that I acknowledge that your writings to be the kind

4. That neither Man nor Muse can commend them more than they deserve.

5. It's true, and all men can testify to this. But this kind of praise

6. Is not the course of action I had in mind with which to honor you.

7. For the most feebly ignorant people may read these lines,

8. Which, at the time that their ignorance examines/proves these lines to be good, they are really only/merely imitations of what is true.

9. Or you might be praised with "blind affection" (people who have never actually seen you in person but love your works), which never gets any closer to or promotes

10. The truth, but only searches for it uncertainly and asserts what it does by accident (but not by honesty).

11. Or with cunning ill will, some might use this praise as a pretext to elevate someone

12. But actually intend to destroy/demolish that person in a place (such as this eulogy) where it gives the appearance of putting someone in a higher position.

13. These are the sorts of tricks with which some notorious pimp or whore

14. Might praise a respectable elderly lady of the upper class. What could actually hurt her more?

15. But you are impervious to these tricks and, to be sure,

16. You are far above the unfortunate destiny they plan for you, or the necessity of it.

17. I, accordingly, will lay the true foundation: Soul of the Age!

18. You are the acclaimed, the source of pleasure, and the prodigy/astonishment of our theatres!

19. My "Shakspeare," ascend from the grave; I will not have you dwell at the side of

20. Geoffrey Chaucer *(writer, about 1343–1400, d.57 y.o.)* or Edmund Spenser *(poet, about 1552–1599, d.47 y.o.)*, nor will I request that Francis Beaumont *(playwright, about 1584–1616, d.32 y.o.) (each of these men is buried in Poets Corner in Westminster Abbey)*

21. Scoot over a little in their graves to make room for you in Westminster Abbey.

22. You yourself are an enduring edifice, enduring beyond and outside of any tomb,

23. And you are in the world still, as long as your written works are in print,

24. And as long as the rest of us have the intellectual/creative capacity to understand/learn/discover/guess/perceive your work and have the glorification to attribute/bestow on it.

25. That I not mix thee so, my brain excuses,

26. I mean with great, but disproportion'd Muses

27. For, if I thought my judgment were of years,

28. I should commit thee surely with thy peers,

29. And tell, how far thou didst our Lily outshine,

30. Or sporting Kid, or Marlowe's mighty line.

31. And though thou hadst small Latin, and less Greek,

32. From thence to honour thee, I would not seek

33. For names; but call forth thund'ring Æschilus,

34. Euripides, and Sophocles to us,

35. Paccuvius, Accius, him of Cordova dead,

36. To life again, to hear thy Buskin tread,

37. And shake a Stage: Or, when thy Socks were on,

38. Leave thee alone, for the comparison

39. Of all, that insolent Greece, or haughty Rome

40. Sent forth, or since did from their ashes come.

25. In as much as I should not mingle you with such company as mentioned above, my thoughts ask pardon/have justification because

26. I have in mind to place you in the same company as other powerful Muses, even though you are disproportionately greater

27. Because, if I considered that my opinion here was only to last these few years (rather than for all time)

28. I would be inclined to ensconce you undoubtedly/certainly with your fellow writers here in England

29. And explain to what degree you surpassed our playwright John Lyly (*c.1554–1606, d.60 y.o.; he did not write after 1590; letters of his complained of failure and neglect; most of his plays were written for child actors or select audiences with Queen Elizabeth*)

30. Or the amusing/contemptuous/mocking playwright Thomas Kyd (*1558–1594, d.36 y.o.; imprisoned for supposed atheism, tortured, died broken and sad in poverty shortly thereafter*)

    or playwright Christopher Marlowe's illustrious/potent/powerful written works (*1564–1593, d.29 y.o.; murdered supposedly over a bar tab*)

31. And even though you wrote few works in Latin and even fewer in Greek

32. For which we can honor you, I do not need to solicit

33. Names for comparison, but summon powerful Aeschylus (*pronounced ees' kil us, c.525–456 BC, d.69 y.o., playwright known as "the father of Greek Tragedy"*),

34. Euripedes (*pronounced you rip' uh deez, c.480–406 BC, d.74 y.o., Greek tragic playwright*)

    and Sophocles to us, (*soe' fuh kleez, c.495–406 BC, d.91 y.o., Greek tragic playwright*)

35. Marcus Pacuvius (*c.130–220, d.90 y.o., painter, playwright, greatest of the Roman tragic poets*)

    and Lucius Accius (*170–c.86 BC, d.84 y.o., Roman poet, playwright, and scholar*)

    and Lucius Annaeus Seneca (*the Younger*), him of Cordova (*about 3 BC–65 AD; a Roman born in Cordova, Spain, like his father, although Seneca lived and died in Rome; tutor to Nero; poet, tragedian, philosopher; forced to commmit suicide at about 68 years old*)

    all these who are dead,

36. I would like to bring them all to life again so they could hear your tragedies (*tragic actors wore heavy-soled half boots called buskins*)

37. And see how you inspire the acting profession. Or, when your comedies are played (*comic actors wore soft slippers called socks*)

38. They would realize you are so far above them as to be alone, compared

39. With everything that the overbearing Greek playwrights or the arrogantly proud Roman playwrights

40. Have ever written or anything that has been discovered from there since the destruction of their civilizations.

Mary was several times suggested, by other writers, to be the tenth Muse. The Muses are all women.

Why did Jonson compare the author to these three playwrights in 1623, each of whom was either murdered, tortured, or neglected, and who were not contemporaries of "Shakespeare's" greatest works, but had all been dead for quite a while, and none had written anything since 1594 at the latest?

41. Triumph, my Britaine, thou hast one to show,

42. To whom all Scenes of Europe homage owe.

43. He was not of an age, but for all time!

44. And all the Muses still were in their prime,

45. When like Apollo he came forth to warm

46. Our ears, or like a Mercury to charm!

47. Nature herself was proud of his designs,

48. And joy'd to wear the dressing of his lines!

49. Which were so richly spun, and woven so fit,

50. As, since, she will vouchsafe no other Wit.

51. The merry Greeke, tart Aristophanes,

41. Exult, Britain, for you have one writer to brag of

42. To whom all the theaters of Europe owe respect and reverence.

43. This writer was not limited to this one short time period in history, but will endure forever.

44. It is as if all the Muses even yet were at their heights of perfection,

45. At the same time that, resembling/in the manner of/indicative of Apollo *(Greek god who loved poetry and music; his weapon a bow, his plant the laurel)*

46. Make us a receptive audience, or in the manner of Mercury to charm us *("charm" meant a magic spell, bewitchment, pretending one thing over another).*

    Mercury's primary function is the protection of thieves and businessmen.

    "On any view, his cult was old, and it had close links with shopkeepers and transporters of goods, notably grain . . . . Mediator between gods and mortals, between the dead and the living, and always in motion, Mercury is also a deceiver, since he moves on the boundaries and the intervening space; he is patron of the shopkeeper as much as the trader, the traveller as well as the brigand." [2]

    Mercury (also known as Hermes) was the god of thieves. Almost immediately after he was born, he killed a tortoise and made the first lyre out of it. Using the lyre, he sang a lullaby that put his mother, the nymph Maia, to sleep. Then he went out into the world where he stole a herd of fifty cattle that belonged to Apollo; clever newborn that he was, he placed improvised shoes on the cows' feet and made them walk backward so it looked like they had gone in the opposite direction.

    Is this the sort of charm William Shakespeare cast? Why does Ben Jonson say that William Shakespeare charmed us in the manner of Mercury, patron god of thieves and businessmen?

47. Nature—the creative power herself—had a high opinion of the author's enterprises

48. And delighted to bear/carry/have/own the costumes of his poetry,

49. Which were created so abundantly and appropriately

50. That, ever since she's known these, she will not condescend to participate in the works of any other learned person.

51. The merry Greek *(perhaps Socrates,[3] 469–399 BC, d.70 y.o., who had an infant son, was condemned to death, and drank poisonous hemlock tea; Socrates never actually wrote anything)* . . .

    Perhaps an interesting parallel? Socrates was an "Athenian public figure and central participant in the intellectual debates so common in the city in the middle and late 5th century. His influence has been enormous, although he himself wrote nothing. . . . Socrates' philosophy and personality reached a broad ancient audience mainly through the dialogues a number of his associates wrote with him as protagonist. . . . This is the root of 'the Socratic problem,' the question whether we can ever capture the personality and philosophy of the historical Socrates [or Shakespeare?] or whether we must limit ourselves to the interpretation of one or another of his literary representations." [4]

    Or perhaps Democritus, the laughing philosopher, whose portrait hangs in Mary's Wilton home?

    . . . cynical Aristophanes *(c.448–386 BC, d.62 y.o., master of ancient Greek comedy)*

52. Neat Terence, witty Plautus, now not please;

53. But antiquated, and deserted lie

54. As they were not of Nature's family.

55. Yet must I not give Nature all: Thy Art,

56. My gentle Shakespeare, must enjoy a part.

57. For though the Poets matter, Nature be,

58. His Art doth give the fashion. And, that he,

59. Who casts to write a living line, must sweat,

60. (such as thine are) and strike the second heat

61. Upon the Muses anvil: turn the same,

62. (And himself with it) that he thinks to frame;

63. Or for the laurel, he may gain a scorn,

64. For a good Poet's made, as well as born.

52. Precise and pithy Terence (*c.189–159 BC, a freed slave and Roman playwright who is said to have put his name on works written by noblemen*)

    "It is commonly said that Scipio [Scipio Africanus the Younger, a Roman aristocrat] and Laelius [Caius Laelius Sapiens, tribune, legate, governor, c.138 AD/CE] assisted the author in his plays; and indeed, Terence himself increased that suspicion by the little pains he took to refute it. . . . To wipe off the aspersion of plagiarism . . ." Terence took a boat to Greece and was never heard from again. "Some ancient writers relate that he died at sea." He was 25 or 30 years old.[5]

    . . . clever and amusing Titus Maccius Plautus don't even please us anymore, (*c.254–184 BC, d.70 y.o., comic playwright*)

53. Their works only rest here quietly, obsolete and abandoned

54. As if they were not in the same category of natural creative power.

55. But I must not give natural creativity (raw talent or genius) all the credit. Your skill, as the result of study and practice . . .

    Jonson "had always championed the cause of art [study] and had repeatedly chastised the popular playwrights of his day for relying on their own raw talent."[6] Here he emphasizes that the author has spent a good deal of time studying and practicing.

56. My well-born author, must possess a share of the credit

    Jonson was the first person ever to call Shakespeare "gentle," seven years after he died.

57. Even though the subject/substance/theme for writers is Nature,

58. It is a writer's learned skill that shows/proclaims/publishes/delivers/represents the shape/form of literature. In addition, it is true that he

59. Who forms in a mold (as for bronzing)/attempts to compose a line of poetry that is full of life and animation, must toil and labor (*pun on sweating in a blacksmith's shop*)

60. (Of the same sort as the lines you have written) and work again (strike the second heat)

61. Upon the Muse's anvil: shape the lines, transform/work with the words in a different way

62. (And himself he must reshape/think through again) that which he plans to create a mold of for casting,

63. Or if he doesn't strive to improve his work, he may receive scorn instead of the honor of the poet's laurel wreath

    Or: he will be scorned for wearing the laurel wreath and pretending to be a poet,

64. For a good Poet is made—by hard work and study—as well as born naturally gifted.

65. And such wert thou. Look how the father's face

66. Lives in his issue, even so, the race

67. Of Shakspeare's mind, and manners brightly shines

68. In his well turned, and true filed lines:

69. In each of which, he seems to shake a Lance,

70. As brandish't at the eyes of Ignorance.

71. Sweet Swan of Avon! what a sight it were

72. To see thee in our waters yet appear,

73. And make those flights upon the banks of Thames,

74. That so did take Eliza, and our James!

75. But stay, I see thee in the Hemisphere

76. Advanc'd, and made a Constellation there!

77. Shine forth, thou Star of Poets, and with rage,

78. Or influence, chide, or cheer the drooping Stage;

79. Which, since thy flight from hence, hath mourn'd like night,

80. And despairs day, but for thy Volume's light.

Ben: Jonson

Benjamin Jonson
1623

65. And such a good Poet are you, my beloved Author. Notice how the features in a father's face

66. Appear in the face of his son; even in this manner, the natural disposition

   Might this be a reference to Mary's brother Philip Sidney, and his skill naturally appearing in Mary's hand?

67. Of the author's intellect and behavior can be clearly seen

68. In his well-rounded and finely tuned lines.

69. In each of which, he seems to contemptuously shake a spear

70. As if threatening the people who don't understand/are ignorant/lack any culture of the mind or lack experience and skill.

71. Fragrant/pleasing/delightful/lovely/kind/meek/mild/dear/term of endearment/luscious Swan of Avon!

72. To see you still emerge/appear in London

73. And create/beget those soaring excursions of imagination along the banks of the Thames (in our playhouses and the court)

74. That so captivated/delighted Queen Elizabeth and King James!

75. But wait, you have been promoted to the heavens

76. And designated there as a constellation! (*Cygnus, the Swan*)

77. Radiate into the open view, you Star of Poets, and with headlong passion/ intensity

78. Or with divine power/force, either rebuke or comfort the languishing theatre world

79. Which, since that time when you hastily departed (*flight = secret departure*) from here, has been as gloomy as night is dark

80. And hopeless in the day, if it wasn't for the brilliance of this collection of your Work.

Benjamin Jonson

1623

Appendix D
The Narrative Poems

She trembles at his tale,
And on his neck her yoking arms she throws.
She sinketh down, still hanging by his neck,
He on her belly falls, she on her back.

Venus and Adonis, lines 591–94

SIXTEEN YEARS BEFORE THE SONNETS were published and five years before a play was printed under William Shakespeare's name, two lengthy poems attributed to Shakespeare were published: *Venus and Adonis* (1593) and *The Rape of Lucrece* (1594). They are the only printed works in the Shakespearean canon that include a dedication from the author.

Documentation exists verifying that William Shakespeare composed and published these two overwrought and melodramatic poems.

Experts agree the poet apparently took the poems to press and watched them through the printing process, judging by the mistakes that were corrected along the way. "In the 1,194 lines of *Venus and Adonis* there are only two clear errors—errors which have been recognized as such by practically all editors of the poem; in the 1,855 lines of *The Rape of Lucrece* there are only three: a rate of about one and two-thirds errors per 1,000 lines."[1]

Contrast this to the plays printed during Shakespeare's lifetime, called quartos, where "the rate of error in one of the very best quartos is about one hundred sixty per 1,000 lines . . . ."[2]

As Colin Burrow states in the Oxford edition of the sonnets, "He was, after all, principally known as the author of *Venus and Adonis* [rather than as a dramatist] in the early years of the seventeenth century."[3]

Shakespeare's True Voice?

Below are excerpts from these narrative poems.

> *If he had spoke, the wolf would leave his prey*
> *And never fright the silly lamb that day.*

Venus and Adonis, lines 1097–98

> *Even as an empty eagle, sharp by fast,* [hungry from fasting]
> *Tires* [ravenously tears] *with her beak on feathers, flesh and bone,*
> *Shaking her wings, devouring all in haste,*
> *Til either gorge be stuffed or prey be gone,*
> *Even so* [in this manner] *she* [Venus] *kissed his brow,*
> *his cheek, his chin,*
> *And where she ends she doth anew begin.*

Venus and Adonis, lines 55–60

> *He wrings her nose, he strikes her on the cheeks,*
> *He bends her fingers, holds her pulses hard,*
> *He chafes her lips; a thousand ways he seeks*
> *To mend the hurt that his unkindness marred.*
> *He kisses her, and she, by her good will,*
> *Will never rise, so he will kiss her still.*

Venus and Adonis, lines 475–80

> *Or, as the snail, whose tender horns being hit,*
> *Shrinks backward in his shelly cave with pain,*
> *And there, all smothered up, in shade doth sit,*
> *Long after fearing to creep forth again;*
> *So, at his bloody view, her eyes are fled*
> *Into the deep dark cabins of her head.*

Venus and Adonis, lines 1033–38 (compares the eyes of a goddess with the slimy horns of a snail)

> *Her two blue windows faintly she up-heaveth.*

Venus and Adonis, line 482 (this means she opened her blue eyes)

> *If children predecease progenitors,*
> *We are their offspring, and they none of ours.*

The Rape of Lucrece, lines 1756–57

If "overwrought" and "melodramatic" seems harsh, consider the passage below from *Venus and Adonis*, where Adonis manages to escape the amorous clutches of Venus to go hunting boar and is killed by the boar. I've added a paraphrase below because it's hard to keep track of whom each "he" and "his" refers to.

> But this foul, grim, and urchin-snouted boar,
> Whose downward eye still looketh for a grave,
> Ne'er saw the beauteous livery that he wore—
> Witness the entertainment that he gave.
>   If he did see his face, why then I know
>   He thought to kiss him, and hath killed him so.
>
> 'Tis true, 'tis true! Thus was Adonis slain:
> He ran upon the boar with his sharp spear,
> Who did not whet his teeth at him again,
> But by a kiss thought to persuade him there;
>   And, nuzzling in his flank, the loving swine
>   Sheathed unaware the tusk in his soft groin.
>
> Had I been toothed like him, I must confess,
> With kissing him I should have killed him first.

[paraphrase]

But this wicked, threatening boar with a demonic snout
Whose eyes are always looking at the ground, as if searching for graves
*   in which to bury its victims,*
This boar never saw the beautiful face and appearance of Adonis—
As we can tell by the reception/treatment the boar gave Adonis.

*   If the boar did happen to see the face of Adonis before it killed him,*
*   why then I am positive*
*   The boar meant to kiss Adonis, but accidentally killed him instead.*

It's true, it's true! [Venus is trying to convince herself.] This is how Adonis was killed:
Adonis ran at the boar with his sharp spear,
But the boar did not sharpen his teeth in return;
Instead the boar was so impressed with the beauty of Adonis
*   that he thought he [the boar] would win Adonis to himself with a kiss;*
*   And, as the affectionate pig nuzzled Adonis's side,*
*   It accidentally shoved its tusk into Adonis's soft genital area and killed him.*

If I had that boar's tusks, I must say,
The way I was kissing Adonis, I would have accidentally killed him myself.

Many scholars have dared to wonder whether the author who wrote lines such as, "So, at his bloody view, her eyes are fled/Into the deep dark cabins of her head," is the same author who wrote the plays.

Even Harold Bloom remarks, "The only works Shakespeare ever proofread and stood by were *Venus and Adonis* and *The Rape of Lucrece*, neither of them worthy of the poet of the Sonnets, let alone of *Lear, Hamlet, Othello, Macbeth*." [4]

Hallett Smith in *The Riverside Shakespeare* admits that "*Venus and Adonis* . . . is an Ovidian poem that does not fully succeed. . . . Unfortunately, Shakespeare's hunter seems rather less a creature of myth than a bashful country boy from Stratford. . . . Here for eighty lines [Venus] discusses Mars, her own charms, Narcissus, torches . . . so that instead of realizing evoked physical beauty we are listening to a lecture." [5]

Gary Waller reluctantly describes *Venus and Adonis* in *English Poetry of the Sixteenth Century*: "Alongside Marlowe's masterpiece [*Hero and Leander*], Shakespeare's is regretfully static, with just too much argument and insufficient flowing sensuality to make it pleasurable reading. Its treatment of love relies too heavily upon Neoplatonic and Ovidian commonplaces, and (unlike *Hero and Leander*) upon heavy moralizing allegory, with Venus representing the flesh and Adonis something like spiritual longing." [6]

Regarding the "graver labor" of *The Rape of Lucrece*, Professor Waller states, "There are some fine local atmospheric effects, which in their declamatory power occasionally bring the directness and power of the stage into the verse. But overall it is less impressive than might be expected from Shakespeare." [7]

Waller admits that these poems "are interesting primarily because it was Shakespeare who wrote them." [8]

William Hazlitt, a distinguished Shakespearean critic writing in the early nineteenth century, doesn't bother to equivocate: "Our idolatry of Shakespeare (not to say our admiration) ceases with his plays. . . . In a word, we do not like Shakespeare's poems, because we like his plays; the one, in all their excellencies, are just the reverse to the other. It has been the fashion of late to cry up our author's poems, as equal to his plays: this is the desperate cant of modern criticism." [9]

Hazlitt complains that in these two narrative poems, "The author seems all the time to be thinking of his verses, and not of his subject, not of what his characters would feel, but of what he shall say; and as it must happen in all such cases, he always puts into their mouths those things which they would be the last to think of, and which it shows the greatest ingenuity in him to find out. The whole is laboured, up-hill work." He deplores the detached metaphors and similes, the "patchwork" of images, the cold lack of emotion: "Sentiment is built up upon plays of words; the hero or heroine feels, not from the impulse of passion, but from the force of dialectics." [10]

But That Means . . .

However, here is the problem scholars face if they dare to suggest that Shakespeare wasn't the author of these poems: These two poems are the only works in the canon most clearly attributable to the man named William Shakespeare. They are the only works supervised through the press while he was alive and the only works that have a dedication from the author. Also, they are clearly attributed to William Shakespeare on the title pages of every one of the many editions, and Shakespeare was more famous for these narrative poems during his lifetime than he was for the plays.

As Gerald Bentley points out:

> Not only Spenser and Milton, but most of the other poets of the time either published statements about their poetry or left statements in manuscript letters or comments showing their interest in getting their works into the hands of readers and having them understood. *But no such evidence exists for a single one of Shakespeare's thirty-eight plays.* No play of his, printed during his lifetime, had a dedication, or an author's preface, or an address to the reader. There is no known comment in print or in manuscript made by Shakespeare on any of his plays. None of them ever appeared in print with anything which could be attributed to Shakespeare . . . . [11]
> [emphasis added]

Bentley goes on to say:

> For though he never used prefaces, dedications, or
> addresses to the reader for his plays, he did use them
> when he published non-dramatic verse —*Venus and
> Adonis* and *The Rape of Lucrece*.[12]

This is the dedication from Shakespeare to Henry Wriothesley, Earl of
Southampton, in *Venus and Adonis*:

> *Right Honourable, I know not how I shall offend in dedicating my
> unpolished lines to your lordship, nor how the world will censure
> me for choosing so strong a prop to support so weak a burden: only
> if your honour seem but pleased, I account myself highly praised,
> and vow to take advantage of all idle hours, til I have honoured
> you with some graver labour. But if the first heir of my invention
> prove deformed, I shall be sorry it had so noble a godfather, and
> never after ear so barren a land, of fear it yield me still so bad a
> harvest. I leave it to your heart's content; which I wish may always
> answer your own wish and the world's hopeful expectation.*
>
> *Your honour's in all duty,*
> *William Shakespeare.*

About the dedication, David Bevington remarks that William
Shakespeare "speaks of *Venus and Adonis* as 'the first heir of my
invention,' as though he had written no plays earlier . . . ."[13] Why would
Shakespeare call this poem "the first heir of my invention," when seven
or eight plays by "William Shakespeare" had already appeared on stage
and several of those had been printed (albeit anonymously)?

These narrative poems were Shakespeare's most commercially successful
printed works. *Venus and Adonis* outsold the best-selling Shakespearean
play by four editions.[14] Hallett Smith remarks, "Of all Shakespeare's
works, *Venus and Adonis* was the most popular during his lifetime. It
was printed in at least nine editions (with half a dozen more by 1636);
there are more allusions to it than to any other work of the author; and
in the decade after its publication a swarm of imitations, of it and *Hero
and Leander* [by Christopher Marlowe], appeared."[15]

Echoing Colin Burrow's statement quoted at the beginning of this
chapter, Bevington writes that "Shakespeare's belief in their importance

to his literary career is confirmed by the reports of his contemporaries,"[16] in that they more often refer to these poems rather than to the plays.

> Richard Barnfield [a contemporary of Shakespeare's who wrote homoerotic pornography] singled them out as the works most likely to assure a place for Shakespeare in "fame's immortal book." Francis Meres, in his *Palladis Tamia: Wit's Treasury*, exclaimed in 1598 that "the sweet witty soul of Ovid lives in mellifluous and honey-tongued Shakespeare: witness his *Venus and Adonis*, his *Lucrece*, his sugared sonnets among his private friends, etc." Gabriel Harvey, although preferring *Lucrece* and *Hamlet* as more pleasing to "the wiser sort," conceded that "the younger sort takes much delight in Shakespeare's *Venus and Adonis*." John Weever and still others add further testimonials to the extraordinary reputation of Shakespeare's nondramatic poems.[17]

Although these narrative poems were considered by his contemporaries to be Shakespeare's most important and best work, they were not included in the First Folio, the printed collection of his work after Shakespeare died. They weren't even mentioned. (The book of Sonnets wasn't mentioned either, but its publication was suppressed even while Shakespeare was alive.)

The scholars who justify including these poems in the Shakespearean canon end up with some curious writing. For instance, Bevington insists that

> The story itself [*Venus and Adonis*] is relatively uneventful, and the characters are static. For two-thirds of the poem, very little happens other than a series of amorous claspings, from which Adonis feebly attempts to extricate himself. Even his subsequent fight with the boar and his violent death are occasions for rhetorical pathos rather than for vivid narrative description.[18]

Yet he tells us that "we must not expect psychological insight or meaningful self-discovery."[19]

He also justifies the bookish writing: "These pyrotechnics may at first seem mechanical, but they, too, have a place in a work of art that celebrates both the erotic and the spiritual in love. Decoration has its function and is not mere embellishment for its own sake."[20]

Or in regard to *The Rape of Lucrece*, "we must recognize its conventions and not expect it to be other than what it professes to be."[21]

And, "In a poem on a serious subject, these devices may seem overly contrived to us. We should nevertheless recognize them as conventional in the genre to which *The Rape of Lucrece* belongs."[22]

To Stoop So Low

By the time *The Rape of Lucrece* went to press in 1594, these Shakespearean plays had already been written: *Titus Andronicus, Richard III*, all three parts of *Henry VI, The Comedy of Errors, The Taming of the Shrew*, and possibly *Love's Labor's Lost* and *King John*.

It seems rather odd that this extraordinary genius, the most significant writer ever to live, would stoop to common devices and platitudes for these two lengthy poems.

But perhaps these poems were not written by the same author who wrote the plays. Perhaps *Venus and Adonis* and *The Rape of Lucrece* were written by the man named William Shakespeare—documented evidence leads us to believe these were his works.

Appendix E
Literary Allusions

Following are every one of the literary references to William Shakespeare that appeared during his lifetime.[1] These are the items that Shakespeareans refer to when they say his "friends" talked about him. But notice that not one is a personal reference to the *man*; they are all references to the *work*, like book reviews. We have no documented evidence that any of these reviewers met the man named William Shakespeare. Most of these writers spell the name as it was spelled on the printed quartos, not as Shakespeare himself spelled his name.

1. Anonymous (registered 1594)
   From the prefatory poem in *Willobie his Avisa.*

   Though Collatine have dearly bought,
   To high renown, a lasting life,
   And found, that most in vain have sought,
   To have a Fair, and Constant wife,
   Yet Tarquin plucked his glistering grape,
   And **Shake-speare,** paints poore Lucrece rape.

2. William Covell (1595)
   A marginal note to a laudation of Spenser and Daniel.

   All praiseworthy. Lucrecia Sweet **Shakspeare.** Eloquent Gaveston. Wanton Adonis. Watsons heyre.

3. Francis Meres (1598)
   From *Palladis Tamia: Wits Treasury,* in the section titled "A comparative discourse of our English Poets with the Greek, Latin, and Italian Poets."

   ... The English tongue is mightily enriched, and gorgeously invested in rare ornaments and resplendent habiliments by Sir Philip Sidney, Spencer, Daniel, Drayton, Warner, **Shakespeare**, Marlow and Chapman. ...

   As the soul of Euphorbus was thought to live in Pythagoras: so the sweet witty soul of Ovid lives in mellifluous & honey-tongued **Shakespeare,** witness his *Venus and Adonis,* his *Lucrece,* his sugared Sonnets among his private friends, &c.

As Plautus and Seneca are accounted the best for Comedy and Tragedy among the Latins: so *Shakespeare* among the English is the most excellent in both kinds for the stage; for Comedy, witness his *Gentlemen of Verona*, his *Errors*, his *Loves Labors Lost*, his *Love Labors Won*, his *Midsummer Night's Dream*, & his *Merchant of Venice*: for Tragedy his *Richard the 2, Richard the 3, Henry the 4, King John, Titus Andronicus* and his *Romeo and Juliet.*

As Epius Stolo said, that the Muses would speak with Plautus tongue, if they would speak Latin: so I say that the Muses would speak with *Shakespeare's* fine filed phrase, if they would speak English. . . .

As Ovid saith of his work . . . as Horace saith of his . . . so say I severally of Sir Philip Sidney's, Spencer's, Daniel's, Drayton's, *Shakespeare's,* and Warner's works;

> Non Iouis ira, imbres, Mars, ferrum, flamma, senectus,
> Hoc opus vnda, lues, turbo, venena ruent . . . .

As Pindarus, Anacreon and Callmachus among the Greeks; and Horace and Catullus among the Latins are the best Lyric Poets: so in this faculty the best among our Poets are Spencer (who excels in all kinds), Daniel, Drayton, *Shakespeare,* Bretton . . . .

These are our best for Tragedy, the Lord Buckhurst, Doctor Legge of Cambridge, Doctor Edes of Oxford, Master Edward Ferris, the Author of the *Mirror for Magistrates*, Marlowe, Peele, Watson, Kid, *Shakespeare,* Drayton, Chapman, Decker, and Benjamin Johnson . . . .

The best for Comedy amongst us is, Edward Earl of Oxford, Doctor Gager of Oxford, Master Rowley once a rare Scholar of learned Pembroke Hall in Cambridge, Master Edwards one of her Majesty's Chapel, eloquent and witty John Lyly, Lodge, Gascoine, Greene, *Shakespeare,* Thomas Nash, Thomas Heywood, Anthony Munday our best plotter, Chapman, Porter, Wilson, Hathaway, and Henry Chettle . . . .

These are the most passionate among us to bewail and bemoan the perplexities of Love, Henry Howard Earl of Surrey, Sir Thomas Wyatt the elder, Sir Francis Brian, Sir Philip Sidney, Sir Walter Raleigh, Sir Edward Dyer, Spencer, Daniel, Drayton, *Shakespeare,* Whetstone, Gascoine, Samuel Page sometime fellow of Corpus Christi College in Oxford, Churchyard, Breton.

4. Richard Barnfield (1598)
From *Poems in Divers Humors*.

A Remembrance of some English Poets.

And *Shakespeare,* thou, whose honey-flowing Vein,
(Pleasing the World) thy Praises doth obtain.
Whose Venus, and whose Lucrece (sweet, and chaste)
Thy Name in fame's immortal Book have plac't.
Live ever you, at least in Fame live ever:
Well may the Body die, but Fame dies never.

Note: *When Meres updated this book in 1634 and again in 1636, he did not include any other plays from Shakespeare than those he mentioned in 1598.*

5. Gabriel Harvey (1598)
From marginalia in a copy of Speght's *Chaucer*.

Amongst which, the *Countess of Pembroke's Arcadia*, & the *Faerie Queene* are now freshest in request: & *Astrophil*, & *Amyntas* are none of the idlest pastimes of some fine humanists. The Earl of Essex much commends Albions *England*: and not unworthily for diverse notable pageants, before, & in the Chronicle, Some English & other Histories nowhere more sensibly described, or more inwardly discovered. The Lord Mountjoy makes the like account of Daniel's piece of the Chronicle, touching the Usurpation of Henry of Bullingbrooke. Which indeed is a fine, sententious, & politique piece of Poetry: as profitable, as pleasurable. The younger sort takes much delight in **Shakespeare's** *Venus, & Adonis*: but his *Lucrece*, & his tragedy of *Hamlet, Prince of Denmark*, have it in them, to please the wiser sort. Or such poets: or better: or none.

> Vilia miretur vulgus: mihi flavus Apollo
> Pocula Castaliae plena ministret aquae:

quoth Sir Edward Dyer, between jest, & earnest. Whose written devises far excell most of the sonnets, and cantos in print. His *Amaryllis*, & Sir Walter Raleigh's *Cynthia*, how fine & sweet inventions? Excellent matter of emulation for Spencer, Constable, France, Watson, Daniel, Warner, Chapman, Silvester, **Shakespeare**, & the rest of our flourishing metricians.

6. John Weever (1599)
From *Epigrammes in the oldest Cut, and newest Fashion*.

Ad Gulielmum **Shakespeare**.

Honey-tongued **Shakespeare** when I saw thine issue
I swore Apollo got them and none other,
Their rosy-tainted features cloth'd in tissue,
Some heaven born goddess said to be their mother:

Rose-checked Adonis with his amber tresses,
Fair fire-hot Venus charming him to love her,
Chaste Lucretia virgin-like her dresses,
Proud lust-stung Tarquin seeking still to prove her:
Romea Richard; more whose names I know not,
Their sugared tongues, and power attractive beauty
Say they are Saints although that Saints they show not
For thousands vow to them subjective duty:
They burn in love thy children **Shakespeare** het them,
Go, wo thy Muse more Nymphish brood beget them.

7. John Manningham (March 13, 1602)
From his diary.

Upon a time when Burbidge played Rich. 3. there was a citizen grew so far in liking with him, that before she went from the play she appointed him to come that night into her by the name of Ri: the 3. **Shakespeare** overhearing their conclusion went before, was entertained, and at his game ere Burbidge came. Then message being brought that Rich. the 3.[d] was at the door, **Shakespeare** caused return to be made that William the Conqueror was before Rich. the 3. **Shakespeare's** name William. (Mr. Curle.)

8. Francis Davison (1602)
   In manuscript "Catalog of the Poems contained in Englands Helicon,"
   made in preparation for editing *A Poetical Rhapsody*.

   W. **Shakespeare** (handwritten)

9. Anonymous (1603)
   From *A Mournful Ditty, entitled Elizabeth's Loss*.

   You Poets all brave **Shakspeare,** Johnson, Greene,
   Bestow your time to write for England's Queen.
   Lament, lament, lament you English Peers,
   Lament your loss possessed so many years.
   Return your songs and Sonnets and your says:
   To set forth sweet Elizabeth's praise.

   This poem begs Shakespeare, Jonson, and Greene to write poems in honor of Queen Elizabeth's death. The writer didn't even know that Robert Greene had been dead for eleven years.

10. John Cooke (1604)
    From *Epigrams,* in response to the ditty above.

    some other humbly craves
    For help of Spirits in their sleeping graves,
    As he that called to **Shakespeare,** Johnson, Greene,
    To write of their dead noble Queen.

11. Sir John Davies of Hereford (1610)
    An epigram published in *The Scourge of Folly*.

    To our English Terence, Mr. Will. **Shake-speare.**

    Some say (good *Will*) which I, in sport, do sing,
    Had'st thou not played some Kingly parts in sport,
    Thou hadst bin a companion for a *King;*
    And, been a King among the meaner sort.
    Some others raile; but, raile as they think fit,
    Thou hast no rayling, but, a raigning Wit:
    And honesty *thou sow'st which they do reap;*
    So, to increase their Stock which they do keep.

12. Anthony Scoloker (1604)
    From *Epistle to Daiphantus, or the Passions of Love*.

    It should be like the Never-too-well read *Arcadia*, where the Prose and
    Verse (Matter and Words) are like his Mistress's eyes, one still excelling
    another and without Co-rival: or to come home to the vulgars Element,
    like Friendly **Shakespeare's** Tragedies, where the Comedian rides, when the
    Tragedian stands on Tip-toe: Faith it should please all, like Prince Hamlet.
    But in sadness, then it were to be feared he would run mad: Insooth I will
    not be moon-sick, to please: nor out of my wits though I displeased all.

13. William Camden (1605)
    From *Remains of a Greater Work concerning Britain, Poem 8*.

    These may suffice for some Poetical descriptions of our ancient Poets, if I
    would come to our time, what a world could I present to you out of Sir
    Philip Sidney, Edmund Spencer, Samuel Daniel, Hugh Holland, Ben

Jonson, Thomas Campion, Michael Drayton, George Chapman, John Marston, William **Shakespeare,** & other most pregnant wits of these our times, whom succeeding ages may justly admire.

14. William Barksted (1607)
From end of *Myrrha, the Mother of Adonis; or Lusts Prodigies.*

But stay my Muse in thine own confines keep,
 & wage not war with so dear loved a neighbor,
But having sung thy day song, rest and sleep
 preserve thy small fame and his greater favor:
His Song was worthy merit (**Shakspeare** he)
sung the fair blossom, thou the withered tree
  Laurel is due to him, his art and wit
  hat purchased it, Cypress thy brow will fit.

15. John Webster (1612)
From *Epistle* to *The White Devil.*

Detraction is the sworn friend to ignorance: For mine own part I have ever truly cherished my good opinion of other men's worthy Labors, especially of that full and heightened style of Master Chapman: The labor'd and understanding works of Master Johnson; The no less worthy composures of the both worthily excellent Master Beamont & Master Fletcher: And lastly (without wrong last to be named), the right happy and copious industry of M. **Shake-speare,** M. Decker, & M. Heywood, wishing what I write may be read by their light: Protesting, that, in the strength of mine own judgment, I know them so worthy, that though I rest silent in my own work, yet to most of theirs I dare (without flattery) fix that of Martiall.
—non norunt, Haec monumenta mori.

16. Richard Carew (1614)
From *Epistle* in *The Excellency of the English Tongue,* added to the 2^d edition (1614) of Camden's *Remains of a Greater Work concerning Britain.*

Add hereunto, that whatsoever grace any other language carrieth in verse or Prose, in Tropes or Metaphors, in Echos and Agnominations, they may all be lively and exactly represented in ours: will you have Plato's vein? read Sir Thomas Smith, the Ionic? Sir Thomas Moore. Cicero's? Ascham, Varro? Chaucer, Demosthenes? Sir John Cheeke (who in his treatise to the Rebels, hath comprised all the figures of Rhetoric). Will you read Virgil? take the Earl of Surrey. Catullus? **Shakespheare** and Barlowes (Marlows) fragment, Ovid? Daniel. Lucan? Spencer, Martial? Sir John Davies and others: will you have all in all for Prose and verse? take the miracle of our age, Sir Philip Sidney.

17. Thomas Freeman (1614)
From *Runne and a Great Cast* (the second part of *Rubbe, and a Great Cast*).

To Master W. **Shakespeare.**

Shakespeare, that nimble Mercury thy brain,
Lulls many hundred Argus-eyes asleep,
So fit, for all thou fashionest thy vain,

At the horse-foot fountain thou has drunk full deep,
Virtues or vices theme to thee all one is:
Who loves chaste life, there's *Lucrece* for a Teacher:
Who list read lust there's *Venus* and *Adonis*,
True model of a most lascivious lecher.
Besides in plays thy wit winds like Meander:
Whence needy new-composers borrow more
Than Terence doth from Plautus of Menander.
But to praise thee aright I want thy store:
Then let thine own works thine own worth upraise,
And help t' adorn thee with deserved Baies.

horse-foot fountain: The fountain of Hippocrene (literally "fountain of the horse"), which is a source of inspiration to poets. It's on Mt. Helicon, where the Muses lived, and was formed by a kick from the foot of Pegasus, the winged horse. Since Pegasus was the flying horse of the Muses, it is a symbol of high-flying imagination.

18. Edmund Howes (1615)
From an emendation to John Stow's *Annals*.

Our modern, and present excellent Poets which worthily flourish in their own works, and all of them in my own knowledge lived together in this Queen's reign, according to their priorities as near as I could, I have orderly set down (viz) George Gascoigne Esquire, Thomas Churchyard Esquire, Sir Edward Dyer Knight, Edmund Spencer Esquire, Sir Philip Sidney Knight, Sir John Harrington Knight, Sir Thomas Challoner Knight, Sir Francis Bacon Knight, & Sir John Davie Knight, Master John Lillie gentleman, Master George Chapman gentleman, M.W. Warner gentleman, M. Willi. **Shakespeare** gentleman, Samuel Daniel Esquire, Michael Drayton Esquire, of the bath, M. Christopher Marlo gen., M. Benjamin Johnson gentleman, John Marston Esquire, M. Abraham Francis gen., master Frauncis Meers gentle., master Josua Silvester gentle., master Thomas Decker gentleman, M. John Flecher gentl., M. John Webster gentleman, M. Thomas Heywood gentleman, M. Thomas Middleton gentleman, M. George Withers.

19. Possibly Francis Beaumont (possibly 1615)
From a manuscript with varying author initials.

To M^r B: J:

    . . . here I would let slip
(If I had any in me) scholarship,
And from all Learning keep these lines as clear
as **Shakespeares** best are, which our heirs shall hear.
Preachers apt to their auditors to show
how far sometimes a mortal man may go
by the dim light of Nature, tis to me
an help to write of nothing . . . .

20. Anonymous, ascribed to Edmund Bolton (c. 1616)
Assumed to be a draft for the *Hypercritica* of Bolton.

The books also out of which we gather the most warrantable English are not many to my Remembrance, of which in regard they require a particular and curious tract, I forbear to speak at this present. But among the chief, or rather the chief are in my opinion these . . . **Shakespere,** M^r. Francis Beamont, and innumerable other writers for the stage and press tenderly to be used in this Argument.

21. Thomas Porter (about 1615)
From a book of Latin epigrams.

Gul: *Shakespeare* Poëtam lepidum.

Quot lepores in Atho tot habet tua Musa lepôres
Ingenii vena diuite metra tua.

22. The Parnassus Plays (1598–1601/2)
A series of three anonymous plays were performed at St. John's College, Cambridge, probably during the Christmas seasons of 1598–1601/2: *The Pilgrimage to Parnassus, The Return from Parnassus, Part I,* and *The Return from Parnassus, Part II.* In the dialogue, characters mention Chaucer, Gower, Spenser, Shakespeare, and Samuel Daniel, among others. The narrative poems *(Venus and Adonis, The Rape of Lucrece)* are mentioned by name, as are a couple of plays and several lines from Shakespearean plays.

Appendix F
The History Plays

The following is the rest of the data from Mary Sidney's genealogy and the history plays. For the other plays, please see Chapter 11.

Richard II, Henry IV parts 1 and 2, and Henry V

Character	Relation to Mary Sidney
King Richard II	1C 7R
Queen Isabel	-- (by marriage)
John of Gaunt	6G Grandfather
Eleanor de Bohun, Duchess of Gloucester	7G Aunt
Edmund of Langley, 1st Duke of York	7G Uncle
Duchess of York, mother of Aumerle	7G Aunt
Edward of Norwich, Duke of Aumerle	1C 7R
Henry Bolingbroke, Duke of Hereford, afterward King Henry IV	6G Uncle (half)
Thomas Mowbray, 1st Duke of Norfolk	5G Grandfather
Thomas Holland, Duke of Surrey	2C 5R
John Montacute, 3d Earl of Salisbury	his son married Mary's 2C 5R
Thomas Lord Berkeley	6G Grandfather
Sir Henry Green	4G Uncle
Sir John Bushy	--
Sir William (or John) Bagot	--
Henry Percy, 1st Earl of Northumberland	7G Uncle
Henry Percy, called Hotspur	1C 7R
William Lord Ross	married to 1C 7R
William, 5th Baron Willoughby de Ersby	6G Uncle
Walter Lord Fitzwater	very distantly related
Thomas Marke, Bishop of Carlisle	--
William de Colchester, Abbot of Westminster	--
Thomas Holland, Lord Marshall	2C 5R
Sir Stephen Scroop (Scrope)	unclear
Henry, Prince of Wales (Prince Hal), afterwards King Henry V	1C 6R (half)
Prince John of Lancaster, Duke of Bedford	1C 6R (half)

Ralph Neville, 1ˢᵗ Earl of Westmorland	5G Grandfather
Sir Walter Blunt	7G Grandfather
Lady Percy, wife of Hotspur	2C 6R
Thomas Percy, Earl of Worcester	1C 7R
Edmund Mortimer	2C 6R
Lady Mortimer (Glendower's daughter)	*married to 2C 6R*
Richard Scroop (Scrope), Archbishop of York	*distant relation*
Archibald, 4ᵗʰ Earl of Douglas	--
Owen Glendower	*his daughter married Mary's 2C 6R*
King Henry V	1C 6R (half)
Thomas Beaufort, Duke of Exeter	5G Uncle
Edward of Norwich, 2ᵈ Duke of York	1C 7R
Thomas Montacute, 4ᵗʰ Earl of Salisbury	*married to Mary's 2C 5R*
Richard Plantagenet, Earl of Cambridge	1C 7R
Henry Chichele, Archbishop of Canterbury	--
John Fordham, Bishop of Ely	--
Henry of Masham, 3ᵈ Baron Scrope	*married to 2C 5R*
Sir Thomas Grey	1C 6R
Captain Fluellen (Welsh)	*based on Davy Gam*
Captain Jamy (Scottish)	*probably a reference to King James I of Scotland who went to France with Henry V*
Sir Thomas Erpingham	--
Philip the Good, Duke of Burgundy	*distant relation*
Sir Richard Vernon	--
Thomas Plantagenet, Duke of Clarence	1C 6R (half)
Humphrey Plantagenet, Duke of Gloucester and Earl of Pembroke	1C 6R (half)
Richard Beauchamp, 13ᵗʰ Earl of Warwick	5G Grandfather
Thomas Fitzalan, 5ᵗʰ Earl of Surrey and 11ᵗʰ Earl of Arundel	6G Uncle
Sir Thomas Harcourt (probably)	--
Sir John Blunt	6G Uncle
Lord Chief Justice, Sir William Gascoigne	*very distant*
Margaret Neville, Lady Northumberland	7G Aunt
Thomas Lord Mowbray	4G Uncle
Thomas Lord Bardolph	--
Sir John Coleville	--
Sir John Falstaff	--

mentioned in the plays:
Straight out of Holinshed:

Sir Thomas Blount of Belton	--
Sir Bennet Seely	--
Sir John Norberry	--
Reginald, 2ᵈ Lord Cobham	--
Francis Quoint (or Point)	--
Sir Walter Blunt	7G Grandfather
William le Scrope, Earl of Wiltshire	*unclear*

Thomas of Woodstock, Duke of Glouceſter	7G Uncle
Owen Glendower	*his daughter married Mary's 2C 6R*
Davy Gam	*7G Grandfather of Mary's husband. His daughter became the mother of William Herbert, 1ˢᵗ Earl of Pembroke in the Herbert house.*
Michael de la Pole, 3ᵈ Earl of Suffolk	2C 6R
Gilbert Talbot	5G Uncle
Sir Richard Ketley	--
John Holland, Earl of Huntingdon	1C 6R (half)

Three parts of Henry VI, plus Richard III

Character	Relation to Mary Sidney
King Henry VI	2C 5R (half)
Queen Margaret of Anjou	*-- (by marriage)*
Humphrey Plantagenet, Duke of Glouceſter and Earl of Pembroke	1C 6R (half)
Prince John of Lancaster, Duke of Bedford	1C 6R (half)
Thomas Beaufort, Duke of Exeter	6G Uncle
Henry Beaufort, Bishop then Cardinal of Wincheſter	6G Uncle
John Beaufort, 3ᵈ Earl of Somerset	1C 6R
Richard Plantagenet, 3ᵈ Duke of York	5G Uncle
Cecily Neville, Duchess of York	5G Aunt
Edmund Plantagenet, Earl of Rutland	1C 5R
Richard Beauchamp, 13ᵗʰ Earl of Warwick	5G Grandfather
Thomas Montacute, 4ᵗʰ Earl of Salisbury	*married to Mary's 2C 5R*
William de la Pole, 4ᵗʰ Earl of Suffolk, later 1ˢᵗ Duke of Suffolk	2C 6R
John Lord Talbot, 1ˢᵗ Earl of Shrewsbury	4G Grandfather
John Talbot (son of above), Viscount and 1ˢᵗ Baron Lisle	3G Grandfather
Edmund Mortimer, 5ᵗʰ Earl of March	3C 4R
Edmund Beaufort, 2ᵈ Duke of Somerset	5G Uncle
Edward Plantagenet, 3ᵈ Earl of March (to become King Edward IV)	1C 5R
Humphrey Stafford, Duke of Buckingham	5G Grandfather
Richard Neville, 5ᵗʰ Earl of Salisbury	5G Uncle
Richard Neville, 16ᵗʰ Earl of Warwick, the Kingmaker	1C 5R
Thomas Lord Clifford	*unclear*
John, Young Clifford, later Lord Clifford	*unclear; there is a John Lord Clifford in her geneaology, but it's a mistake*
Edward, Prince of Wales (son of Henry VI)	3C 4R (half)
(Henry &) Edmund Beaufort, (3ᵈ &) 4ᵗʰ Dukes of Somerset	1C 5R
Henry Holland, 2ᵈ Duke of Exeter	2C 5R (half)

Henry Percy, 3ᵈ Earl of Northumberland	1C 5R
Ralph Neville, 2ᵈ Earl of Westmorland	1C 5R
George Plantagenet, Duke of Clarence	1C 5R
Richard Plantagenet, Duke of Gloucester (afterwards Richard III)	1C 5R
Elizabeth Woodville, Lady Grey (afterwards Queen to Edward IV)	GG Aunt
John Neville, Marquess of Montague	1C 5R
William Herbert, Earl of Pembroke (non-speaking part)	Mary's husband's 5G Grandfather
William Lord Hastings	*married to 1C 5R*
John de Vere, 13ᵗʰ Earl of Oxford	*distantly related*
Edward Plantagenet, Prince of Wales, afterward King Edward V	2C 4R
Richard Plantagenet, Duke of York (prince in the Tower)	2C 4R
Margaret, Countess of Salisbury ("Girl")	2C 4R
Edward Plantagenet, Earl of Warwick ("Boy")	2C 4R
Lady Anne Neville	2C 4R
Cardinal Thomas Bourchier	2C 6R
Thomas Scott Rotherham, Archbishop of York	--
Henry Stafford, 2ᵈ Duke of Buckingham	2C 4R
John Howard, Duke of Norfolk (grandson of Mowbray in RII)	1C 5R
Thomas Howard, Earl of Surrey (and 2ᵈ Duke of Norfolk, son of above)	2C 4R
John Mowbray, 3ᵈ Duke of Norfolk	1C 5R
Sir Thomas Grey, 1ˢᵗ Marquess of Dorset	1C 3R
Sir Thomas Stanley, 1st Earl of Derby	*married to 1C 5R*
Sir Thomas Vaughan	--
Fancis, 12ᵗʰ Lord Lovel	2C 4R (his great-grandfather was Mary's 5G grandfather)
Sir Richard Radcliffe	*distantly related*
Sir William Catesby	*distantly related*
Sir James Blunt, grandson of Walter Blunt	5G Uncle
Sir Walter Herbert	her husband's 5G Uncle
Sir William Brandon	--
Sir Robert Brakenbury, Keeper of the Tower	*-- he served under Mary's 2C 4R*
Sir Christopher Urswick, priest	*-- he was personal agent and messenger for Margaret Beaufort, Mary's 1C 5R*
Henry Long of Wrexall, Sheriff of Wiltshire	--
Humphrey Lord Stafford (non-speaking part)	*distant relation*
Sir John Mortimer	*unclear; there are lots of Mortimers in her genealogy*
Sir Hugh Mortimer (non-speaking)	*unclear*
Henry Tudor, Earl of Richmond, afterwards Henry VII	3C 4R
Anthony Woodville, 2ᵈ Earl of Rivers	*brother to Mary's GG Aunt*
William Neville, Lord Falconbridge and Earl of Kent	5G Uncle

Sir Thomas Stanley, 1st Earl of Derby	
(non-speaking parting)	*married 1C 5R*
Sir John (Thomas) Montgomery	2C 3R
Thomas Lord Scales	3C 5R
James Fiennes, Lord Say	*-- (there are other Fiennes and a Sir John Say in Mary's genealogy, but not this one)*
Sir John Stanley	--
Sir William Vaux	--
Matthew Goffe (Gough)	--
Alexander Iden of Kent	--

mentioned in the plays:

Sir Walter Blunt	7G Grandfather
Sir John Blunt	7G Uncle
Lord Walter Hungerford	5G Grandfather
Thomas de Scales, Lord Scales	3C 5R
Lionel of Antwerp, Duke of Clarence	7G Uncle
James Butler, Earl of Wiltshire and 5th Earl of Ormonde	2C 5R
Lord Clifford	*unclear*
Roger Mortimer, 4th Earl of March	2C 6R
Edmund/Edward Brooke, Lord Cobham of Kent	2C 4R
Lord Richard Grey, 8th Baron Ferrers of Groby	4C 3R *(error for Sir John Grey, first husband of QE Woodville)*
George Stanley	2C 4R
Sir John Guildford	3G Grandfather
Sir Richard Guildford	2G Grandfather
Sir Gilbert Talbot	1C 4R (half)
Sir William Stanley	
(brother to Thomas)	4C 2R
Jasper Tudor, Earl of Pembroke, "redoubted Pembroke"	--
Rhys ap Thomas	--
Henry Percy, (melancholy) Lord Northumberland	1C 5R
Walter Devereux, Lord Ferrers	--
Sir John Fastolf	--
Philip the Good, Duke of Burgundy	*distant relation*
Richard Woodville, Lieutenant of the Tower	*distant relation*
Sir Edward Courtenay	--
Bishop of Exeter	--
Sir William Lucy	*distant relation*
Sir William Glansdale	--
Sir Thomas Gargrave	--
Sir Richard Vernon	--

Henry VIII

Character	Relation to Mary Sidney
King Henry VIII	3C 3R
Queen Catharine of Aragon	--
Anne Boleyn, Marchioness of Pembroke	4C 2R
Thomas Howard, 2d Duke of Norfolk	2C 4R
Charles Brandon, Duke of Suffolk	--
Edward Stafford, 3d Duke of Buckingham	3C 3R
Charles Somerset, Lord Chamberlain	Great Grandfather
Sir Thomas More, Lord Chancellor	--
Stephen Gardiner, Bishop of Winchester	--
John Longland, Bishop of Lincoln	--
George Neville, Lord Abergavenny	1C 4R
Lord Sandys, Sir William Sandys	*distantly related*
Sir Henry Guildford	Great Uncle (half)
Sir Thomas Lovel	--
Sir Anthony Denny	--
Sir Nicholas Vaux	*his sister is Mary's 2G Grandmother*
Cardinal Wolsey	--
Cardinal Campeius	--
Thomas Cranmer, Archbishop of Canterbury	--
Thomas Cromwell	--

Appendix G
English Peerage

Below is the order of the British peerage (those holding a hereditary or honorary title). A Duke is the highest peer next to a King or Queen. These are *not* titles of royalty. One is *born* into royalty; a title can be *acquired* (if you're born in the right circles).

When George Villiers was made Duke of Buckingham in 1623, there had been no Dukes since the Duke of Norfolk had his head chopped off in 1572. Villiers was assassinated in 1628 during the reign of King James' son, Charles I.

Duke and Duchess

Marquess (*mar KESS*) **and Marchioness** (*MAR shuh ness*)

Earl and Countess

Viscount (*VIE count,* rhymes with *PIE count*) **and Viscountess**

Baron and Baroness

Knight is not a peerage title, and in Mary Sidney's time, you could be given the honor of Knight by titled peers without the Queen's or King's permission.

If your father had no peer title, you were a **commoner.** Philip Sidney was a commoner. The Queen Mother (Queen Elizabeth II's mother) was called a commoner, even though she was descended from kings and grew up in Glamis Castle; she was a commoner because at the time she married, her father did not have a title (he later became Earl of Strathmore and Kinghorne).

To distinguish "commoners" such as the Queen Mother or Winston Churchill (born in Blenheim Palace) from the rest of us, we are called **baseborn,** of low birth or origin, as opposed to **highborn** people who are born into the ruling class or aristocracy. In Mary Sidney's time, it was believed that God ordained you to be born into a particular class, just as He ordained some creatures to be snails and some lions.

Appendix H
Real Money

The following is a list of the approximate equivalents in money values from the Elizabethan/Jacobean eras. I have used the formula developed by John J. McCusker[1] based on the composite commodity price indices in Great Britain from 1600 to 2001.

Below, the price in pounds is an approximation of the value in 2001; the price in U.S. dollars is what that price translates to in early 2006.

One pound = £1 (1*l*)
£1 = 20 shillings (20*s*)
20*s* = 12 pence (12*d*)

Year	Item	Amount	Today
1585*	London journeyman annual wages, including meat and drink[2]	£4	£535.09 $951.44
1585*	London journeyman wages, not including meat and drink	£8	£1,070.17 $1,902.87
1597*	Shakespeare paid for the deed to his house, New Place	£60	£8,026.29 $14,271.55
1600	Typical wage earner	£2/year	£267.54 $475.13
1600	Price paid to a playwright for a play	£5	£668.86 $1,189.30
1602	Shakespeare paid cash for land	£320	£41,617.78 $74,000.58
1605	Shakespeare paid cash for a share of the tithes in Stratford	£440	£60,590.59 $107,736.13
1610	Price paid to a playwright for a play	£10	£1,232.10 $2,190.80

*Although these are for the years 1585 and 1597, the nearest I could get was 1600 using McCusker's price indices.

Year	Item	Amount	Today
1613	Shakespeare's share of buying the Blackfriars gatehouse	£140 altogether	£15,606.67
			$27,750.22
		£80 of it in cash	£8,918.10
			$15,857.27
1623	Price of the finished First Folio	£2 each	£208.09
			$370.01

"Working six days a week, a journeyman [or player] near the top end of the scale with an £8 yearly wage would find his pay amounting to something under sixpence per day. In a world of annual wages where the bottom range was £3 to £4, a worker earning £8 to £10 a year should have been able to live quite adequately, perhaps even comfortably."[3]

Shown below, as a comparison, are some of the monetary amounts in the world of the Herbert boys, Mary's sons.

Year	Item	Amount	Today
1603	Philip Herbert and two others given a grant for transport of cloth	£10,000 per year	£1,377,058.82
			$2,448,548.29
1610	William Herbert's gift to Ben Jonson every New Year's Day	£20	£2,464.21
			$4,381.61
1611	Gift to Philip Herbert from King James	£6,000	£802,628.57
			$1,427,153.86
1615	William Herbert's annual income	£5,000	£544,418.60
			$968,030.71

The Endnotes

Prologue

1. Robert McCrum, William Cran, Robert MacNeil, *The Story of English,* new and rev. ed. (New York and London: Penguin Books, 1993), p. 85.

   Jeffrey McQuain and Stanley Malless, *Coined by Shakespeare* (Springfield: Merriam-Webster, Inc., 1998), p. viii, claim Shakespeare had a vocabulary of 20,000 words.

2. Bernard Levin, in *The Story of English,* pp. 81–82.

   Many of the words and phrases quoted in this statement were not actually used for the first time by Shakespeare, but were popularized through the plays. These include such phrases as it's Greek to me, to play fast and loose, in a pickle, make a virtue of necessity, sleep not one wink, cold comfort, fool's paradise, the long and short of it, your own flesh and blood, teeth set on edge, and give the devil his due. All were used by other authors in print prior to Shakespeare; see *Brush Up Your Shakespeare!,* by Michale Macrone (New York: Harper and Row, 2000), pp. 204–211.

3. David Linton, "Shakespeare as Media Critic: Communication Theory and Historiography," *Mosaic* (June 1996).

4. Russ McDonald, *The Bedford Companion to Shakespeare* (Boston: Bedford Books, 1996), p. 25.

5. Caroline Spurgeon, *Shakespeare's Imagery and What It Tells Us* (1935; reprint, Cambridge: Cambridge University Press, 1996).

6. Ibid., p. 47.

7. Ibid., p. 119.

8. Ibid., p. 124.

9. Ibid., p. 129.

10. Ibid., p. 136.

11. Ibid., p. 137.

12. Ibid., p. 184.

13. All of the hawking information is from Emma Ford, *Falconry: Art and Practice,* rev. ed. (London: Blandford, 1995).

14. M.B. Friedman, "Shakespeare's 'Master Mistris': Image and Tone in Sonnet 20," *Shakespeare Quarterly,* XXXII.2 (Spring 1971), pp. 189-91. Quoted in Stephen Booth, ed., *Shakespeare's Sonnets* (New Haven and London: Yale Univ. Press, 1977), p. 163.

15. Lyndy Abraham, *A Dictionary of Alchemical Imagery* (Cambridge University Press: Cambridge, 1998), p. 173.

16. Charles Nicholl, *The Chemical Theatre* (The Akadine Press: New York, 1997), p. 18.

17. Ibid., p. xii.

18. Abraham, *Dictionary,* p. 179.

19. The four plays with original plots are *The Merry Wives of Windsor, A Midsummer Night's Dream, The Tempest,* and *Love's Labor's Lost.*

20. Michael Dobson and Stanley Wells, eds., *The Oxford Companion to Shakespeare* (Oxford: Oxford University Press, 2001), p. 441.

21. Ibid., p. 441.

22. Sources are condensed from:

   Geoffrey Bullough, *Narrative and Dramatic Sources of Shakespeare,* vols. 1–8 (London: Routledge and Kegan Paul; New York: Columbia University Press, 1960).

   The Riverside Shakespeare, 2d ed., *The Complete Works* (Boston, New York: Houghton Mifflin Company, 1997).

   David Bevington, ed., *The Complete Works of Shakespeare,* 4th ed. (New York: Longman, 1997).

   Stuart Gillespie, *Shakespeare's Books, A Dictionary of Shakespeare's Sources* (London, New York: Continuum, 2004).

Chapter 1: The Man Named William Shakespeare

1. Michael Keevak, *Sexual Shakespeare: Forgery, Authorship, Portraiture* (Detroit: Wayne State University Press, 2001), p. 25.

2. These facts are in every biography about Shakespeare. My traditional favorite is S. Schoenbaum's *William Shakespeare, A Compact Documentary Life* (Oxford: Oxford University Press, 1987) because he usually sticks closer to facts than most biographers.

   My favorite brutally honest biography is by Diana Price, *Shakespeare's Unorthodox Biography: New Evidence of an Authorship Problem* (Westport, CT, London: Greenwood Press, 2001).

   Be particularly wary when reading anything by A. L. Rowse as he tends to present his invented ideas as if they are facts. In general, read any biography of Shakespeare with a discerning mind (and a yellow highlighter).

3. Shakespeare's oldest daughter, Susanna, was able to sign her name (the others signed with marks), but she was not able to read or even recognize her husband's handwriting, indicating a signature was the limit of her literacy. Schoenbaum, *William Shakespeare,* p. 291.

4. Stephen Orgel and A.R. Braunmuller, "Shakespeare, the Stage, and the Book," in the digital edition of *William Shakespeare: Comedies, Histories, & Tragedies* (Oakland, California: Octavo, 2001), p. 27. www.Octavo.com.

   I would think this comment would offend millions of students and professors—five years (average time of attendance) of schooling from ages 5 to 10 in a village grammar school would daunt college graduates today?

5. Charles Knight, *William Shakespere, A Biography* (New York: Routledge, 1865), p. 15.

6. Oscar James Campbell, ed., *The Reader's Encyclopedia of Shakespeare* (New York: MJF Books, 1966), p. 358.

7. E.K. Chambers, *William Shakespeare: A Study of Facts and Problems,* vol. 2 (Oxford: Clarendon Press, 1930), Appendix D. The plays that Henslowe mentions are *Titus Andronicus, Henry VI, King Lear, Hamlet,* and *The Taming of a Shrew.*

8. John Michell, *Who Wrote Shakespeare?* (London: Thames and Hudson, 1996), p. 53.

9. Katherine Duncan-Jones, *Sir Philip Sidney, Courtier Poet* (New Haven and London: Yale University Press, 1991), p. ix.

10. Price, *Unorthodox Biography,* p. 150.

11. Three years after Shakespeare died, a poet named William Drummond wrote down a conversation he had with Ben Jonson in which Jonson mentioned that Shakespeare "wanted art" (lacked any trained skill). Jonson complained of *The Winter's Tale* shipwreck in Bohemia where there is no coast, and criticized a line in *Julius Caesar.*

12. Rosalind Miles, *Ben Jonson: His Life and Work* (London and New York: Routledge & Kegan Paul, 1986), p. 77.

13. John Berryman and John Haffenden, eds., *Berryman's Shakespeare* (New York: Farrar, Straus and Giroux, 1999), p. 34.

14. Please see Appendix H for a comparison of money from then to now.

15. Schoenbaum, *Compact Documentary Life,* p. 234.

16. Ibid., pp. 271–72.

    The title-deed lists three co-purchasers, but "Shakespeare was evidently the sole buyer. He put up the purchase money; the others merely acted as trustees in his interest." Why? "The practical effect would be to deprive Shakespeare's widow of presumed dower right to a third share for life in this part of the estate. . . ."

17. Price, *Unorthodox Biography,* p. 103.

18. Gerald Eades Bentley, *The Profession of Dramatist in Shakespeare's Time, 1590–1642* (Princeton: Princeton University Press, 1971), p. 97.

19. Price, *Unorthodox Biography,* p. 149.

20. Chambers, *William Shakespeare,* vol. 2, p. 215.

21. Ibid., p. 219.

22. Ibid., p. 220.

23. Price, *Unorthodox Biography,* p. 139.

24. Ibid., pp. 139–141.

25. Berryman, *Shakespeare,* p. 34.

26. Michael Brennan, *Literary Patronage in the English Renaissance: The Pembroke Family* (London, New York: Routledge, 1988), p. 78.

27. Linton, "Shakespeare as Media Critic: Communication Theory and Historiography," p. 9.

28. Bentley, *The Profession of Dramatist,* p. 89.

29. Charlotte Stopes, *Life of Henry, Third Earl of Southampton, Shakespeare's Patron* (AMS Press, Inc.).

30. G.P.V. Akrigg, *Shakespeare and the Earl of Southampton* (Cambridge: Harvard University Press, 1968).

31. Berryman, *Shakespeare,* p. 33.

32. Campbell, *Reader's Encyclopedia,* p. 741.

    "In 1900, a Mr. Pearson showed Sidney Lee a document he discovered in the Tixall Library that listed 23 persons who reportedly got their coats-of-arms under false pretenses. Under a drawing of a coat-of-arms were the words, 'Shakespeare Ye Player.'" The herald was accused of "elevating base persons" to the class of gentleman. Notice Shakespeare is identified as a *player,* not a dramatist or poet.

33. Price, *Unorthodox Biography,* p. 52.

34. Schoenbaum, *Shakespeare's Lives,* new ed. (Oxford, New York: Oxford University Press, 1993), pp. 61–65.

35. E.K. Chambers, *William Shakespeare: A Study of Facts and Problems,* vol. 2 (Oxford: Clarendon Press, 1930), p. 212.

36. Campbell, *Reader's Encyclopedia,* p. 213.

37. Ibid., p. 187.

38. Alden Brooks, *Will Shakspere, Factotum and Agent* (New York: Round Table Press, Inc., 1937), p.14.

39. A.L. Rowse, ed., *The Annotated Shakespeare* (New York: Greenwich House, 1988), p. 1943.

40. Don Foster, *Author Unknown: On the Trail of Anonymous* (New York: Henry Hold and Company, 2000), p. 70.

41. Margaret P. Hannay, et al., eds., *The Collected Works of Mary Sidney Herbert, Countess of Pembroke,* vols. 1 and 2 (Oxford: Clarendon Press, 1998), p. 120.

42. One of the reasons we have so many documents from this era is that paper made from wood pulp hadn't been invented yet—and wouldn't be until the mid-1800s in America. People wrote either on parchment (sheep skin), vellum (calf, goat, or lamb skin), or 100 percent "rag" paper, which was literally made of rags of linen or cotton cloth, all of which is much more durable than wood-pulp paper.

    Dard Hunter, *Papermaking: The History and Technique of an Ancient Craft,* 2d ed. (New York: Dover Publications, Inc., 1978), pp. 13–14. In 1666, "To save linen and cotton for the papermakers a decree was issued in England prohibiting the use of these materials for the burial of the dead; only wool could be used for this purpose. In England at this time 200,000 pounds of linen and cotton were saved annually in this manner." p. 482.

43. Margaret P. Hannay, *Philip's Phoenix, Mary Sidney, Countess of Pembroke* (New York: Oxford University Press, 1990), p. 122.

44. Twenty-three years after William Cory wrote about the letter, the "Lady Herbert, then not in very good memory, believed that a copy was at the B.M. [British Museum], or possibly the R.O. [Royal Observatory]. Nothing has since been heard of it." In Chambers, *William Shakespeare,* vol. 2, p. 329.

45. E.K. Chambers, *The Elizabethan Stage*, vol. 4 (Oxford: Clarendon Press, 1923), p. 168.

> There is documentation that the Kings Men were payed £30 to perform before the King [who was at Wilton] on December 2, 1603.

Chapter 2: Mary Sidney as a Young Woman

1. Margaret P. Hannay, *Philip's Phoenix: Mary Sidney, Countess of Pembroke* (New York: Oxford University Press, 1990), p. 145.

2. The following are the only biographies about Mary Sidney Herbert (note—these are written by academics for academics, which means they're not much fun to read and they assume you already know all the people and current events of the times):

> Margaret P. Hannay, *Philip's Phoenix: Mary Sidney, Countess of Pembroke* (New York: Oxford University Press, 1990).
>
> Gary F. Waller, *Mary Sidney, Countess of Pembroke: A Critical Study of Her Writings and Literary Milieu* (Salzburg: Universität Salzburg, 1979). No index.
>
> Frances Berkeley Young, *Mary Sidney, Countess of Pembroke* (London: David Nutt, 1912).
>
> Margaret P. Hannay, et al., eds., *The Collected Works of Mary Sidney Herbert, Countess of Pembroke,* vols. 1 and 2 (Oxford: Clarendon Press, 1998).

3. Hannay, *Philip's Phoenix*, p. 22.

4. Brennan, *Literary Patronage*, p. 99.

5. *The Rare SECRETS of the English Countess Mary of Pembroke* (Nuremberg: Gabriel Nicolaus Raspe, 1763), p. 116.

6. Peter Holman, *Four and Twenty Fiddlers: The Violin at the English Court, 1540–1690* (Oxford: Clarendon Press, 2002), p. 125.

7. J. Alan B. Somerset, *Records of Early English Drama, Shropshire*, vol. 2: *Editorial Apparatus* (Toronto: University of Toronto Press, 1994), p. 645.

8. Hannay, *Philip's Phoenix*, p. 27.

9. Ibid.

10. Ibid., p. 124.

11. Somerset, *Records of Early English Drama*, p. 395.

12. Hannay, *Philip's Phoenix*, p. 124.

13. Alexander Maclaren Witherspoon, *The Influence of Robert Garnier on Elizabethan Drama* (New York: Phaeto Press, 1968), p. 69.

14. As quoted in Hannay, *Philip's Phoenix*, p. 31.

15. Hannay, *The Collected Works of Mary Sidney Herbert*, vol. 1, p. 65.

16. William Dugdale, *The Antiquities of Warwickshire, Illustrated* (1656; reprint, Manchester: E.J. Morten, Ltd., 1730), p. 166.

17. Hannay, *Philip's Phoenix*, p. 35.

18. Anne Somerset, *Elizabeth I* (New York: St. Martin's Griffin, 1991), p. 368.

19. Hannay, *Philip's Phoenix*, p. 35.

> Henry Herbert had an earlier marriage at 19 years old to Katherine, age 14, the sister of Lady Jane Grey, reluctant queen for nine days in 1553. The marriage was unconsummated and annulled before Lady Jane's head was smit off.

20. Adrian Gilbert, Mary, her brother Philip, his dear friend Edward Dyer, as well as Mary's mother, were good friends with and students of Dr. John Dee, the astrologer and "magician." See Peter French, *John Dee, the World of an Elizabethan Magus* (London: Routledge, 1972).

> Giordano Bruno was also close to her brother; Bruno dedicated two major philosophical works to Philip; see Duncan-Jones, *Sir Philip Sidney, Courtier Poet*, p. 271.

21. Roy Strong, *The Renaissance Garden in England* (London: Thames & Hudson, 1998) pp. 122–23.

22. John Aubrey, *Aubrey's Natural History of Wiltshire* (originally written between 1656 and 1691) (Wiltshire: David & Charles Reprints, 1969), p. 86.

23. Juliana Berners' book was the first book in England printed on paper in which colored inks were used in the illustrations. Hunter, *Papermaking*, p. 477.

24. Alan Stewart, *Philip Sidney: A Double Life* (New York: St. Martin's Press, 2000), p. 202.

25. Duncan-Jones, *Sir Philip Sidney*, p. x.

26. From Philip Sidney's *Astrophil and Stella,* sonnet 21, line 8.

27. Tucker Brooke and Matthias A. Shaaber, *A Literary History of England*, vol. 2, *The Renaissance (1500–1660)*, 2d ed. (New York: Appleton-Century-Crofts, 1967), p. 472.

28. Katherine Duncan-Jones, ed., *The Oxford Authors—Sir Philip Sidney, A Critical Edition of the Major Works* (Oxford, New York: Oxford University Press, 1989), p. ix.

29. James M. Osborn, *Young Philip Sidney, 1572–1577* (New Haven and London: Yale University Press, 1972), p. 503.

> When Queen Elizabeth was negotiating marriage with the French Catholic Duc d'Anjou (Alençon), the great Protestant Earls (including Leicester and Pembroke), Sir Frances Walsingham, Sir Christopher Hatton, and others met at the Pembroke's Baynard's Castle in London. They chose Philip Sidney to represent them; he wrote a formal letter to the Queen frankly condemning the proposed marriage. There is no record of the Queen's response, but Philip shortly thereafter retired to Wilton House with his sister.
>
> When John Stubbs, a man of lower class, published a protest against the marriage, the Queen had both the printer's and Stubbs' right hands cut off (the distributor's hand was scheduled to be cut off, but it was saved due to his advanced age).

30. Duncan-Jones, *Sir Philip Sidney*, p. 167.

31. S.P. Cerasano and Marion Wynne-Davies, eds., *Renaissance Drama by Women: Texts and Documents* (London and New York: Routledge, 1996), p. 13.

32. The original work, titled *Arcadia*, was available in manuscript only. After Philip died, Mary edited and added to the book; this more highly involved and ornate version is titled *The Countess of Pembroke's Arcadia* and was published in 1590. The two books are often designated as the *Old Arcadia* and the *New Arcadia*. This book was used as a source for *King Lear* and three other Shakespearean plays; however, it is virtually impossible that William Shakespeare would have had a copy of the original handwritten manuscript.

33. Merriam-Webster and Encyclopedia Britannica, eds., *Merriam-Webster's Encyclopedia of Literature* (Springfield: Merriam-Webster, 1995), p. 1030.

34. Brooke and Shaaber, *A Literary History of England*, p. 472.

35. Merriam-Webster, *Encyclopedia of Literature*, p. 1030.

36. Hardin Craig and David Bevington, eds., *The Complete Works of Shakespeare*, rev. ed. (Glenview, IL: Scott, Foresman and Company, 1973), p. 468.

37. Duncan-Jones, *Oxford Authors*, p. xvii.

38. Roma Gill, ed., *The Taming of the Shrew* (Oxford: Oxford University Press, 1996), p. 120.

39. Duncan-Jones, *Sir Philip Sidney*, p. 143.

40. John Buxton, *Sir Philip Sidney and the English Renaissance* (New York and London: St. Martin's Press, 1966), p. 31.

41. Katherine J. Roberts, *Fair Ladies: Sir Philip Sidney's Female Characters* (New York: Peter Lang Publishing, Inc., 1993), p. 121.

42. Ibid., p. 122.

43. Waller, *Critical Study*, p. 39. Waller is comparing Mary and Wilton House with Marguerite de Navarre's palace academy, which was a source for *Love's Labor's Lost*.

44. Albert C. Baugh, ed., *A Literary History of England* (New York: Appleton-Century-Crofts, Inc., 1948), p. 472.

45. Hannay, *Philip's Phoenix*, p. 55.

    "The death of the same La. Katherine . . . being threyeare old and one daie, a child of promised much excellencie if she mought haue lived . . . ."

46. Pearl Hogrefe, *Women of Action in Tudor England: Nine Biographical Sketches* (Ames, Iowa: Iowa State University Press, 1977), p. 120.

47. Hannay, *Philip's Phoenix*, pp. 59–60.

Chapter 3: Mary Sidney's Life of Literature

1. Hannay, *Philip's Phoenix*, p. vix.

2. Waller, *Critical Study*, p. 45.

3. Ibid., p. 17.

4. Ibid., p. 71.

5. Ibid., p. 66.

6. Ibid., p. 18.

7. Witherspoon, *Influence of Robert Garnier*, p. 68.

8. Waller, *Critical Study*, p. 29.

9. Young, *Mary Sidney*, p. 174.

10. Ibid., p. 164.

11. Ibid., p. 181.

12. Hannay, *Collected Works*, vol. 1, p. 22.

13. Francis Meres, *Palladis Tamia*, (1598; reprint, New York: Scholars' Facsimilies & Reprints, 1978), p. 285.

14. Mary Ellen Lamb, "The Cooke Sisters: Attitudes toward Learned Women in the Renaissance," in *Silent but for the Word: Tudor Women as Patrons, Translators, and Writers of Religious Works*, ed. Margaret P. Hannay (Ohio: Kent State University Press, 1985), p. 116.

15. Waller, *Critical Study*, p. 101.

16. Ibid., p. 181.

17. Ibid., p. 190.

18. Cerasano and Wynne-Davis, *Renaissance Drama*, p. 15.

19. Hannay, *Collected Works*, vol. 1, p. 57.

20. Ibid., p. 57, n.5.

21. Wendy Wall, *The Imprint of Gender: Authorship and Publication in the English Renaissance* (Ithaca and London: Cornell University Press, 1993), p. 313.

22. Young, *Mary Sidney*, p. 139.

23. R. E. Pritchard, ed., *Mary Sidney (and Sir Philip Sidney): The Sidney Psalms* (England: Fyfield Books, 1992), p. 18.

24. Diane Bornstein, "The Style of the Countess of Pembroke's Translation of Philippe de Mornay's 'Discours de la vie et de la mort,'" in *Silent but for the Word*, p. 134.

25. Waller, *Critical Study*, p. 108.

26. S.P. Cerasano and Marion Wynne-Davies, eds., *Readings in Renaissance Women's Drama: Criticism, History, and Performance, 1594–1998* (London and New York: Routledge, 1998), p. 16.

27. Ibid., p. 34.

28. Margaret P. Hannay, "'Bearing the livery of your name': The Countess of Pembroke's Agency in Print and Scribal Publications," *Sidney Journal* 18:1 (2000), p. 41.

29. Waller, *Critical Study*, p. 89.

30. Ibid., pp. 146–149.

31. Hannay, *Collected Works*, vol. 1, p. 265.

32. Gavin Alexander, a modernised edition on the Sidneiana website: www.english.cam.ac.uk/ceres/sidneiana/triumph.htm

33. Cerasano and Wynne-Davies, *Readings*, p. 33.

34. Hannay, *Philip's Phoenix*, p. 165.

35. Josephine A. Roberts, *The Poems of Lady Mary Wroth* (Baton Rouge and London: Louisiana State University Press, 1983), p. 15. Three letters are included in *A Collection of Letters by Sir Tobie Matthew*, ed. John Donne, 1660.

36. Waller, *Critical Study*, p. 198.

37. Cerasano and Wynne-Davies, *Renaissance Drama*, p. 17.

38. Hannay, *Philip's Phoenix*, p. x.

39. Cerasano and Wynne-Davies, *Renaissance Drama*, p. 13.

40. Louise Schleiner, *Tudor & Stuart Women Writers* (Bloomington and Indianapolis: Indiana University Press, 1994), p. 81.

41. Waller, *Critical Study*, p. 31.

42. Sir Peter Hall, *Cities in Civilization* (New York: Pantheon Books, 1998), p. 125.

43. Buxton, *Sir Philip Sidney*, p. 233.

Chapter 4: Mary Sidney as an Older Woman

1. Brennan, *Literary Patronage*, p. 101.

2. Hannay, *Philip's Phoenix*, p. 169.

3. Ibid., p. xi.

4. Lady Newdigate, ed. and transcriber, *Gossip from a Muniment Room, being Passages in the Lives of Anne and Mary Fytton, 1574–1618* (London: David Nutt in the Strand, 1897), p. 36.

5. Hannay, *Philip's Phoenix*, pp. 173–84.

6. Ibid., p. 212.

7. Duncan-Jones, *Sir Philip Sidney*, p. 174.

   Contrary to the belief of many Oxfordians, Philip never did reconcile with Oxford. Oxfordians claim that Philip was Oxford's second in the "Callophisus" tournament as the White Knight, but Duncan-Jones proves Philip was the Blue Knight. The White Knight was Oxford's nephew, Edward, Lord Windsor. *Courtier Poet,* pp. 202–03.

8. Francis Osborne, *Historical Memoirs of the Reigns of Queen Elizabeth and King James* (London: T. Robinson, 1658). Quoted in Hannay, *Philip's Phoenix*, p. 212.

9. Michael G. Brennan and Noel J. Kinnamon, *A Sidney Chronology, 1554–1654* (Basingstoke and New York: Palgrave Macmillan, 2003), p.187.

10. Ibid., pp. 214–15.

11. Hannay, *Philip's Phoenix*, p. 198.

12. It is thought that Houghton House is the "House Beautiful" that John Bunyan refers to in *The Pilgrim's Progress.* Outside the town of Ampthill is a hill that is thought to be his "Hill Difficulty."

13. Hannay, *Philip's Phoenix*, p. 140; I modernized the spelling.

Chapter 5: Introduction to the Sonnets

1. Hyder Edward Rollins, ed. *A New Variorum Edition of Shakespeare: The Sonnets,* vol. 1 (Philadelphia & London: J.B. Lippincott Company, 1944), p. vi.

2. Harold Bloom, *Shakespeare: The Invention of the Human* (New York: Riverhead Books, 1998), p. 731.

3. Donald Foster, "Master W.H., R.I.P.," in *Shakespeare's Sonnets, Critical Essays,* ed. James Schiffer (New York: Garland Publishing, Inc., 1999), p. 15.

4. Brooke and Shaaber, *A Literary History of England,* vol. 2, p. 482.

5. In the 1821 edition of *The Plays and Poems of William Shakespeare,* ed. Edmond Malone.

6. Peter Stallybrass, "Editing as Cultural Formation," in *Shakespeare's Sonnets,* p. 77.

7. James Schiffer, "Reading New Life into Shakespeare's Sonnets," in *Shakespeare's Sonnets,* p. 46.

8. Bevington, *Complete Works,* p. 1662.

9. Ibid., p. 1663.

10. Keevak, *Sexual Shakespeare,* pp. 30–31.

11. Ibid., p. 39.

12. Joseph Pequigney, "Such Is My Love: A Study of Shakespeare's Sonnets," in *Shakespeare's Sonnets,* p. 13.

13. E.K. Chambers, *William Shakespeare,* vol. 1, p. 595.

14. J. Dover Wilson, *The Sonnets* (Cambridge: Cambridge University Press, 1969), p. l (that's an "el," or page 50 in the intro).

15. Ibid., pp. l–li.

16. Colin Burrow, ed., *The Complete Sonnets and Poems* (Oxford, New York: Oxford University Press, 2002), p. 100.

17. Schiffer, "Reading New Life," in *Shakespeare's Sonnets,* p. 30.

18. Stanley Wells, "Objects of Desire," *Around the Globe, The Magazine of Shakespeare's Globe* 22 (Autumn 2002), p. 16.

19. Ibid., p. 16.

20. L.P. Smith, "On Reading Shakespeare," quoted in Schiffer, *Shakespeare's Sonnets,* p. 30.

21. Antonia Fraser, ed., *The Lives of the Kings & Queens of England* (Berkeley: University of California Press, 1998), pp. 87–93.

22. Ibid., pp. 216–23.

23. George T. Wright, "The Silent Speech of Shakespeare's Sonnets," in *Shakespeare's Sonnets,* pp. 157–58.

24. Ibid., p. 140.

25. Ibid., p. 148.

Chapter 6: The Love Sonnets

1. Katherine Duncan-Jones, ed., *The Arden Shakespeare, Shakespeare's Sonnets* (Walton-on-Thames: Thomas Nelson and Sons Ltd., 1997), p. 10.

2. Somerset, *Elizabeth I,* p. 347.

3. Alexander Schmidt, *Shakespeare Lexicon and Quotation Dictionary* (New York: Dover Publications, Inc., 1971), p. 135. And dozens of books on the sonnets; please see the bibliography.

4. Mary Wroth was the first English woman to write an original (as opposed to translated) dramatic comedy, a prose romance, a sonnet sequence, and an original pastoral drama.

5. The manuscript (handwritten) copy of "Love's Victory" is in the Huntington Library in San Marino, California. It was probably written in the early 1620s for private performance. The entire play is reproduced in *Renaissance Drama by Women: Texts and Documents,* pp. 91–125.

6. Cerasano and Wynne-Davies, *Renaissance Drama by Women,* p. 91. If the character named Rustic in the play represents Mary Wroth's husband, Robert Wroth, as the scholars say, Mary Wroth certainly does despise him and so does everyone else.

7. Gary Waller, *Sidney Family Romance* (Detroit: Wayne State University Press, 1993), p. 242.

8. Also in the play, Mary Sidney berates Lister for being fickle, for professing vows of love to another woman, and for reviling a particular woman to Mary's face but wooing her behind Mary's back.

9. Schleiner, *Tudor & Stuart Women Writers,* p. 143.

10. M.A. Beese, "A Critical Edition of the Poems Printed by John Donne the Younger in 1660, As Written by William Herbert, Earl of Pembroke, and Sir Benjamin Ruddier," unpublished dissertation, Oxford University, 1935. Discussed in *The Sidney Family Romance,* p. 122.

> Some scholars think Mary Wroth, through her illegitimate daughter with William Herbert, may be the grandmother of the writer Aphra Behn. Ms. Behn is the first woman to make a living by writing in English. She had seventeen plays produced on the London stage in seventeen years, among many other amazing accomplishments in and out of the literary world. Yet Aphra Behn also "constitutes an example of almost every technique men have used to abuse, devalue, and erase women." Dale Spender, *Women of Ideas & What Men Have Done To Them* (London: Routledge, 1982), p. 34.

11. Waller, *Sidney Family Romance,* p. 122.

> William Herbert had no living children with his own wife—after twelve years of marriage, their first baby died at birth, and five years later another baby died as an infant.
>
> Mary Wroth's only child with her husband was born ten years into her marriage, one month before her husband died. The baby died when two years old.

Chapter 7: The Procreation Sonnets

1. Craig and Bevington, *Complete Works,* 1973, p. 468.

2. Brennan and Kinnamon, *A Sidney Chronology,* p. 130.

3. Brooke and Shaaber, *A Literary History,* p. 480.

4. Hannay, *Philip's Phoenix,* pp. 162–163.

5. Ibid., p. 117.

> Samuel Daniel wrote this to Mary's son, William Herbert, in the dedication to "A Defence of Rhyme."

6. Wilson, *The Sonnets,* p. 89.

7. Ibid., p. 90.

8. C.S. Lewis, *English Literature in the Sixteenth Century* (New York: Oxford University Press, 1954), pp. 503–05.

9. Wilson, *The Sonnets,* p. 92.

10. Duncan-Jones, *Shakespeare's Sonnets,* p. 146.

11. Anne Ferry, *The "Inward" Language: Sonnets of Wyatt, Sidney, Shakespeare, Donne* (Chicago, London: The University of Chicago Press, 1983), p. 170.

12. Ibid., p. 172.

13. Ibid., p. 192.

14. Ibid., pp. 177–78.

15. Ibid., p. 198.

16. Ibid., p. 205.

Chapter 8: Sonnet Miscellany

1. David Honneyman, *Shakespeare's Sonnets and the Court of Navarre* (Lewiston: The Edwin Mellen Press, 1997), p. 3.

2. Duncan-Jones, *Shakespeare's Sonnets,* p. 69.

3. J.D. Wilson, *An Introduction to Shakespeare's Sonnets for Historians and Others* (New York: Cambridge Univ. Press, 1964), p. 30.

4. James Schiffer, "Introduction," in *Shakespeare's Sonnets,* p. 16.

5. Wilson, *The Sonnets,* p. xli.

6. Schiffer, "Introduction," in *Shakespeare's Sonnets,* p. 16.

7. Campbell, *Reader's Encyclopedia,* p. 872.

8. Alfred Bates, *The Drama, Its History, Literature and Influence on Civilization,* vol. 2 (London: Historical Publishing Company, 1906), pp. 205–207.

> The Elizabethans knew Terence's reputation, as evidenced by the writings of Robert Ascham and John Florio. Terence was about 25 or 30 years old when he disappeared.

9. Waller, *Sidney Family Romance,* p. 9.

10. Price, *Unorthodox Biography,* p. 64.

11. The epigram continues:

> Some others raile; but raile as they think fit,
> Thou hast no rayling, but, a raigning Wit:
>
> And honesty thou sow'st, which they do reap;
> So, to increase their Stock which they do keep.

Chapter 9: The Sources of the Plays

1. There were no public libraries in England until September, 1852, when one was opened in Manchester. The first public library in America opened in 1848 in Boston.

2. Unless otherwise noted, the sources are from:

> Bevington, *The Complete Works of Shakespeare,* pp. A-22–58.
>
> Also see *The Riverside Shakespeare,* pp. 78–87.

3. **French only:** Francois de Belleforest's French transla-tion of Bandello's Italian Novelle, titled *Histoires Tragiques;* two eyewitness accounts of Richard II in unpublished French manuscript; Montaigne's *Essays;* the author of the plays is thought to have possibly known the French and Italian versions of Boccaccio's *Decameron, Novel 38,* for *All's Well That Ends Well.*

> **Italian only:** *Il Pecorone (The Dunce),* by Ser Giovanni Fiorentino; *Il Novellino* by Masuccio; Matteo Bandello's *Novelle; Gl'Ingannati* (anonymous versions were avail-able in Italian, French, Latin, and Spanish); *Epitia,* a play, and *Hecatommithi,* a collection of novels, both written by Giraldi Giambattista (known as Cinthio); Boccaccio's *Decameron, Day 2, Tale 9.*

Latin only: Plautus's *Menaechmi*; Ovid's *Metamorphoses* (details for *A Midsummer Night's Dream* are not found in Golding's translation); *Wakefield Chronicle* in manuscript; Mathew Paris's *Historia Maior*; Gabriel Harvey's *Ciceronianus*; Erasmus's *Adagia*; *Henrici Quinti Angliae Regis Gest* by a chaplain in Henry V's army; *Vita et Gesta Henrici Quinti,* erroneously attrituded to Thomas Elmham; *A Golden Ass* by Apuleius (plus a translation by Addlington); George Buchanan's *Rerum Scoticarum Historia;* John Leslie's *De Origine, Moribus, et Rebus Gestis Scotorum; Timon: Comoedia Imitata,* by Jakob Gretser, a German playwright; Geoffrey of Monmouth's *Historia Regum Britanniae.*

Lucian's *Timon, or the Misanthrope* was originally in Greek, with translations available in Latin, Italian, and French, but no English.

4. *King John; Richard II; Richard III; Henry IV parts 1 and 2; Henry V; Henry VI parts 1, 2, and 3; Henry VIII; Macbeth; Cymbeline.*

5. *King Lear; Two Gentlemen of Verona; Midsummer Night's Dream; Twelfth Night; Pericles.*

6. Bevington, *Complete Works,* p. A-48.

7. Aubrey, *Natural History,* p. 89.

8. *Romeo and Juliet; Antony and Cleopatra; Richard II; Henry IV parts 1 and 2.*

9. Waller, *Critical Study,* p.72.

10. Buxton, *Sir Philip Sidney,* p. 200.

   Navarre was a small kingdom that straddled the Pyrenees mountains on the border between France and Spain. Its capital was Pamplona.

   Henri III of Navarre (later Henry IV of France) was Marguerite de Navarre's grandson. His wife was also named Marguerite, but of Valois.

11. Bevington, *Complete Works,* p. A-51.

12. Ibid., p. A-51.

13. Hannay, *Collected Works,* vol. 1, p. 39.

14. Ibid., p. 40.

15. Bullough, *Narrative and Dramatic Sources of Shakespeare,* vol. 5, p. 229.

16. John Wilders, ed., *The Arden Shakespeare, Antony and Cleopatra* (New York: Routledge, 1995), p. 63.

17. Alvin Kernan, *Shakespeare, the King's Playwright* (New Haven: Yale University Press, 1995), p. 174.

18. Campbell, *Reader's Encyclopedia,* p. 813.

19. *Titus Andronicus; Midsummer Night's Dream; Merry Wives of Windsor; The Tempest.*

20. Bullough, *Sources,* p. 232.

21. Hannay, *Collected Works,* vol. 1, p. 41.

22. Ibid., p. 34.

23. *Henry VI parts 1, 2, and 3; King John; Henry VIII.*

24. Hannay, *Collected Works,* vol. 1, p. 211.

25. *Much Ado About Nothing; Twelfth Night; Hamlet.*

26. Bevington, *Complete Works,* p. 217.

27. Duncan-Jones, *Sir Philip Sidney,* pp. 29–30.

28. *Henry IV parts 1 and 2; Richard III.*

29. Osborn, *Young Philip Sidney,* p. 515.

30. Stewart, *Philip Sidney, A Double Life,* p. 303.

31. Hannay, *Collected Works,* vol. 1, p. 33 n.48.

32. H. R. Woudhuysen, *Sir Philip Sidney and the Circulation of Manuscripts, 1558–1640* (Oxford: Oxford University Press, 1996), p. 344.

33. *The Tempest; Midsummer Night's Dream; Henry VI plays.*

34. Hannay, *Collected Works,* vol. 1, p. 122.

35. Ibid., p. 140.

36. Alister E. McGrath, *In the Beginning: The Story of the King James Bible and How It Changed a Nation, a Language, and a Culture* (New York: Doubleday, 2001), p. 129.

37. Brennan and Kinnamon, *Sidney Chronology,* p. 181.

38. Campbell, *Reader's Encyclopedia,* p. 598.

39. Brennan and Kinnamon, *Sidney Chronology,* p. 38

40. Stewart, *Philip Sidney, A Double Life,* p. 305.

41. Millicent V. Hay, *The Life of Robert Sidney, Earl of Leicester (1563–1626)* (Washington: The Folger Shakespeare Library, 1984), p. 127.

42. Campbell, *Reader's Encyclopedia,* p. 460.

43. "The names of the persons appearing below are those listed on the Charters of 1606, 1609, 1612, and a list of stockholders in 1620." www.Jamestowne.org/adv.htm

44. Hannay, *Philip's Phoenix,* p. 42.

45. Charles Boyce, ed., *Shakespeare A to Z* (New York: Roundtable Press, 1990), pp. 156 and 568.

46. Hannay, *Philip's Phoenix,* p. 123.

47. *The Riverside Shakespeare,* pp. 82 and 83.

48. Campbell, *Reader's Encyclopedia,* p. 851.

49. Duncan-Jones, *Sir Philip Sidney,* p. 148.

50. Hannay, *Philip's Phoenix,* p. 124.

51. *Julius Caesar; The Tempest.*

52. Bevington, *Complete Works,* p. A-43.

53. Peter Ure, ed., *The Arden Shakespeare, King Richard II* (Surrey: Thomas Nelson & Sons Ltd., 1998), p. xlv.

54. Waller, *Critical Study,* p. 57.

55. Bevington, *Complete Works,* p. A-24.

56. Campbell, *Reader's Encyclopedia,* p. 558.

57. Hannay, *Philip's Phoenix,* pp. 115–16.

58. Campbell, *Reader's Encyclopedia,* p. 558.

59. Schoenbaum, *A Compact Documentary Life,* pp. 115–16.

60. Hannay, *Philip's Phoenix,* pp. 33–35.

61. Chambers, *William Shakespeare,* vol. 1, p. 358.

62. Campbell, *Reader's Encyclopedia,* p. 471.

63. Hannay, *Philip's Phoenix,* p. 22.

64. Katherine Duncan-Jones, "Liquid Prisoners: Shakespeare's Re-writings of Sidney," *Sidney Journal* 15:2 (Fall 1997), p. 10.

65. Brennan, *Literary Patronage,* pp. 77–78.

66. Campbell, *Reader's Encyclopedia,* p. 575.

67. Hannay, *Philip's Phoenix*, p. 27, referencing the L'Isle family papers.

68. Woudhuysen, *Circulation of Manuscripts*, p. 61.

69. Claes Schaar, *An Elizabethan Sonnet Problem* (Lund: Håkan Ohlssons Boktryckeri, 1960), p. 7.

70. Hannay, *Philip's Phoenix*, p. 72.

71. McQuain and Malless, *Coined by Shakespeare*, p. viii.

72. Hannay, *Collected Works*, vol. 1, p. 27.

73. J. Madison Davis and A. Daniel Frankforter, *The Shakespeare Name Dictionary* (New York, London: Garland Publishing, Inc., 1995), p. 170.

74. Baugh, *A Literary History of England*, p. 475 n.8.

75. Michell, *Who Wrote Shakespeare?*, p. 215.

76. Campbell, *Reader's Encyclopedia*, p. 215.

77. Bevington, *Complete Works*, p. A-31.

78. Brennan and Kinnamon, *Sidney Chronology*, p. 177–78.

79. Nicholl, *The Chemical Theatre*, p. xii.

Alchemy includes a "quintessence," the fifth spiritual element after earth, water, fire, and air. It is involved with vessels, distillation, volatile vapors, smoke, spirits being liberated from solid matter, probing, purifying, transforming, transmuting, "the capacity of chemical experiments to mirror both physic and cosmic meanings" (p. 6), crystals, "good angels" (p. 20), fire, death and rebirth, loss and restoration of form, purity, and the search for the "Universal Medicine," or Elixir, which fully perfects metals or imperfect bodies (this is also called the Philosopher's Stone). Out of pairs of the four qualities (cold, hot, moist, dry) arise the four elements: earth (cold and dry), water (cold and wet), fire (hot and dry) and air (hot and wet) (p. 25). (See the sonnets 44 and 45.)

80. John Aubrey, *Brief Lives* (1680; reprint, Rochester, New York: The Boydell Press, 1997), p. 140.

81. Nicholl, *The Chemical Theatre*, p. 15.

82. Duncan-Jones, *Sir Philip Sidney*, p. 271.

83. Michael White, *The Pope and the Heretic* (London: Little, Brown and Company, 2002), p. 180.

84. Ibid., p. 92.

85. Philip also traveled to Paris, Strasbourg, Basle, Dresden, Leipzig, Frankfurt, Heidelberg, Cologne, Bruges, Antwerp, Zutphen (the Netherlands), among other places.

86. Duncan-Jones, *Sir Philip Sidney*, p. xi.

87. Hay, *The Life of Robert Sidney*, pp. 34–35 and throughout.

88. Gilbert Slater, *Seven Shakespeares* (Oxford: Kemp Hall Press, Ltd., 1931), p. 106.

89. Frederick J. Harries, *Shakespeare and the Welsh* (London: T. Fisher Unwin, Ltd., 1919), p. 5.

90. Bloom, *The Invention of the Human*, p. 695.

91. Brennan, *Literary Patronage*, pp. 157–58.

92. Hannay, *Philip's Phoenix*, p. 101.

93. Mary is known to have owned *The Book of Hawking and Hunting*, by Dame Juliana Berners, printed in 1486. Mary Queen of Scots often hunted with her merlins. Katherine Duncan-Jones reports in *Philip Sidney: Courtier, Poet*, p. 74, that Catherine Howard, sister of the executed Duke of Norfolk, was "so addicted to falconry that her dresses were covered with bird-droppings."

94. Ure, *King Richard II*, p. l (el, 50).

95. Hannay, *Philip's Phoenix*, p. 49.

96. Davis and Frankforter, *Shakespeare Name Dictionary*.

97. Brennan and Kinnamon, *Sidney Chronology*, p. xxii.

98. Ibid., p. 39.

99. Ibid., p. 39.

Chapter 10: The Sources and How They Were Changed

1. Barton, *The Riverside Shakespeare* (Boston, New York: Houghton Mifflin Company, 1997), p. 399.

2. Bevington, *Complete Works*, p. A-30.

3. This was from *The Riverside Shakespeare*. In Bevington's *Complete Works*, he says the chapbook has now been shown to be an expansion of the story based on a ballad of 1594, which was in turn modeled on the play. It's very interesting, whether the play was based on the chapbook or the chapbook on the play, that the author of the play as we know it softened various elements, and the author of the chapbook took out the softening elements.

4. Barton, *The Riverside Shakespeare*, p. 138.

5. Bevington, *Complete Works*, p. A-25.

6. H. R. Woudhuysen, *Circulation of Manuscripts*, p. 61.

7. Bevington, *Complete Works*, p. A-23.

8. Ibid., p. A-23.

9. Ibid., p. A-32.

10. Ibid., p. A-48.

11. Ibid., p. A-57.

12. Frank Kermode, *The Riverside Shakespeare*, p. 1441.

13. Bevington, *Complete Works*, p. A-49.

14. Ibid., p. A-52.

15. Barton, *Riverside Shakespeare*, p. 322.

16. Tina Krontiris, *Oppositional Voices: Woman as Writers and Translators of Literature in the English Renaissance* (London and New York: Routledge, 1992), p. 69.

17. Wilders, *Antony and Cleopatra*, p. 62.

Chapter 11: The Plays and Mary's Life

1. Waller, *Critical Study*, p. 100.

2. John Klause, "Politics, Heresy, and Martyrdom in Shakespeare's Sonnet 124 and *Titus Andronicus*," in *Shakespeare's Sonnets*, p. 234.

3. Campbell, ed., *Reader's Encyclopedia*, p. 881.

4. "That the countess herself had some responsibility for the players is indicated by the will of the actor Simon Jewell, which bequeathed 'my share of such money as shalbe givenn by my ladie Pembrooke or by her means.'" Hannay, *Collected Works*, vol. 1, p. 38.

5. Campbell, ed., *Reader's Encyclopedia*, p. 677.

6. M.C. Bradbrook, "Shakespeare and Elizabethan Poetry," reprinted in the Signet Classic edition of *All's Well That Ends Well* (New York: New American Library, 1965), p. 182.

7. Ibid., p. 181.

8. Hannay, *Philip's Phoenix*, pp. 171 and 184.

9. The source is one of the stories in a section of Boccaccio's Decameron (Day III), "Gigletta di Nerbona" (1313–1375).

10. Bevington, *Complete Works*, p. A-23.

11. Richard David, ed., *The Arden Shakespeare, Love's Labour's Lost* (London: Routledge, 1994), p. xxx.

12. Waller, *Critical Study*, p. 39.

13. Hannay, *Collected Works*, vol. 1, p. 208.

    Also see Brennan and Kinnamon, *Sidney Chronology*, p. 91.

14. A.H. Upham, *The French Influence in English Literature: From the Accession of Elizabeth to the Restoration* (New York: Columbia University Press, 1911), p. 58.

15. Hannay, *Collected Works*, vol. 1, p. 24.

16. A. H. Upham, *The French Influence*, p. 60.

17. Aubrey, *Natural History*, p. 89.

18. Bevington, *Complete Works*, p. A-23.

19. Hannay, *Philip's Phoenix*, p. 141.

20. Campbell, *Reader's Encyclopedia*, p. 471.

21. Hannay, *Philip's Phoenix*, p. 73.

22. P.J. Croft, *The Poems of Robert Sidney, Edited from the Poet's Autograph Notebook with Introduction and Commentary* (Oxford: Clarendon Press, 1984), p. 4.

    Discovered in the Warwick Castle Library in the late 1960s and properly attributed to Robert Sidney in the early 1970s.

23. Bevington, *Complete Works*, p. 498.

    There is argument among scholars over whether the anonymous play published in 1591, *The Troublesome Raigne of John, King of England*, was earlier and used as a source or perhaps it was a bad quarto. E.A.J. Honigmann believes *Troublesome Raigne* was based on the Shakespearean play, *King John*. *Troublesome Raigne* was reprinted in 1611 with "by W.Sh." on the title page, and the 1622 reprint attributed the play to "W. Shakespeare."

24. Hannay, *Collected Works*, vol. 1, p. 39.

25. W.G. Boswell-Stone, *Shakespeare's Holinshed: The Chronicles and the Historical Plays Compared* (1896; reprint, New York, London: Benjamin Blom, Inc., 2003), p. 119.

26. Ure, *King Richard II*, p. xxxiii.

27. Ibid., p. xxxiv.

28. John Julius Norwich, *Shakespeare's Kings: The Great Plays and the History of England in the Middle Ages: 1337–1485* (New York: Touchestone, Simon & Schuster, 1999), p. 145.

29. Bevington, *Complete Works*, p. A-35.

Chapter 12: Do You Not Know I Am a Woman?

1. From the introduction to the article by Wendy Greenhill and Paul Wignall, "Shakespeare's Froward Females: Women Who Defy Male Domination," *Shakespeare* 2:2 (Spring 1998), p. 7.

2. Jeanne Addison Roberts, "Are Shakespeare's Women Unruly?" *Shakespeare* 2:2 (Spring 1998), p. 11.

3. Barton, *The Riverside Shakespeare* (Boston: Houghton Mifflin, 1974), p. 107. Except for this citation, all other references to The Riverside Shakespeare are to the 2d ed., 1997 printing.

4. Slater, *Seven Shakespeares*, p. 218.

5. Juliet Dusinberre, *Shakespeare and the Nature of Women*, 2d ed. (New York: St. Martin's Press, Inc., 1996), p. 308.

Chapter 13: The Imagery in the Plays

1. Spurgeon, *Shakespeare's Imagery*.

2. Ibid., p. 114.

3. Ibid., pp. 119–120.

4. Ibid., p. 205.

5. Ibid., Chart VII.

6. Ibid., pp. 124–125.

7. Ibid., p. 137.

8. Ibid., pp. 110–111.

9. Craig and Bevington, *Complete Works*, rev. ed., p. 1237, n.339.

10. John Bold with John Reeves, *Wilton House and English Palladianism, Some Wiltshire Houses* (London: Her Majesty's Stationery Office, 1988), p. 79.

11. Spurgeon, *Shakespeare's Imagery*, p. 27.

12. Ibid., p. 36.

13. Ibid., pp. 28–29.

Chapter 14: The Incomparable Brethren at Court

1. G.P.V. Akrigg, *Jacobean Pageant, or The Court of King James I* (Cambridge: Harvard University Press, 1963), p. 173.

2. Duncan-Jones, *Sir Philip Sidney*, p. 165, quoting Fulke Greville's *Prose Works*, page 39.

3. Duncan-Jones, *Sir Philip Sidney*, p. 165.

4. Hay, *The Life of Robert Sidney*, pp. 38–39.

5. Kernan, *Shakespeare, King's Playwright*, p. 173.

    After 16 years of a fairly happy although financially unstable marriage, Donne's wife, 32-year-old Anne, died after the stillborn delivery of their twelfth child.

6. Brennan, *Literary Patronage*, pp. 16–17.

7. Somerset, *Elizabeth I,* p. 499.

8. Both notes from Hannay, *Philip's Phoenix,* p. 169.

9. All above from Hannay, *Philip's Phoenix,* pp. 170–71.

10. Kernan, *Shakespeare, King's Playwright,* p. 115.

11. David Riggs, *Ben Jonson: A Life* (Cambridge, London: Harvard Univ. Press, 1989) p. 219.

12. Akrigg, *Jacobean Pageant,* pp. 190–204.

> Well, Suffolk's daughter's "scandalous behavior" was pretty horrible—she had Sir Thomas Overbury murdered with a poisoned enema in the Tower of London. Though she and her husband, Robert Carr, were found guilty, they were pardoned—but they did lose their power at court, which was considered punishment enough for people of that social class. They lived in an apartment in the Tower of London for a couple of years, which Carr remodeled with part of the annual income of £4,000 that came from his "office." Then they were banished to an estate in the English countryside. Poor things.
>
> The lower-class "inferiors" involved in the murder plot, however, such as the apothecary who was asked to supply the poison, the dress designer/madame who delivered the poison to the prison, the elderly servingman who unwittingly handed the poisonous enema to Overbury, and even the kind-hearted Lieutenant who substituted fresh food for the obviously poisoned food for months, were hanged.

13. Waller, *Sidney Family Romance,* p. 87.

14. Brennan, *Literary Patronage,* p. 122.

15. Ibid., p. 123.

16. Waller, *Sidney Family Romance,* p. 88.

17. Ibid., pp. 88–89.

18. Kernan, *Shakespeare, King's Playwright,* p. 115.

19. Riggs, *Ben Jonson,* pp. 215–18.

20. Waller, *Sidney Family Romance,* p. 89.

21. Brennan, *Literary Patronage,* p. 160.

> Pembroke College at Oxford was originally called Broadgates Hall but changed its name in 1624 in honor of William Herbert. This Pembroke College is not to be confused with Pembroke College at Cambridge, founded in 1347 by Mary de St. Pol, Countess of Pembroke from 1321. St. John's College at Cambridge was also founded by a woman in 1511—Lady Margaret Beaufort, mother of Henry VII.
>
> The statue in the courtyard of the Bodleian Library at Oxford is of William Herbert.

22. Brennan, *Literary Patronage,* p. 163.

23. Miles, *Ben Jonson, His Life and Work,* p. 206.

24. Kenneth R.H. MacKenzie, *Royal Masonic Cyclopaedia,* vol. 1 (1877; reprint, Montana: Kessinger Publications, 2002), p. 285.

25. Waller, *Sidney Family Romance,* p. 123.

26. Hannay, *Philip's Phoenix,* quoting "William Herbert's Nativity" (Bodleian Library, MS Ashmole 394, ff.76–81), p. 211.

27. Waller, *Sidney Family Romance,* p. 56.

28. Edward Hyde, the Earl of Clarendon, *History of the Rebellion,* ed. W. Dunn Macray (Oxford, 1888), pp. 71–73, quoted in *An Introduction to Shakespeare's Sonnets for the Use of Historians and Others* by John Dover Wilson (New York: Cambridge University Press, 1964), p. 108.

29. Hannay, *Silent but for the Word,* p. 10.

30. Cerasano and Wynne-Davies, *Renaissance Drama by Women,* p. 15.

31. Wall, *The Imprint of Gender,* p. 281.

32. Louise Bernikow, ed., *The World Split Open: Four Centuries of Women Poets in England and America, 1552–1950* (New York: Random House, 1974), p. 19.

33. Lamb, "The Cooke Sisters: Attitudes toward Learned Women in the Renaissance," in *Silent but for the Word,* p. 115.

34. Wall, *The Imprint of Gender,* p. 280.

35. Hannay, *Silent but for the Word,* p. 9.

36. Hannay, "'Bearing the livery of your name': The Countess of Pembroke's Agency in Print and Scribal Publication," p. 17.

37. Cerasano and Wynne-Davies, *Renaissance Drama,* p. 93.

38. Axel Erdman, *My Gracious Silence: Women in the Mirror of 16th Century Printing in Western Europe* (Luzern: Gilhofer & Ranschburg, Switzerland, 1999), p. xvii.

39. Cerasano and Wynne-Davies, *Renaissance Drama,* p. 13.

40. Waller, *Sidney Family Romance,* p. 230.

41. E.E. Willoughby, *A Printer of Shakespeare* (London: Philip Allan & Co. Ltd, 1934), p. 166.

42. Lawrence Stone and Jeanne C. Fawtier Stone, *An Open Elite? England 1540–1880,* abridged ed. (1986; reprint, Oxford: Clarendon Press, 2001), p. 165.

43. Ibid., p. 185.

44. Brennan, *Literary Patronage,* p. 119.

45. Hannay, *Philip's Phoenix,* p. 212.

46. Brennan, *Literary Patronage,* p. 119.

47. Ibid., p. 106.

48. Kernan, *Shakespeare, King's Playwright,* p. 11.

49. Brennan, *Literary Patronage,* pp. 107–09.

> Bucephalus was the horse belonging to Alexander the Great. It was high-spirited and difficult to control, but as a young boy Alexander was the only one able to ride it. At the spot where the horse later died in battle in India, Alexander founded the city of Bucephala.

50. In a letter from Dudley Carleton to Winwood, quoted in Waller, *Sidney Family Romance,* p. 83.

51. Brennan, *Literary Patronage,* p. 106.

52. Hannay, *Philip's Phoenix,* p. 191.

53. Kernan, *Shakespeare, King's Playwright,* p. 118.

54. Akrigg, *Jacobean Pageant,* p. 52.

55. Brennan, *Literary Patronage,* p. 167.

Chapter 15: The Publication of the Plays

1. Ann Jennalie Cook, *The Privileged Playgoers of Shakespeare's London, 1576–1642* (Princeton: Princeton University Press, 1981), p. 176.

2. Riggs, *Ben Jonson*, p. 24.

3. William Ingram, "The Economics of Playing," in *A Companion to Shakespeare,* ed. David Scott Kastan, (Oxford: Blackwell Publishers, 1999), p. 314.

4. Bentley, *Profession of Dramatist*, p. 25.

5. Ibid., p. 17.

6. Somerset, *Elizabeth I*, p. 368.

7. Riggs, *Ben Jonson*, p. 24.

8. Hall, *Cities in Civilization*, p. 115.

9. Bentley, *Profession of Dramatist*, p. 199.

10. Ibid., p. 16.

11. Hall, *Cities in Civilization*, p. 115.

12. Bentley, *Profession of Dramatist*, p. 100.

13. Besides the six other plays published in the Third Folio, there are three plays that Humphrey Moseley entered in the Stationers' Register as Shakespeare's: *Duke Humphrey, Iphis and Iantha,* and *King Stephen.*

    In the library of King Charles (reigned 1660–85), there was a volume titled *Shakespeare Volume I* that included *Mucedorus, Fair Em,* and *The Merry Devil of Edmonton.*

14. Campbell, *Reader's Encyclopedia*, p. 621.

15. Ibid., p. 313.

16. These plays are thought by scholars to have been sold to a printer and reproduced through memorial reconstruction: *Richard II, Henry V, Merry Wives of Windsor, Romeo and Juliet, Hamlet, King Lear, Pericles.*

17. Campbell, *Reader's Encyclopedia*, p. 520.

18. Berryman, *Shakespeare*, p. 36.

19. Price, *Unorthodox Biography*, p. 130.

20. Ibid., p. 130.

21. Ibid., p. 131.

22. Chambers, *William Shakespeare,* vol. 2, pp. 323–325.

23.

Locrine	1595	"Newly set forth, overseen, and corrected by W.S." Included in the Third Folio (second edition) and in the Fourth Folio of Shakespeare's works.	
The Puritan	1607	"Written by W.S."	
A Yorkshire Tragedy	1608, 1619	"Written by W. Shakespeare"	
Sir John Oldcastle	1600	Anonymous	
	1619	Printed in a collection along with *King Lear, Merry Wives,* and others as "Written by William Shakespeare"	
Thomas Lord Cromwell	1602, 1613	"By W.S." Von Schlegel regards this play as among Shakespeare's masterpieces.	
Mucedorus	1598 1610	Anonymous Anonymous; acted by Shakespeare's company. Found in a volume titled *Shakespeare,* vol. 1, in the library of King Charles II.	

24. Chambers, *William Shakespeare,* vol. 2, p. 210.

    In Ben Jonson's papers called *Timber, or Discoveries,* he wrote, "I remember, the Players have often mentioned it as an honor to Shakespeare that in his writing (whatsoever he penned), he never blotted out a line. My answer hath been, would he had blotted a thousand. Which they thought a malevolent speech. I had not told posterity this, but for their ignorance, who choose that circumstance to commend their friend by, wherein he most faulted."

    In the First Folio, the epistle supposedly by Heminge and Condell states, "And what he thought, he uttered with that easiness, that we have scarce received from him a blot in his papers."

25. The sixth signature is on his will and is illegible. It is assumed that he spelled it Shakspere as on the other page.

26. The anomalies:
    Love's Labor's Lost in 1598, "by W. Shakespere."
    King Lear in 1608, "by William Shak-speare."

Chapter 16: The Publication of the First Folio

1. Campbell, *Reader's Encyclopedia*, p. 620.

2. Paul Werstine, "Plays in Manuscript," in *A New History of Early English Drama,* eds. John D. Cox and David Scott Kastan (New York: Columbia University Press, 1997), p. 482.

3. Ibid., p. 493. Specifically, the Malone Society found *Tom A Lincoln* in 1992; six manuscripts were found at the Warwickshire Record Office and Arbury Hall "constituting the canon of the amateur playwright John Newdigate III"; in 1977 at Castle Ashby, William P. Williams found thirteen manuscript plays of Cosmo Manuche, three of which were in multiple drafts.

4. Bentley, *Profession of Dramatist*, p. 20.

5. Woudhuysen, *Circulation of Manuscripts*, p. 212.

6. Ibid., p. 92.

7. Ibid., p. 95.

8. Charlton Hinman, *The Printing and Proof-Reading of the First Folio of Shakespeare,* vol. 1 (Oxford: Clarendon Press, 1963), p. 4.

9. According to *The Reader's Encyclopedia of Shakespeare* and E.K. Chambers, the following printed plays used original manuscripts for the First Folio:

> *Titus Andronicus,* originally printed in 1594, used the original manuscript in 1622, almost 30 years later.

> *The Taming of the Shrew,* originally printed in 1594, used the original manuscript.

> *Henry IV, part 2,* originally printed in 1600, used the original manuscript.

> *Troilus and Cressida,* originally printed in 1609, was set in conjunction with the original manuscript.

> *Henry V,* originally printed in 1600, used the foul papers.

> *Hamlet,* originally printed in 1603, *The Merry Wives of Windsor,* originally printed in 1602, and *King Lear,* originally printed in 1608, used prompt books.

10. Woodhuysen, *Circulation of Manuscripts,* pp. 386–87.

11. Miles, *Ben Jonson,* p. 171.

12. Ibid., p. 172.

13. Riggs, *Ben Jonson,* p. 3.

14. W. David Kay, *Ben Jonson, A Literary Life* (New York: St. Martin's Press, 1995), p. 141.

15. E.E. Willoughby, *The Printing of the First Folio of Shakespeare* (Great Britain: Oxford University Press, 1932), p. 28. I don't find Hinman's challenge to Willoughby's timeline to be convincing.

16. Willoughby, *A Printer of Shakespeare,* p. 21.

17. Bevington, *Complete Works,* p. lxxxvii.

18. Waller, *Sidney Family Romance,* p. 230.

19. *The Tempest, Two Gentlemen of Verona, The Merry Wives of Windsor,* and *Measure for Measure.* (Perhaps also *The Winter's Tale* and *Cymbeline.*)

20. Bevington, *Complete Works,* p. lxxxix.

21. Willoughby, *A Printer,* p. 166.

22. Hannay, *Philip's Phoenix,* p. 205.

23. Michell, *Who Wrote Shakespeare?,* p. 80.

24. Charlton Ogburn, *The Mysterious William Shakespeare: The Myth and the Reality* (McLean, Virginia: Dodd, Mead & Co./EPM Publications, Inc., 1984), p. 219.

25. Campbell, *Reader's Encyclopedia,* p. 407.

26. Riggs, *Ben Jonson,* p. 277–78.

27. Miles, *Ben Jonson,* p. 87–88.

28. Kay, *Ben Jonson,* p. 117.

29. Riggs, *Ben Jonson,* p. 180.

30. Campbell, *Reader's Encyclopedia,* pp. 229–30.

31. Riggs, *Ben Jonson,* p. 276.

32. Ibid., p. 276.

33. In Jonson's *Timber, or Discoveries,* which was published posthumously in 1641, he wrote this of Shakespeare:

> "Many times he fell into those things, could not escape laughter: As when he said in the person of Caesar, one speaking to him; Caesar, thou dost me wrong. He replyed: Caesar did never wrong, but

> with just cause: and such like; which were ridiculous."

> The line in the First Folio has been changed to the logical "Caesar doth not wrong, nor without cause will he be satisfied."

Chapter 17: The Sweet Swan of Avon

1. Riggs, *Ben Jonson,* p. 13 (spelling modernized).

2. Ibid., p. 277.

3. Buxton, *Sir Philip Sidney,* p. 106 n.1.

4. Ibid., frontispiece.

5. Quoted in Buxton, *Sir Philip Sidney,* p. 48.

6. Christopher Marlowe also refers to Mary as Delia. In a dedication to "Mary Countess of Pembroke," Marlowe begins, "Delia born of a laurel-crowned race, true sister of Sidney the bard of Apollo...."

7. Hannay, *Philip's Phoenix,* p. 117. Today the Wilton House estate encompasses only 21 acres. When Mary Sidney lived at Wilton House with its 14,000 acres, the Avon River ran through her property.

8. Quoted in Young, *Mary Sidney, Countess of Pembroke,* pp. 175–76.

Chapter 18: Mary Sidney, alias Shakespeare

1. Hannay et al., *Collected Works,* vol. 1, p. 49. Davies wrote this in regard to Mary's refusal to publish her Psalms.

2. Willoughby, *A Printer of Shakespeare,* p. 166.

3. "[William Herbert, Earl of] Pembroke showed considerable generosity in settling his mother's estate, avoiding the sibling quarrels that so often occur when a parent dies intestate: 'the Lord Chamberlain [William Herbert] hath geven the earle of Montgomerie [Philip Herbert] all her personall estate, contenting himself with her joynter, for she died without [a] will.'" Hannay, *Philip's Phoenix,* p. 206.

Appendix A: Old School

1. Witherspoon, *Influence of Garnier,* p. 182.

2. Hannay, *Philip's Phoenix,* p. 129.

3. Hannay, *Collected Works,* vol. 1, pp. 36–37.

4. Cerasano and Wynne-Davies, *Renaissance Drama,* p. 16.

5. Duncan-Jones, *Sir Philip Sidney,* p. 148.

6. Sir John Harington, *Nugae Antiquae,* ed. Henry Harington (London: Vernon and Hood, 1804), 1:173; quoted in Hannay, *Philip's Phoenix,* p. 134, although it is unclear whether Hannay is actually referring to Sir John Harington (Mary's contemporary, 1561–1612) as the author of the quote or to Henry Harington, the editor in 1804, since Hannay simply refers to "Harington." Spelling is modernized.

7. Hannay, *Philip's Phoenix,* pp. 64–65.

8. Ibid., p. 65.

9. Gary Waller, *Critical Study,* p. 267.

10. Ibid., p. 267.

Appendix B: The Other Candidates

1. *Merchant of Venice* (Venice); *All's Well That Ends Well* (partly in Tuscany); *Taming of the Shrew* (Padua); *Romeo and Juliet* (Verona and Mantua); *Othello* (partly in Venice); *Two Gentlemen of Verona* (Verona, Milan); plus the four Roman history plays. Sicily was not part of Italy until 1861.

2. Brenda James and William D. Rubinstein, *The Truth Will Out: Unmasking the Real Shakespeare* (London: Pearson Longman, 2005), p. 158.

Appendix C: Jonson's Eulogy

1. Chambers, *William Shakespeare*, vol. 2, p. 226.

   In a book of John Donne's titled *Poems*, published in 1633, was a short poem that started with:

   > Renowned Spencer, lie a thought more nigh
   > To learned Chaucer, and rare Beaumont lie
   > A little nearer Spenser to make room
   > For Shakespeare in your threefold fowerfold Tomb.

   This poem was later ascribed to William Basse.

2. Simon Hornblower and Antony Spawforth, eds., *The Oxford Classical Dictionary*, 3d ed. (Oxford, New York: Oxford University Press, 1996), p. 962.

3. In Plato's *Dialogues:*
   PHAEDRUS: Indeed, you are pleased to be merry.
   SOCRATES: Do you mean that I am not in earnest?

4. Hornblower and Spawforth, *Oxford Classical Dictionary,* p. 1419.

5. Bates, *The Drama, Its History, Literature and Influence on Civilization,* vol. 2, pp. 205–07 (all quoted material in this paragraph).

6. Riggs, *Ben Jonson,* p. 277.

Appendix D: The Narrative Poems

1. Gerald Eades Bentley, *Shakespeare and His Theatre* (Lincoln: University of Nebraska Press, 1964), p. 14.

2. Ibid., p. 15.

3. Burrow, *The Complete Sonnets and Poems,* p. 151.

4. Harold Bloom, *The Western Canon: The Books and School of the Ages* (New York: Riverhead Books, 1994), p. 49.

5. Hallett Smith, in *The Riverside Shakespeare*, p. 1798.

6. Gary Waller, *English Poetry of the Sixteenth* Century (London, New York: Longman Group, 1986), p. 217.

7. Ibid., p. 218.

8. Ibid., p. 218.

9. R.S. White, ed., *Hazlitt's Criticism of Shakespeare: Studies in British Literature,* vol. 18 (Lewiston: The Edwin Mellen Press, 1996), pp. 189–190.

10. Ibid., p. 190.

11. Bentley, *Shakespeare and His Theatre*, pp. 3–4.

12. Ibid., p. 8.

13. Bevington, *Complete Works*, p. 1608.

14. Peter W. M. Blayney, "The Publication of Playbooks," in *A New History of Early English Drama*, p. 388.

15. Hallett Smith, in *The Riverside Shakespeare,* p. 1798.

16. Bevington, *Complete Works,* p. 1608.

17. Ibid., p. 1608.

18. Ibid., p. 1608.

19. Ibid., p. 1608.

20. Ibid., p. 1609.

21. Ibid., p. 1626.

22. Ibid., p. 1627.

Appendix E: Literary Allusions

1. All quotes are from Chambers, *William Shakespeare, A Study of Facts and Problems,* vol. 2, pp. 192–225.

Appendix H: Real Money

1. John J. McCusker, *How Much Is That in Real Money? A Historical Commodity Price Index for Use as a Deflator of Money Values in the Economy of the United States, Second Edition, Revised and Enlarged* (Worcester: American Antiquarian Society, 2001), Table D-1: Commodity Price Indexes, Great Britain, 1600–2000.

2. Ingram, "The Economics of Playing," in *A Companion to Shakespeare,* p. 314.

3. Ibid., p. 314; information about a player earning the same wage as a journeyman is on p. 320.

Index

COLOPHON

I drafted this book on a Mac in Mariner Write,
my favorite word processor (MarinerSoftware.
com). I poured the draft into Adobe InDesign
(Adobe.com) on a Mac to continue the development process. I designed the book, indexed it,
and created the table of contents in InDesign.
I uploaded PDFs to my editor and my proofer.

I set the body copy in Brioso Pro, an OpenType
font, and the script face in Voluta Script, both
from Adobe Systems and available at Veer.com.
The sans serif font is ITC Officina Sans from
ITCfonts.com. The ornaments throughout the
book are from a font called Type Embellishments
from Linotype.com.

To find the old and rare books I need, I love to
use FetchBook.info.

To create the timelines, I used Bee Docs' Timeline
from BeeDocuments.com.

To keep track of visual and textual details in
production, I used iClip from Inventive.us.

I entered Mary Sidney's genealogy into Reunion
from LeisterPro.com.

To organize my personal library that holds more
than 5,500 books, I use Delicious Library from
Delicious-Monster.com.

John Tollett used Corel Painter to create the
illustrations of Mary Sidney and Wilton House
(Corel.com) and Adobe Photoshop to create
the cover background. I finished the cover in
InDesign.

And John and I use GarageBand and iWeb
from Apple to create and post the Mary
Sidney Society podcasts and blog at
web.mac.com/marysidney/iWeb.

It's so much fun to live in this world. ;-)